SANTA CLARA JOURNAL

The UTS Law Review No. 7

The Mind
The Body and
The Law

HALSTEAD PRESS

SYDNEY MMVI
Published by Halstead Press
300/3 Smail Street,
Broadway, New South Wales, 2007

© Copyright: Faculty of Law, University of Technology, Sydney, 2006. Not to be copied whole or in part without authorisation. Typeset by Network Printing Studios, Kensington NSW. Printed by Shannon Books, Melbourne.

ISBN 1920831274
ISSN 14424959

CONTENTS

Introduction
The Mind, the Body and the Law

11 Marketing Humanity: Should we Allow the Sale of Human Body Parts?
Alexandra George

62 Sounds Suspiciously Like Property Treatment: Does Human Tissue Fit Within The Common Law Concept of Property?
Imogen Goold

87 Regulating Human Biological Enhancements: Questionable Justifications and International Complications
Henry T. Greely

111 Surrogacy in Israel: A Model of Comprehensive Regulation of New Technologies
Jacqueline Hand

117 Prophecy with Numbers: Prospective Punishment for Predictable Human Behaviour?
Brad Johnson

134 Human Clones and International Human Rights
Kerry Lynn Macintosh

157 If I Only Had a Heart! The Australian case of Annetts and the Internationally Confounding Question of Compensation in Nervous Shock Law
Yega Muthu, Ellen Geraghty and Barbara Hocking

184 The Trials of Tenofovir: Mediating the Ethics of Third World Research
Peter J. Hammer & Tammy Sue Lundstrom

Review—*Law in Perspective: Ethics, Society and Critical Thinking*

Santa Clara Journal of International Law Volume IV
Board Of Editors

Editor-in-Chief
Shannon Ghadiri-Asli

Managing Editor
Alan Upton

Senior Technical Editor
Eric Berquist

Senior Comments Editor
Lauren Shaman

Senior Articles Editor
Yvette Garfield

Technical Editors
Robert Stamps
Ekaterina Petkova
Dai Tan

Articles/Comments Editors
Utpal Donde
Jonathan Collins
Celeste Kelly
Eric Ortner

Symposium Director
Thomas Howe

Business/Web Editor
Peter Hoang

This journal may be cited as (2005) 7 UTS Law Review, (2005) 7 UTSLR or 4 Santa Clara Journal of International Law (2006)

UTS Law Review Editorial Board for Volume 7

Editors
June Carbone
Anita Stuhmcke
Patrick Keyzer

Editorial Board
Joseph Azize
Karen Bubna-Litic
Jennifer Burn
Bill Childs
Geoff Holland
Helen Kiel
Stathis Palassis
Michelle Sanson

Faculty Advisory Committee
Joseph Azize
Roberto Buonamano
Geoff Holland
Vicki John
Francis Johns
Patrick Keyzer (Chair)
Jill McKeough (Dean)
Robert Watt

Abbreviations

ADRDM	American Declaration of the Rights and Duties of Man
Adver. & Commc'ns	Advertising and Communications
AM. J. HUM. GENET.	American Journal of Human Genetics
AM. J. INT'L L.	American Journal of International Law
AM. J. MED.	American Journal of Medicine
AM. J. BIOETHICS	American Journal of Bioethics
CAL. ADVISORY COMM. ON HUMAN CLONING	California Advisory Committee on Human Cloning
CAL. BUS. & PROF. CODE	California Business and Professions Code
CDC	Centers For Disease Control and Prevention
CIOMS, GUIDELINES	Council for International Organizations of Medical Sciences, International Ethical Guidelines For Biomedical Research Involving Human Subjects
COLUM. L. REV.	Columbia Law Review
Conn. Public Act	Connecticut Public Act
COUNCIL FOR INT'L ORGS. OF MED. SCIS.	Council for International Organizations of Medical Sciences
Ctrs. For Disease Control	Centers for Disease Control and Prevention
Div. of Drug Mktg.	Division of Drug Marketing
DRUG WK.	Drug Week
ENG'G & PUB. POLICY	Engineering and Public Policy
EUR. CT. H.R.	European Court of Human Rights
G.A.	General Assembly
GENETICS & PUB. POLICY CTR	Genetics And Public Policy Center
HASTINGS L.J.	Hastings Law Journal
HUM. RTS. Q	Human Rights Quarterly
ICCRR	International Covenant on Civil and Political Rights
ICESCR	International Covenant on Economic, Social, and Cultural Rights
INT'L ORGS. OF MED. SCI.	International Organizations of Medical Sciences
INTER-AM. C.H.R.	Inter-American Commission on Human Rights
Mass. Adv. Legis. Serv.	Massachusetts Advisory Legislative Service
MED. HUMAN. REV.	Medical Humanities Review
MICH. L. REV.	Michigan Law Review
MORBIDITY & MORTALITY WKLY. REP.	Morbidity and Mortality Weekly Report

N.J. Stat. Ann.	New Jersey Statutes annotated
NAD	National Association of the Deaf
NAS Report	The National Academies, Scientific and Medical Aspects of Human Reproductive Cloning
Nat'l Acads.	The National Academies
Nat'l Ass'n of the Deaf	National Association of the Deaf
Nat'l Bioethics Advisory Comm'n	National Bioethics Advisory Commission
New Eng. J. Med.	New England Journal of Medicine
PGA	Professional Golfers' Association
Proc. Nat'l Acad. Sci. U.S.	Proceedings of the National Academy of Sciences of the United States of America
Project Inform. Persp.	Project Inform Perspective
Pub. Libr. Sci. Biology	Public library of science biology
R.I. Gen. Laws	Rhode Island General Laws
Reg'l	Regional
S.F. Chron.	San Francisco Chronicle
Sask. L. Rev.	Saskatchewan Law Review
Stan. L. & Pol'y Rev.	Stanford Law and Policy Review
Tex. L. Rev.	Texas Law Review
The Am. Soc'y of Human Genetics Bd. of Dirs.	The American Society of Human Genetics Board of Directors
U.N. Gen. Assembly, Sixth Comm.	United Nations General Assembly Sixth Committee
U.N. Integrated Reg'l Info. Networks	United Nations Integrated Regional Information Networks
U.N.GAOR	United Nations General Assembly Official Record
U.N.T.S.	United Nations Treaty Series
UDHR	Universal Declaration of Human Rights
UNESCO	United Nations Educational, Scientific and Cultural Organization
Univ. of Ind.	University of Indiana
Utah L. Rev.	Utah Law Review
Va. Code Ann.	Virginia Annotated Code
Wall St. J.	The Wall Street Journal
Wash. L. Rev.	Washington Law Review
WHO	World Health Organization
WMA	World Medical Association
WNU	Women's Network for Unity
Yale J. Health Pol'y L. & Ethics	Yale Journal of Health Policy, Law, and Ethics

THE MIND, THE BODY AND THE LAW
Introduction

Given the theme of this journal it is perhaps unsurprising that the articles in it deal with the challenging and complex issue of the law's accommodation of change. Whether the law has responded appropriately and the twin question how should the law respond are recurring themes in each of these papers. Contributions come from Australia, the United Kingdom and the United States.

The four articles from Australia and the United Kingdom each deal with the theme of legal change. Alexandra George examines the cases for and against the sale of human body parts from a philosophical perspective. The paper by Imogen Goold 'Sounds Suspiciously like Property Treatment: Does Human Tissue Fit within the Common Law Concept of Property?' examines whether human tissue as an object fits within the common law concept of property. The article by Yega Muthu, Ellen Geraghty and Barbara Hocking 'If I Only Had a Heart! The Australian Case of Annetts and the Internationally Confounding Question of Compensation in Nervous Shock Law' provides insight into how Australian case law has dealt with psychiatric illness. It goes on to examine legislative change and international case law. Brad Johnson has provided an insightful, critical analysis of Queensland's post-sentence preventive detention legislation, interrogating the 'scientific' basis of risk prediction in this context.

The papers from the United States similarly address the issue of legal change in the context of comparative and international bioethics. These papers consider the challenges globalisation presents to the regulation of emerging technology that changes reproduction, medicine, and treatments in the context of different legal and social cultures. The first paper, 'Regulating Human Biological Enhancements: Questionable Justifications and International Complications', by Henry T. Greely, considers whether human *biological* enhancement is meaningfully different from other forms of human enhancement and, if so, whether it can effectively be regulated within an international realm. 'The Trials of Tenofovir: Mediating the Ethics of Third-World Research', by Peter J. Hammer and Tammy Sue Lundstrom, examines the controversy that arose when Western researchers sought to test the effectiveness of a drug in preventing the transmission of HIV/AIDS among Cambodian prostitutes. They explore the difficulties of exporting ethical standards developed in the context of Western countries to the different circumstances in which the drugs may be tested and used. Kerry Macintosh, in her article 'Human Clones and International Human Rights', provides a provocative argument that human clones will someday be born, and that the current efforts to ban their existence serve primarily to stigmatise the resulting children in violation of the fundamental principle of nondiscrimination in international human rights law. Finally, Jacqueline Hand provides a review of Kelly Weisberg's book, *Surrogacy in Israel*, a richly detailed case study of the adoption of the strongest surrogacy legislation in the world.

The importance of an international joint edition of the journal on these topics is that it reflects the increasing recognition of the global nature of the debates over the issues discussed in these papers.

The concept of this edition, two years in the making, began with a suggestion by Professor June Carbone from Santa Clara University that has after much work at Santa Clara and UTS, evolved into a truly international journal.

We would like to thank the Center for Global Law and Policy at Santa Clara University, the student editors at Santa Clara and UTS, and Matthew Richardson from Halstead Press, who have made this edition possible. We hope this joint edition of the *Santa Clara Journal of International Law* and the *UTS Law Review* will make a lasting contribution to the legal, ethical and moral debates about the mind, the body and the law.

Professor June Carbone
Associate Professor Anita Stuhmcke
Associate Professor Patrick Keyzer

MARKETING HUMANITY
Should we Allow the Sale of Human Body Parts?
Alexandra George*

I. Introduction

"Fully functional Kidney for sale". The advertisement appeared on an Internet auction site on 2 September 1999. Bidding opened at US$25,000 and reached over US$5.75 million in the several days before site managers removed the offer.[1] Later attempts to e-auction human body parts were similarly thwarted,[2] but it is still easy to find human kidneys for sale on the Internet. One online "message board" has numerous postings from people advertising their organs for sale,[3] and another Internet site claims to have many potential donors waiting to sell kidneys.[4] A domain name registration site offered the domain names Kidneysales.com, kidney4sale.

---

* Lecturer in Intellectual Property Law, Queen Mary, University of London. The author would like to thank Chris Birch, Tom Campbell and the anonymous reviewers for their very helpful comments on earlier drafts of this paper.

1 J Sayfer, "Million-Dollar Kidney: eBay Shuts Down Bidding on Body Part After it Hits $5.7 Million" *Associated Press*.

2 On 4 December 2003, eBay removed an advertisement to auction a kidney with a reserve price of £50,000 (US$85,000). The advertisement had been placed by Peter Randall, a British man who described himself as a "49-year-old non-smoking male who drinks only socially and who is in good health." Randall said he was trying to raise money to pay for treatment for his six-year-old daughter who suffers from cerebral palsy. See "EBay removes ad for sale of human kidney" (2003) <http://www.cnn.com/2003/TECH/internet/12/05/britain.kidney.ap/> at 19 June 2005.
On 25 February 2003, a US man from Rossville, Georgia, posted an advertisement to eBay that read, "I am a white male, 44 years old, in excellent health and wish to sell one of my kidneys for $250,000 plus all expenses. My blood type is O-negative. Serious inquiries only." eBay removed the advertisement before any bids were placed. See "Kidney for Sale on eBay quickly removed" (2003) <http://www.thekcrachannel.com/news/2011004/detail.html> at 19 June 2005.

3 <http://www.ait-cec.com/jebhe10mesg/5171.html> at 19 June 2005. The message board contains threads such as "I want to sell my kidney for cash" (posted 11 September 2004), "Kidney for sale" (posted 7 September 2004), "Re: Kidney for Sale 24 healthy, none smoker British A Rh+ type blood" (posted 9 January 2004), "20 year old selling kidney" (posted 4 December 2003), "Re: Indian guy wants to sell his kidney" (posted November 4, 2003), "Re: Kidney for Sale 23 healthy American O type Blood" (posted 31 October 2003), "I sell my kidney for $100,000" (posted 27 June 2003), and "Who wants My kidney" (posted 21 March 2003).

4 <http://llogic.www3.50megs.com/> at 19 June 2005. The site calls itself "The Life keepers" and states:

> We are looking for new donors! Our primary goals: Daily in the world many people are loosing their kidneys and then suffer from health problems, which could be solved with money! Our Solution To This Problem. We have a lot of donors who are ready to sell a kidney for money!! The reasons for this people to sell theyr kidneys are different. In the most of cases these are the big money which we give to them and exactly the better conditions of living with this money. In Bulgaria have a lot of familyes who can't aford to by themselves anything different from food!! **We will find you kidney for no longer than 7 days. Just contact us and say what you want!!Then we'll send you a donor's medicine file and his/her picture.** *Then remain only the price and conditions for exporting the donor to YOU* . [Emphasis and poor spelling in original]

11

com, kidneysaleoffer.com, buyakidney.com and bodyparts4sale.com,[5] presumably in anticipation of a surge in enthusiasm to sell human body parts over the Internet. The same organisation offered the name kidney-for-sale.co.uk for US$500, even though the sale of kidneys is illegal in the United Kingdom.

Just as the market for kidneys was generated by medical developments that made it possible to transplant human organs from one person to another, evolving scientific discoveries are creating new demands for human bodily products. Technological advances promise innovative solutions such as the growth of test tube kidneys from stem cells and xenotransplantation of organs from sheep or pigs that have been genetically adapted to grow humanised body parts.[6] Scientific dreams are becoming medical realities, but they remain too far off into the future to benefit the people in need of replacement tissue and organs today. Just as fast as one miracle treatment does away with the need for supplies of one sort of human body part, further scientific discoveries such as reproductive and gene therapies are creating a demand for new body parts to transplant or experiment upon.[7] These days it is not just human kidneys, corneas, livers and hearts that are wanted for transplantation; the growing list now includes stem cells, oocytes, embryos, and so on.[8] If the sale of human body parts is not already big business, or legitimate business, there are clearly some who believe that it should or will become so.

Among those who advocate the creation of a legitimate market in human body parts are libertarian theorists and some economists.[9] They

---

5 <http://www.greatdomains.com> at 22 April 2001.
6 Sylvia Pagán Westphal, *Humanised Organs Can be Grown in Animals* (2003) New Scientist Online News <http://www.newscientist.com/article.ns?id=dn4492> at 19 June 2005, reporting that "human" embryonic stem cells have been harvested from cloned embryos created by fusing human cells with rabbit cells. See also, Natasha McDowell, *Mini-pig Clone Raises Transplant Hope* (2003) New Scientist Online News <http://www.newscientist.com/article.ns?id=dn3257> at 19 June 2005, describing how the cloning of a genetically modified miniature pig brings the prospect of transplanting pig organs into humans closer to fruition.
7 For example, Chinese scientists have recently reported the growth of rabbit-human hybrid embryos using donor cells from the foreskins of a five-year-old boy and two men, and from a woman's facial tissue: Philip Cohen, "Human-rabbit Embryos Intensify Stem Cell Debate", 15 August 2003, New Scientist Online News <http://www.newscientist.com/article.ns?id=dn4060> at 19 June 2005. The donation of such tissue invokes many of the traditional arguments about the transplant and sale of human body parts, with the added complication that the "recipient" in this circumstance would be a clone of the donor.
8 For an indication of how interwoven some of this research is, see Sylvia Pagán Westphal, "Cloned Human Embryos Are Stem Cell Breakthrough", New Scientist Online News, 12 February 2004. This research used 242 eggs donated by 16 women, from which human embryos were grown.
9 Examples include libertarians Richard A Epstein (University of Chicago) and Tim O'Brien (Chairman of the Libertarian Party of Michigan). See, *eg*, Richard A Epstein, *Mortal Peril: Our Inalienable Right to Health Care?* (1997). Clause XI(8) of the Libertarian Party of Michigan's official platform, as updated on 20 May 2000, states: "Recognizing that the only way supply can be brought up to satisfy demand is through the free market system, we favor repeal of the existing prohibition on the commercial sale and purchase of body parts and organs for transplant." It is interesting to note that the US Libertarian Party's National Director Steve Dasbach made a statement condemning eBay's decision to withdraw a kidney

believe that compensated trade would overcome the existing shortages of human tissue and organs available for transplant, and that regulated trade would be a more effective way of protecting the vulnerable than an outright prohibition of such sales. Advocates of a market in body parts are countered by opponents who represent the normative voice of liberal democracies. A recent history of shameless and tragic exploitation of the Third World poor in places where the "body bazaar" has not been effectively controlled by law has prompted these opponents to recommend a conservative policy of caution characterised by prohibitions on the sale of human body parts.

Set against this backdrop, this article examines the cases for and against the sale of human body parts from a philosophical perspective. It is a debate that has been around for some time: scientific developments in the mid- to late twentieth century made the transplant of organs between unrelated donors and recipients a viable treatment option. While these advances and new treatments gave fresh hope to many patients, they spawned a Pandora's box of ethical dilemmas. It was one thing to make transplantation scientifically possible, but how would sufficient donor organs be found to meet the demand generated by this innovative new treatment? As so often in medicine, the problem was one of scarce resources. However, this time it was a scarcity of human resources—a lack of human kidneys, livers, corneas, and so on available for transplantation—rather than a simple lack of funds. Throwing money at the problem would not solve it.

Or would it? If people could be paid to sell their body parts, would the operation of the market eventually resolve the scarcity problem? Would market conditions lead to organs and other bodily material ending up with those who value them the most? Or would it just create even greater conundrums?[10]

The current biotech revolution[11] means this dilemma remains at least

---

from sale: <http://www.bmstahoe.com/Libertarian/onlineorgans.html> at 19 June 2005. A clear expression of an economic analysis of the issue can be found in W Barnett II, M Saliba and D Walker, "A Free Market in Kidneys: Efficient and Equitable" (2001) 3 *The Independent Review*, 373–85. This article contains a useful list of references (at 384–85) of other economic analyses of the topic.

10 The issue of how to compensate those who "donate" human tissue is considered in Charlotte H Harrison, "Neither Moore nor the Market: Alternative Models for Compensating Contributors of Human Tissue" (2002) 28 *American Journal of Law and Medicine* 77. In examining this topic, the article discusses the case of *Moore v Regents of the University of California*, 793 P.2d 479 (Cal. 1990) in which Mr Moore, a patient whose tissue had been used by researchers after being removed when he was undergoing a routine operation, was denied the ability to profit from the use made of his body part. See also, Donna M Gitter, "Ownership of Human Tissue: A Proposal for Federal Recognition of Human Research Participants' Property Rights in their Biological Material" (2004) 61 *Washington and Lee Law Review* 257, arguing that as a market in human tissue already exists, the law should entitle plaintiffs to invoke a property right if they have negotiated in advance for rights in their tissue, and to invoke a liability rule if researchers have hindered their ability to bargain for such rights.

11 For a précis of the advances associated with the biotechnological revolution of the late twentieth and early twenty-first centuries, see Nathan A Adams, IV, "Creating Clones,

as fraught now as it was in 1980 when the introduction of the immuno-suppressant drug Cyclosporin-A made it much more viable to transplant organs between unrelated people. After many years and dozens of medical, ethical and legal journal articles dealing with various aspects of this problem,[12] an acceptable solution still seems elusive. But while progress in this debate appears almost to have stood still,[13] science and medical research have surged forward. While various proposals for increasing the supply of donor organs have been being debated and tested and debated some more, the biotechnological revolution is well underway. It is a revolution that is making ever more medical and scientific techniques possible, and this is leading to an intensification of the ethical quandaries about how the raw materials—the tissue (such as blood, hair and placentas), the genes, the stem cells, the DNA, and the reproductive cells (sperm and ovum)—needed to develop and make use of these technologies will be obtained.[14] The technologies are innovative and new, but the dilemmas have a ring of familiarity. Often, it seems, it is not (or not only) a lack of money that is hindering progress; there is also a lack of a human raw materials that money cannot—or is not permitted to—buy. Just as the progress of science might be drawing us closer to the day when replacement organs will be grown in test tubes, thus negating the need for human donors to provide organs for transplantation, other biotechnological developments are leading us into an age when donated parts of humans are increasingly being sought for new purposes. The specifics and the contexts might be changing but the original practical and ethical problem of how to obtain more donor body parts has not only not gone away, it is now being multiplied by the challenges swept in by the biotechnological revolution.

The purpose of this article is therefore twofold. Its primary and central theme is to use classical liberal philosophical theory to explore the relative strengths and weaknesses of arguments for and against the sale of human body parts in the hope that this approach might help policy makers to

---

Kids and Chimera: Liberal Democratic Compromise at the Crossroads" (2003) 17 *Notre Dame Journal of Law, Ethics and Public Policy* 71. The article looks at the challenges that biotechnology presents to the "prevailing liberal democratic consensus pertaining to health and welfare", 71. See also the interesting discussions in "Life Sciences, Technology, and the Law Symposium" (2003) 10 *Michigan Telecommunications and Technology Law Review* 175.
12 For a good summary of many of the issues and references to the literature, see, eg, Russell Scott, "The Terrible Imbalance: Human Organs and Tissues for Therapy—A Review of Demand and Supply" (1993) 9 *Journal of Contemporary Health Law and Policy* 139. See also, Lynden Griggs, "The Ownership of Excised Body Parts: Does an Individual Have the Right to Sell?" (1994) 1 *Journal of Law and Medicine* 223; R Scott, *The Body as Property* (1981); E W Nelson, et al, *Financial Incentives for Organ Donation: A Report of the United Network for Organ Sharing Ethics Committee* (1993): <http://www.unos.org/Resources/bioethics.asp?index=3> at 19 June 2005.
13 For a discussion of this, see Michael H Shapiro, "On the Possibility of 'progress' in Managing Biomedical Technologies: Markets, Lotteries, and Rational Moral Standards in Organ Transplantation" (2003) 31 *Capital University Law Review* 13.
14 See discussion of developing uses of parts of the human body in Dorothy Nelkin and Lori B Andrews, "Symposium on Legal Disputes over Body Tissue: Introduction: The Body, Economic Power and Social Control" (1999) 75 *Chicago-Kent Law Review* 3.

resolve the problem. In doing so, it draws together a variety of pro and con arguments and presents them methodically as a single case for and a case against the sale of human body parts. This culminates in a conclusion that offers a philosophically consistent approach to resolving the dilemma that has persisted for so long.

The article's subsidiary task is to acknowledge the ongoing relevance of many of those old arguments: they will continue to be significant even after alternatives to transplant kidneys have become a standard treatment for renal disease, even after artificial corneas can be implanted, and so on. The paper suggests that the familiar old arguments are likely to keep reappearing in new contexts as a result of ongoing biotech developments. It thus seems urgent and important that a resolution to the ethical and jurisprudential debate about the sale and appropriation of human body parts is found before the biotechnology, and the black markets that traditionally accompany legal prohibitions, leave law makers far behind in an unregulated wake.

To set the scene, Part II provides some background and context to the debate about a legal market in human body parts by offering a brief overview of the kinds of laws that have been developed in response to the sorts of scientific and medical advances just outlined. In keeping with the liberal philosophical perspective examined by this article, the jurisdictions surveyed are primarily those hosting liberal democratic political systems.

The case against a legal market in human body parts is then presented in Part III. Drawing on liberal philosophical precepts, the anti-market ("Opponents") viewpoint consists of several overlapping arguments that comprise the normative response in contemporary liberal societies. These include the avoidance of exploitation, the avoidance of sales of human body parts by people lacking adequate knowledge or consent, the minimisation of wealth inequalities, the avoidance of slavery and/or the commodification of the body, and the avoidance of moral repugnance.

Part IV explains the liberal philosophy that underpins the argument just put for the Opponents. It analyses the liberal philosophical principles underlying the normative anti-market case and explores the merits and weaknesses of the Opponents' main contentions. By drawing conclusions about how convincing (or otherwise) the Opponents' various arguments are, this section demonstrates that not all of the Opponents' arguments can be supported by fundamental liberal theory; it thereby builds a platform from which to examine the approach of those who advocate a market in human bodily materials.

In Part V, a pro-market ("Advocates") case is presented using a framework based on many of the philosophical principles identified in the anti-market case. This challenges the dominant, anti-market, prohibitionist approach generally found in the legal systems of industrialised, technologically advanced, liberal societies. By showing how effectively the Advocates draw on the same foundational ideals as the Opponents, this section of the paper demonstrates the inherent strength of the Advocates' case.

The conclusion in Part VI explains why the Advocates nevertheless fail to persuade society that human body parts should be able to be bought and sold in a free market. It shows that this is due to the prior failure of existing laws to improve and regulate social conditions to the degree that a market in human body parts could operate in accordance with the requirements of classical liberalism. Thus, the sale of human body parts remains prohibited throughout much of the world and persists as a topic of lively political debate. While utopian liberal conditions[15] remain elusive, the most basic criteria required to validate a free market in human body parts have not been met. In these circumstances, any market in human body parts would need to be strictly regulated and limited according to the liberal principles set out in the Opponents' case below.

Prior to entering and assessing the debate, it is useful to understand the sorts of empirical legal provisions that law makers in liberal democracies have instituted to regulate the use and sale of human body parts. These illustrate the ways in which law makers have grappled with the issues thus far, and provide a helpful context from which to observe the unfolding policy debate.

II. Legal Responses to the Removal and Transplantation of Human Bodily Material

When kidney transplantation became a viable treatment for renal failure, law makers reacted with legislation to regulate the circumstances surrounding the procedure. The UK's *Human Tissue Act 1961* was thus introduced to "make provision with respect to the use of bodies of deceased persons for therapeutic purposes and purposes of medical education and research" in England, Scotland and Wales.[16] This law allowed the use of a dead body for therapeutic purposes or for medical education or research if the deceased person had given consent while alive.[17] Alternatively, so long as the deceased person had not voiced objections prior to death, and so long as the surviving spouse or relatives did not object, authorisation for such use of the body could be given by the person lawfully in possession of the dead body.[18] The *Human Organ Transplants Act 1989* (UK) then made it a criminal offence to engage in commercial dealings in human organs for

---

15 *Utopia* is used throughout this article in its general sense to mean a place of ideal perfection in laws, government and social conditions. It would be a place with a perfect market, no exploitation, perfect knowledge and sufficient basic resources that are evenly and fairly distributed to provide everyone with an adequate minimum standard of living. It does not imply that everyone would have perfect health, but everyone would have access to adequate health care resources.
16 *Human Tissue Act 1961* (UK), Chapter 54, Preamble. The equivalent legislation in Northern Ireland was the *Human Tissue Act (Northern Ireland) 1962*.
17 Ibid, s1(1).
18 Ibid, s1(2).

transplant, or to advertise the buying or selling of organs. It also made it illegal to transplant an organ between a living donor who was unrelated to the recipient unless the Unrelated Live Transplant Regulatory Authority (ULTRA) had approved the operation under the *Human Organ Transplants (Unrelated Persons) Regulations 1989*. These regulations required ULTRA to ensure that no payment or inducement had been offered or made to the donor, that no coercion or pressure had been placed on the donor to undergo the procedure, that the donor was aware of the nature of the operation and the risks involved, and that the donor understood that he or she could withdraw at any time prior to the operation.

This collection of UK laws was similar to those that have been established in many other jurisdictions around the world.

The United States, for example, enacted the *National Organ Transplant Act* in 1984.[19] Under this law, it is a federal crime to "knowingly acquire, receive, or otherwise transfer any human organ for valuable consideration for use in human transplantation if the transfer affects interstate commerce." Similar prohibitions are contained in various pieces of state legislation based on the earlier *Uniform Anatomical Gift Act 1968*.[20] These had been adopted by the District of Columbia and all states by 1973.

The relevant Australian legislation is also state based.[21] These laws are largely derived from model legislation drafted by the Australian Law Reform Commission in conjunction with its 1977 Report, *Human Tissue Transplants*.[22] They regulate issues such as blood and tissue donation by live adults and children, post-mortem examinations and the removal of tissue and organs from the deceased. They also prohibit the trade in human tissue. Scientific developments in the areas of tissue and organ donation, genetics and human reproduction have led to discussions as to how these laws might best be updated to keep up with contemporary needs, and various amendments have ensued.[23] This is typical of trends worldwide.[24]

---

19 *National Organ Transplant Act,* 42 USC § 274e (2002). This law is commonly referred to as "NOTA".
20 *Uniform Anatomical Gift Act,* 8A ULA 15 (1983). This law is known as "UAGA". For further details, see Table 1 in Robin S Shapiro, "Legal Issues in Payment of Living Donors for Solid Organs" (2002) 7 *Current Opinion in Organ Transplantation* 375.
21 See, eg, the *Human Tissue Act 1983* (NSW), the *Human Tissue Amendment Act 1987* (NSW), and the *Human Tissue Regulation Act 2000* (NSW), the *Transplantation and Anatomy Act 1979* (Qld), the *Transplantation and Anatomy Act 1983* (SA), the *Human Tissue Act 1985* (Tas) the *Human Tissue Amendment Act 1987* (Tas), the *Human Tissue and Transplant Act 1982* (WA) and the *Anatomy Act 1930* (WA). The Victorian *Human Tissue Act 1982* was amended by the *Infertility Treatment Act 1995* and the *Human Tissue (Prescribed Institutions) Regulation 1997*. In the territories, these issues are governed by the *Human Tissue Transplant Act 1995* (NT) and the *Transplantation and Anatomy Act 1978* (ACT).
22 Australian Law Reform Commission, *Human Tissue Transplants*, Report No 7 (1977).
23 See, eg, the *Human Tissue Act 1983* (NSW), which was amended in response to Bret Walker SC, *Report of the Inquiry into Matters Arising from the Post-Mortem and Anatomical Examination Practices of the Institute of Forensic Medicine* (Sydney: NSW Department of Health, August 2001). Also referred to as the "Walker Report".
24 A summary of such responses is provided in D Gareth Jones and Kerry A Galvin, "Retention of Body Parts: Reflections from Anatomy" (2002) 115 *Journal of the New Zealand Medical Association* 1155.

As a market in kidneys and other human body parts grew, jurisdictions throughout the world introduced laws to regulate transplantation, and those with established laws have tended to strengthen their provisions to outlaw the sale of human organs and cover newly developing areas of concern.

For example, the Indian *Transplantation of Human Organs Act 1994* was passed in response to the country's notorious market in human body parts. In Indian states adopting the *Act*, organs were only permitted to be donated by a parent or sibling, or by unrelated donors if the state transplantation authorisation committee found that the person was donating purely as a result of emotional attachment to the patient and not for monetary or material gain.[25] The law outlawed trade in or transactions involving human organs, with penalties such as fines and prison terms for agents involved in such deals. Doctors found to have violated the law faced the suspension or cancellation of their medical practice licences. The *Act* also redefined "death" to include the point at which doctors certified a patient as brain stem dead (instead of the moment the heartbeat ceased), thus paving the way for more transplants from deceased people rather than living donors.[26]

Following numerous reports of a brisk trade in human kidneys in China, particularly from the sale of executed prisoners,[27] Chinese legislatures also started to ban the sale of human body parts. For example, the sale of human organs has been illegal in Shenzhen city in China's southern Guangdong province since 1 October 2003. The *British Medical Journal* quoted nephrologist and chair of the Hong Kong Medical Association

---

[25] Doctors have complained that the Act is not strict enough as this provides a loophole, allowing for abuse of the system. See, eg. Ganapati Mudur, "Kidney Trade Arrest Exposes Loopholes in India's Transplant Laws" (2004) 328 *British Medical Journal* 246:

> Dr Sangay Nagral, a gastrointestinal surgeon at the Jaslok Hospital, Mumbai ... said sections of the kidney transplantation community are, at best, turning a blind eye and, at worst, colluding with agents in organ trade. "It should be obvious to the committee about what's going on. There is probably collusion between the committee and the transplant surgeons, but they rationalise it, believing they're helping save lives," he said.

See also, Ganapati Madur, "Indian Doctors Debate Incentives for Organ Donors" (2004) 329 *British Medical Journal* 938.

[26] See report by G Nandan, "India Outlaws Trade in Human Organs" (1994) 308 *British Medical Journal* 1657.

[27] See, eg, Alexandra George, "Australian Woman Travels to China for Executed Man's Kidney", *Reuters*, 5 September 1990:

> Every year hundreds of Australians with kidney disease wait in vain for a transplant. Pauline Mak says she jumped the queue by flying to China to receive a kidney she was told had been taken from a Chinese criminal executed just hours earlier. Ignoring the advice of her doctor in Sydney and family concerns about ethics, the 54-year-old Hong Kong native took what she saw as her last chance for a decent life. "They executed the prisoner and that is a fact nothing can change. Why not utilise that to save other people?" said Pauline's husband, advertising executive S.T. Mak ... Despite official denials, there have been frequent reports in Beijing about such practices. According to one report, police were even willing to remove a kidney from a prisoner before execution. One Beijing health official declined to confirm the stories, saying only: "It is very hard to get organs."

The operation cost Mrs Mak AUD$10,000.

Organ Donation Registry, Dr Ho Chung-ping, as saying: "The central government has always said that it is forbidden to trade in human organs, but this law is putting that on paper."[28]

The Council of Europe has similarly approved a Protocol promoting organ and tissue donation, prohibiting financial gain from the donation of organs or tissue, and outlawing organ and tissue trafficking.[29]

The hegemonic view on this point is thus very clear: the sale of human body parts is unacceptable and illegal. Meanwhile, scientific and medical developments in other areas—such as the field of xenotransplantation, cloning and reproductive technologies—have inspired new policies and laws.

In the UK, for example, the Nuffield Council on Bioethics approved the use of pig organs (but excluded the use of primates organs) for transplantation into humans.[30]

In a separate development, the UK's *Human Tissue Act 1961* and the *Human Organ Transplants Act 1989* has been replaced by the *Human Tissue Act 2004*, with application in England, Wales, Northern Ireland and (in part) Scotland.[31] The new law arose from concerns about the removal, storage and use of organs and tissue from children at the Royal Bristol Infirmary and the Royal Liverpool Children's Hospital. Inquiries showed that body parts had been taken without proper consent, that the practice had been widespread, and that the laws covering this area were not comprehensive, clear or consistent.[32] The new law thus established the Human Tissue Authority to regulate activities involving tissue from both dead and live human bodies. It prohibited commercial dealings for the purposes of transplanting human material consisting of or including human cells, with the exception of gametes, embryos and, in effect,

---

[28] Jane Parry, "Chinese City Outlaws Sale of Human Organs" (2003) 327 *British Medical Journal* 520.
[29] *Additional Protocol to the Convention on Human Rights and Biomedicine Concerning Transplantation of Organs and Tissues of Human Origin* European Treaty Series No 186. See also Rory Watson, "European Parliament Tries to Stamp out Trafficking in Human Organs" (2003) 327 *British Medical Journal* 1009, reporting a European Directive making it a criminal offence for European Community citizens to travel abroad for purchase and transplantation of a kidney and introducing a minimum ten year prison term for anyone trafficking a person into the EC for non-consensual removal of his or her organs.
[30] Luisa Dillner, "Pig Organs Approved for Human Transplants" (1996) 312 *British Medical Journal* 657. For a discussion of the scientific and medical issues involved in transplanting pig organs into humans, see Robin A Weiss, "Science, Medicine, and the Future: Xenotransplantation" (1998) 317 *British Medical Journal* 931.
[31] This law received royal assent on 15 November 2004. Following the introduction of the new UK law, Scottish procedure will additionally be governed by the *Human Tissue (Scotland) Act*. This similarly makes provision for the removal and use of body parts, transplantation from dead and living donors, and for the removal of body parts from a dead person for the purposes of research, education, training, audit or post-mortem.
[32] See HM Inspector of Anatomy, *Isaacs Report: The Investigation of Events that Followed the Death of Cyril Mark Isaacs* (UK Department of Health, 12 May 2003) and *Explanatory Notes to the Human Tissue Act* 2004, ¶5. <http://www.opsi.gov.uk/acts/en2004/2004en30.htm> at 3 July 2005.

patented material.[33] It also defined "consent"[34] and restricted transplants of material from the body of a live donor to those situations in which no reward has been or will be given for the "donation". In doing so, the Act extended the ambit of statutory regulation of scientific research and medical procedures involving the use and transfer of material extracted from the human body. This should also be flexible enough to cover technological advances that are yet to be developed.

Other jurisdictions are similarly amending old laws or closing gaps where activities involving research or transplantation of human bodily products have previously been unregulated.

With much current research involving the use of human embryos and embryonic stem cells,[35] this has been an area of particular legislative attention. A multitude of laws now regulates cloning, embryonic and foetal research in the United States. While no federal legalisation bans cloning, federal funding is not granted for the purposes of research involving human cloning. Numerous state laws address the issues, but they do so in highly variable ways. For example, some states allow research on aborted foetuses or embryos with the consent of the donor; nearly half the states restrict the sale of foetuses or embryos; Louisiana prohibits research on in-vitro fertilised embryos; Illinois and Michigan prohibit research on live embryos; and Nebraska will not permit state funds to be used for embryonic stem cell research. Several states prohibit research on cloned embryos, while others prohibit reproductive cloning but allow cloning for research.[36] The variability of the laws governing this topic within the United States alone is indicative of the unsettled nature of the perspectives, policy and state of technology affecting issues such as cloning and embryonic research.

As in the United States, Australian states have introduced numerous acts, regulations and guidelines, dealing with fertility treatments and reproductive technologies, since the 1980s.[37] In December 2002, Australia's

---

33 *Human Tissue Act 2004*, s32.
34 On 28 June 2004, the UK Parliament's House of Commons debated the proposed legislation in the form of the Human Tissue Bill 2004 (UK). The debate was primarily about the question of consent to donate organs, and included a lengthy discussion about "presumed consent" or "opt out" policies. It also covered the issue of how to treat "residual" or "remnant" tissue (that is, tissue removed lawfully from living patients in the course of diagnosis or surgical investigation) for the purposes of education, training and research. See 423 UK *Hansard* 109, 27–124. These are issues that had not been comprehensively covered by the 1961 legislation.
35 For a summary of the state of research in this area, see Peter Braude, Stephen L Minger and Ruth M Warwick, "Stem Cell Therapy: Hope or Hype?" (2005) 330 *British Medical Journal* 1159.
36 For an overview of the laws, see National Conference of State Legislatures, "State Embryonic and Fetal Research Laws" (2005). This summary provides a useful table summarising state law concerning embryonic and foetal research: <http://www.ncsl.org/programs/health/genetics/embfet.htm> at 1 July 2005. For related information about state legislation concerning the treatment of frozen embryos, see National Conference of State Legislatures, "State Laws and Legislation: use, Storage and Disposal of Frozen Embryos" (2004): <http://www.ncsl.org/programs/health/embryodisposition.htm> at 1 July 2005.
37 See, eg, *Infertility Treatment Act 1995* (Vic), *Infertility Treatment Regulations 1997* (Vic) and *Infertility Treatment (Amendment) Act 1997* (Vic); *Reproductive Technology Act 1988* (SA),

Federal Parliament passed the *Prohibition of Human Cloning Act 2002* and the *Research Involving Human Embryos Act 2002*. These laws took effect in January 2003, establishing a strict framework to prevent human cloning and regulating research on surplus human embryos that had been created during the procedures involved in assisted reproduction. Notably, by 2005 the new legislation was already under review by the "Independent Committee to Review Human Cloning and Embryo Research Legislation". The terms of reference for this Committee included investigating the scope and operation of the laws in light of scientific and medical developments, and reporting back to the Australian Parliament with recommendations about amendments that should be made to the existing laws.[38] Again, the unsettled character of the issues covered by this area of law making are obvious.

Similar dilemmas are being confronted worldwide. Noting that the "transplantation of human cells and tissues is a strongly expanding field of medicine offering great opportunities for the treatment of as yet incurable diseases," a 2004 EC Directive set standards concerning the donation, procurement, use and distribution of human tissues and cells.[39] In addition, Italy's controversial and much-publicised Law 40/2004 introduced regulations concerning medically assisted reproduction. This statute prohibits oocyte and sperm donation, as well as forbidding the cryopreservation of embryos. It also bans medical research on human embryos (such as genetic cloning, eugenic procedures and blending the genes of humans with those from other species) and reproductive cloning.[40] The Italian legislation arose in a particular political climate in which the views of the Roman Catholic Church added an important dimension to debate over how the use of human body parts for research, reproduction and medical therapies should be regulated. As will be seen below, religious and other moral viewpoints can play an influential—if not particularly "liberal"—role in swaying public opinion and policy towards scientific and medical uses of human bodily material.

The laws just surveyed represent just a tiny sample of those affecting the scientific and medical use of human body parts throughout the world. However, they are reasonably representative of those that can be found in

---

Reproductive Technology Code of Ethical Clinical Practices 1995 (SA) and *Reproductive Technology Code of Ethical Research Practice 1995* (SA); *Human Reproductive Technology Act 1991* (WA), *Technology Council (Nominating Bodies) Regulations 1992* (WA) and *Artificial Conception Act 1985* (WA); and *Artificial Conception Act 1985* (ACT).

38 Australian Government National Health and Medical Research Council, "Independent Committee to Review Human Cloning and Embryo Research Legislation" (Press Release, 17 June 2005).

39 *Directive 2004/23/EC of the European Parliament and Council of 31 March 2004 on setting standards of quality and safety for the donation, procurement, testing, processing, preservation, storage and distribution of human tissues and cells*, Official Journal of the European Union (OJ) L series, 102 Fascicle 48, 7.4.2004. Quoting Preamble ¶1.

40 For further details of the law, see Andrea Boggio, "Italy Enacts New Law on Medically Assisted Reproduction" (2005) 20 *Human Reproduction* 1153–57.

most jurisdictions in which legislation about the scientific or medical use of human body parts has been pronounced. This is revealing as it shows that the laws that have been adopted tend to prohibit the compensated alienation of most human body parts, though non-essential or easily regenerable body parts such as blood, hair and sperm are exceptions in some jurisdictions (particularly in the United States). The laws also tend to regulate who can donate human organs and tissue, and in what circumstances (e.g. among living donors, it is common for only relatives or those with demonstrable emotional bonds to be permitted to donate). These principles have been instituted by those who reject the notion of a legal market in human body parts, but they are increasingly challenged by others who believe that a legal market would provide a way of overcoming the chronic shortfall of body parts needed for therapeutic transplantation and scientific research.

It is to this debate that we now turn.

III. The Case against Legalising the Market in Human Body Parts

The normative legal approach to the sale of human body parts in liberal democratic societies is therefore one of prohibition. It is usual for living individuals to be allowed to donate non-essential or regenerable body parts and for body parts to be harvested from cadaveric donors. Sometimes cadaveric harvesting occurs through a state policy of assumed donor consent in which people are taken to have agreed to the post-mortem harvesting of their body parts unless they had taken the required steps to opt out of the system during their lifetimes.[41] It is uncommon for the sale of human body parts to be permitted,[42] although it is not unusual for jurisdictions to have enacted legal prohibitions only after reports of exploitation.[43]

---

41 This is the situation in many countries such as Belgium, Spain, France and Italy. In 1999, the British Medical Association voted to adopt an opt-out policy (policy of presumed consent) for the donation of human organs. See "BMA Backs 'Opt Out' Organ Donation" (1999) *Guardian Unlimited*: <http://www.guardian.co.uk/racism/Story/0,2763,206328,00.html> at 19 June 2005. The system was introduced in Brazil in an attempt to end corruption on official waiting lists and problems of a black market trade in body parts. Many people opted-out due to fear that their deaths could be accelerated by others intent on harvesting their organs. See, eg, Nancy Scheper-Hughes, "The New Cannibalism": "I am not a donor of organs or tissues . . . We were always afraid of crazy drivers, but now we have to worry about ambulance workers who may be paid to declare us 'dead' before our time is really up," said Seu Jose, a house painter: < http://pascalfroissart.online.fr/3-cache/1998-scheperhughes.pdf > at 29 June 2005.
42 Interestingly, by November 1997, the sale of human body parts was still permitted in several states in India where the national 1994 legislation (*Organ Transplantation Act 1994*) outlawing the sale of human body parts had not yet been adopted. See *TED Case Study on the trade of human body parts in India by the Mandala Projects*, (1997): <http://www.american.edu/projects/mandala/TED/KIDNEY.HTM> at 19 June 2005.
43 For example, India's *Organ Transplantation Act* responded to calls for legislation to stem the exploitation of poor Indians. Examples of reported cases included Indians travelling overseas to sell kidneys to foreigners, Indian leprosy patients selling kidneys through agents, and the removal of kidneys from unsuspecting patients in a Bangalore city hospital.

As with prohibition policies generally, the fact that a behaviour is proscribed by law does not mean that it will not occur, and a trade in human organs, tissue, sperm and ova persists nonetheless.[44]

International organisations have made pronouncements against the trade—and particularly the international trade—in human body parts. For example, in 1985 the World Medical Association condemned the purchase and sale of human organs for transplantation. It did so in "due consideration of the fact that in the recent past a trade of considerable financial gain has developed with live kidneys from underdeveloped countries for transplantation in Europe and the United States of America," and it called on governments worldwide to take steps to prevent the commercial use of human organs.[45] At least in societies that consider themselves to be modern liberal democracies, the hegemonic viewpoint has been that the sale of human body parts should be prohibited. Like the unanimous view of United Nations members that there should be a total ban on the creation of cloned human babies,[46] this attitude is underpinned by arguments that it is necessary to forbid the sale of human body parts in order to avoid exploitation, the sale of body parts without true consent—accentuating wealth inequalities—commodification of humanity and slavery, and moral repugnance. Each of these justifications implicates core tenets of liberal philosophy and merits analysis.

A. Avoid Exploitation

The avoidance of exploitation is one of the most pervasive and influential of the arguments against allowing the sale of human body parts. Fear of

---

See, eg, ibid at 2. The British Parliament amended the *Human Tissue Act 1961* after the "kidney for cash" scandal in 1990. See report by the Mandala Project, *Human Body Parts Trade TED Case Study* (1996): <http://www.american.edu/projects/mandala/TED/BODY.HTM> at 19 June 2005.

44 See, eg, Deborah Josefson, "Two Arrested in US for Selling Organs for Transplantation" (1998) 316 *British Medical Journal* 723; Helmut L Karcher, "German Doctors Protest Against 'Organ Tourism'" (1996) 313 *British Medical Journal* 1282; and Judy Siegel-Itzkovich, "Israel Investigates Organ Sales" (1996) 313 *British Medical Journal* 1167.

45 *World Medical Association Statement on Live Organ Trade*, Adopted by the 37th World Medical Assembly (Belgium; 1985). See also the UNHCR report: Office of the United Nations High Commissioner for Human Rights 1996–2000, *Rights of the Child: Sale of Children, Child Prostitution and Child Pornography; Report submitted by V Muntarbhorn, Special Rapporteur, in accordance with Commission on Human Rights resolution 1993/82*: <http://www.unhchr.ch/Huridocda/Huridoca.nsf/TestFrame/3662c5c8967c4768802567320064762f?Opendocument> at 29 June 2005.

46 Andy Coghlan, "Global Therapeutic Cloning Ban Averted", *New Scientist Online News*, (2003): <http://www.newscientist.com/article.ns?id=dn4471> at 29 June 2005, noting the ongoing debate about the ethics of therapeutic and non-therapeutic cloning. The ban on the cloning of human babies is partly due to health and safety fears because cloned animals have tended to suffer from a higher-than-normal variety of medical problems. It is also a result of ethical concerns about allowing a new eugenics in which "designer babies" are the goal. See, Philip Cohen, "Plan to Make Cloning Safe Set Out", *New Scientist Online News* (2003) <http://www.newscientist.com/article.ns?id=dn4334> at 29 June 2005, outlining the risks of cloning and the need to obtain funding to develop safe methods of cloning.

For a detailed discussion of the ethical issues surrounding human tissue cloning, see John A Robertson, "Procreative Liberty in the Era of Genomics" (2003) 29 *American Journal of Law and Medicine* 439–87.

exploitation has been reinforced by experiences in jurisdictions and contexts in which body parts have been permitted to be exchanged for money or the illicit trade in human body parts has not been successfully halted.[47] With the onset of the biotech revolution, the scope for exploitative harvesting of human body parts has been extended. An example is the collection of oocytes (human eggs) from attractive, intelligent female students attending Ivy League colleges in the United States in return for funds with which to pay for their educations.[48] At first glance, the profiles of such donors seem vastly different from those of illiterate rural workers in developing nations who feel compelled to sell their kidneys, but the vulnerability of both groups in their respective societies may be a common factor. Both groups of donors see the sale of a body part as a means—albeit a risky and intrusive one—of obtaining money with which to better their lives and opportunities.

The anxiety is that poverty, need and insecurity will be exploited by body part marketeers who will prey upon the poorest, most vulnerable members of (the global) society,[49] and upon those with the fewest alternative options.[50] Marketeers exploit and reinforce financial inequalities by offering to exchange money for the body parts of the people who most require assistance to raise their living standards. The dichotomous stereotypes of rich and poor, North and South, East and West, First World and Third World, could be reinforced by the invidious exploitation of need. These are scenarios that the Opponents of the sale of human body parts seek to prevent.[51]

---

[47] See, eg, *Extreme Research*, a website documenting research by Nancy Scheper-Hughes and Lawrence Cohen into the sale of human body parts: <http://www.berkeley.edu/news/magazine/summer_99/feature_darkness_scheper.html> at 7 September 2004. Quoting Cohen, it states:
> Crippling debt, he said, has villagers in India lined up to sell kidneys to underground brokers even though it's against the law to provide a kidney to anyone but a relative. The villagers approach the brokers, usually after failing to repay a loan. When loan sharks demand repayment, villagers have no choice but to sell their own kidneys.

[48] For a discussion of the methods and risks involved in oocyte donation, see Curtin E Harris, "To Solve a Deadly Shortage: Economic Incentives for Human Organ Donation" (2001) 16 *Issues in Law and Medicine* 213–33, 230–31. Harris reports advertisements for oocyte donation appearing in Ivy League newspapers, and comments: "Opponents of an organ market point to the current trend of oocyte donation: most are from students at private colleges who are receiving little financial help from family. These women see donation as their only way to cope with the rising costs of a quality education." (231)

[49] Nancy Scheper-Hughes, "Postmodern Cannibalism (Black Market Trade of Human Organs)" (Summer 2000) *Whole Earth*. The article is subtitled: "Organ transplants in the **globalocal** market" (emphasis added).

[50] It is not only the vendors/donors who face limited options, and patients waiting in hope of receiving a life-saving or health-giving transplant may also be exploited in such transactions. A bitter example of exploitation of one such patient was reported in 2001. A Canadian paid for a kidney transplant in India but, upon his return to Canada with poor kidney function, doctors conducted an ultrasound examination and found no evidence of a transplanted kidney (even though the patient had a large scar on his abdomen). See David Spurgeon, "Canadians Seek Kidney Transplants in Poor Countries" (2001) 322 *British Medical Journal* 1446.

[51] See, eg., HumanRightsWatch/Asia Report, 2: because the poor are "induced to sell

An important premise supporting this argument is that any situation in which people alienate parts of their bodies and sell them to other people is presumptively exploitative. This rests on an assumption that rational people would not sell parts of themselves unless their financial needs were so great that they surpassed their needs for health. The sale of a body part in such circumstances might seem to be the most rational option for someone stricken by poverty,[52] but harvesting body parts from indigent people is considered to be exploitative as it physically internalises their poverty. That is, the environmental conditions of poverty that might drive a person to sell a kidney are physically internalised when that person adopts personal responsibility and tries to lessen the effects of poverty by selling an intrinsic—though presumably not imperative—part of his or her body. This fear is entwined with perceptions about the quality of consent that can be made under such conditions.[53]

Regardless of the issue of consent, the Opponents of a legal market consider the sale of body parts to be presumptively exploitative. Those who consider such choices are likely to have large debts and/or limited financial options,[54] and they are likely to be put at further financial risk if removal of a body part incapacitates them. Third World slum dwellers

---

their body parts to meet the transplant needs of high-paying customers, largely from the developed countries, (the trade in human organs) has been widely condemned because of its financially exploitative nature and its abuse of medical ethics." Cited at the American University's Mandala Project website, documenting a case study into the "India Kidney Trade" at <http://www.american.edu/projects/mandala/TED/KIDNEY.HTM> at 29 June 2005. See also *Extreme Research*, above n 47: "The exchanges tend to be poor-to-rich," said Scheper-Hughes. On the black market in India, added Cohen, an impoverished person's kidney, destined for an affluent Indian, can fetch $1,000. "I call it neo-cannibalism," said Scheper-Hughes, "the notion that we can eye each other greedily as a source of spare body parts."
52 J R Richards, "Nephrarious Goings On: Kidney Sales and Moral Arguments" (1996) 21 *Journal of Medicine and Philosophy* 4, 375, 386:
> If the rich who take risks for pleasure or danger money are not misguided, it is difficult to see why the poor, who propose to take risks for higher return, should be regarded as so manifestly irrational as to need saving from themselves. You might think . . . that the poorer you were the more rational it would be to risk selling a kidney.

Cited in Barnett II, Saliba and Walker, above n 9, 381.
53 See discussion in Part IIIB below.
54 See, eg., the reasons given by a random selection of people advertising to sell a kidney: Bobba Venkat Reddy from Rentachintala mandal in the Guntur district of Andhra Pradesh, India, was one of 26 villagers who each sold a kidney to repay debts after receiving poor prices for their crops (V Sridhar, "Distress and Kidney Sale", *Frontline* (2004) 21, 19. <http://www.flonnet.com/fl2113/stories/20040702005901800.htm> at 29 June 2005; "Kantibhai", also from India, is a disabled father of three children who advertised on the internet to sell one of his or his disabled wife's kidneys to help relieve their debts ("Kidney for Sale: Handicapped. Deep in debt. Desperate. Couple offers kidney to highest bidder" *Rediff Guide to the Net* <http://www.rediff.com/search/2002/jan/08kidney.htm> at 29 June 2005; Pauline Williams, a 51 year old pensioner from New Zealand, tried to sell a kidney to pay off her credit card debts. See "Beneficiary wants to sell kidney to pay debt", New Zealand Embassy, *Digest Reports from Mainstream Media* April–June 1999: <http://www.embassy.org.nz/news/digst99c.htm#KIDNEY> at 29 June 2005; and Mike Russel, a 30 year old army officer from Yugoslavia, says he wants to sell a kidney to raise money for his five year old child's heart operation "Kidney for sale, please help me": <http://www.4burialinsurance.com/wwwboard/messages/260.html> at 2001.

would not have the capacity to purchase kidneys or corneas if theirs failed. The First World poor who are not covered by adequate health insurance or a social security safety net might not be much better off. A needy body part vendor who remains healthy is fortunate; one who becomes ill is likely to end up in a far worse situation than before the body part was alienated and is unlikely to have the resources to purchase a life-saving body part in turn from another vendor. Hence, the Opponents conclude, the sale of human body parts is exploitative and should be prohibited.[55]

Fear of exploitation also underpins many of the other arguments against the sale of human body parts, such as exploitation as a result of lack of adequate knowledge or exploitation as a result of lack of consent. These could be described as *secondary* forms of exploitation and will be outlined below.

B. Avoid the Sale of Body Parts without True Consent

Just as those who argue against euthanasia may invoke fears that the elderly will be "killed off" by avaricious friends or relatives[56] who wish to inherit their possessions and/or be relieved of the burden of caring for them, those who argue against a market in human body parts fear that people with ulterior motives might induce the naive or vulnerable to sell body parts in conditions of less than perfect information.[57] It is strongly arguable that a person who sells a body part, without fully understanding the risks involved in the procedure and its consequences has not truly consented to the operation. Likewise, if a person is placed under persuasive moral pressure to sell (or even donate) a body part, the quality of his or her consent to the operation is dubious. Lack of consent implies coercion.

The risk of coercion is a fundamental objection by the Opponents to a market in human body parts. It can be seen to fall into two basic categories: strong and weak coercion, and each deserves thoughtful consideration.

1. Strong Coercion

If a person is physically forced to donate or sell a body part against his or her will, it is a case of *strong coercion*.[58] Such a scenario would arise if a person was kidnapped and sedated and, while unconscious, underwent an operation in which a kidney or other body part was removed without the victim's express or implied consent. This sort of behavior would involve the crimes of unlawful detention or imprisonment, and assault and battery,

---

55 See further discussion in Part IIIC and IIID below.
56 Ronald Dworkin, *Life's Dominion: On Abortion and Euthanasia* (1993) 197, discounts this argument: "Another familiar argument against legalizing euthanasia for conscious people—that old people are vulnerable and can sometimes be persuaded into asking to die—makes the same mistake: it fails to recognize that forcing people to live who genuinely want to die causes serious damage to them."
57 See, eg., Karlheinz Engelhardt, et al, "Correspondence: Organ Donation and Permanent Vegetative State" (1998) 351 *Lancet* 9097. Several correspondents alluded to euthanasia during Nazi and other totalitarian regimes in these letters to the editor in response to an article arguing that organs should be harvested from permanently vegetative people who it has been determined will be allowed to die.
58 Barnett II, Saliba and Walker, above n 9, 382.

and it would be punishable even if the sale of human body parts were to be legalised. Reports of kidnappings of this sort circulate regularly, and authorities repeatedly discount these stories as hoaxes.[59] However, behind the urban myth, cases of "organ theft" have been documented and do involve unacceptable, strong coercion. For example, a Brazilian woman who discovered her kidney had been removed when she was undergoing surgery for the removal of an ovarian cyst did not consent to the "donation" of her organ,[60] and it is her lack of consent that makes this an example of strong coercion.

Indeed, it could be argued that its denial of autonomous decision-making authority over the body—and the associated alienation and loss of identity that this implies—might be akin to slavery, with all the further legal and moral implications that this would entail.[61]

Similar arguments are arising in the context of whether or not "therapeutic babies" (children conceived for the purpose of providing body parts to help or save another human being, and genetically engineered to ensure their biological compatibility for these purposes) should be allowed to be created. The Opponents to a market in human body parts typically say "no", because the therapeutic baby is unable to consent to the procedure. National authorities are currently divided over the ethics of such treatment[62] and, in effect, the concern is that allowing

---

[59] See Red Cross Australia's information about the kidnap myth: "A famous urban myth involves a man who goes to a party and has too much to drink. He wakes up the next day in a bathtub full of ice, with a wound in his side and one of his kidneys missing. This myth has been in circulation since the 1980s and is, of course, not true" <http://www.organ.redcross.org.au/f_faq.html#5> at 29 June 2005. See also the statement by the City of New Orleans Department of Police on 30 January 1997:

> Over the past six months the New Orleans Police Department has received numerous inquiries from corporations and organizations around the United States warning travelers about a well organized crime ring operating in New Orleans. This information alleges that this ring steals kidneys from travelers, after they have been provided alcohol to the point of unconsciousness. After an investigation into these allegations, the New Orleans Police Department has found them to be *completely without merit and without foundation*. The warnings that are being disseminated through the Internet are *fictitious* and may be in violation of criminal statutes concerning the issuance of erroneous and misleading information. [emphasis in original]

<http://www.mardigrasday.com/police1.html> at 29 June 2005. A history of the myth can be found at the *Urban Legends Reference Pages*: <http://www.snopes2.com/horrors/robbery/kidney.htm> at 29 June 2005.

[60] Nancy Scheper-Hughes, "Commodity Fetishism in Organ Trafficking" in Nancy Scheper-Hughes and Loïc Wacquant, eds, *Commodifying Bodies* (2002) 31, 36–37.

[61] Bonnie Steinbock, "Sperm as Property: In the Absence of a Compelling Argument against Posthumous Reproduction, Individual Autonomy Should Prevail" (1995) 6 *Stanford Law and Policy Review* 57, 65.

[62] Shaoni Bhattacharya, "Five 'Designer Babies' Created for Stem Cells" (5 May 2004) *New Scientist Online News*, <http://www.newscientist.com/article.ns?id=dn4965> at 29 June 2005, referring to an article in 291 *Journal of the American Medical Association* 2079. The article reports the birth of five babies conceived to provide stem cells for siblings with serious non-heritable conditions. The babies' embryos were tested for a tissue type match to their siblings, using a technique called preimplantation genetic diagnosis. The children were born in the United States. In one case, a UK couple travelled to the US for treatment after the UK's Human Fertilisation and Embryology Authority ruled they could not use tissue

such procedures would require the toleration of the strong coercion of the therapeutic baby. It would also amount to strong coercion if a child,[63] a person with an intellectual disability, or a person deemed to be incompetent to make informed decisions were to have body parts removed and sold.[64] Clear problems of consent arise in the case of anencephalic infants—babies born without brains but with a brain stem—that have no hope of surviving and who are obviously unable to consent to removal of their organs. Such difficulties are likely to increase rather than disappear as the biotechnological revolution creates ever greater opportunities for using the body parts that could be harvested from such infants.

Another example of strong coercion would arise if someone was tricked or deceived into selling a body part having been provided with misleading information about the procedure. The Opponents fear that brokers eager to close deals would not provide potential vendors of body parts with full or accurate information. For example, the removal of a kidney or cornea involves intrusive surgery and anaesthesia, and carries medical risks. The process involved in donating oocytes can also lead to complications. If providing adequate information might have the consequence of deterring a potential body part vendor, it could be in a broker's interest to err on the side of supplying less information. Decision making in such conditions could be assumed to be flawed and any uninformed "consent" would be invalid.[65] It is imperative for the protection of personal autonomy that people not agree to undergo such operations unless they are well informed

---

matching to create a compatible sibling for stem cell donation to their existing son.
63 This possibility is alluded to in: O Calcetas-Santos (United Nations High Commissioner for Human Rights, 29 January 1999) *The Report of the Special Rapporteur on the Sale of Children, Child Prostitution and Child Pornography*: <http://www.unhchr.ch/pdf/chr60/9AV.pdf> at 29 June 2005. *See also*, "The Corruptive Influence of the Dollar: The Shameful Trade in Mexican Baby Organs" *La Voz de Aztlan* <http://aztlan.net/organs.htm> at 29 June 2005; and Maria M. Morelli, *"Organ Trafficking: Legislative Proposals to Protect Minors"* (1995) 10 *American University Journal of International Law and Policy* 917–54. A report about children being used as sources for organs can be found at the website of PREDA (Peoples Recovery, Empowerment and Development Assistance Foundation Inc, a charitable human rights organization): Father Shay Cullen SSC, "Killing Children for Their Organs", 1 March 1995 <http://www.preda.org/archives/1993-94-95-96/r9503011.htm> at 29 June 2005, first published by the *Philippine Daily Inquirer*. A Columbia University Task Force found no reliable evidence that any such kidnappings had ever occurred: See, D J Rothman, et al, *The Bellagio Task Force Report on Transplantation, Bodily Integrity, and the International Traffic in Organs*, 1 January 1997, Part V <http://66.102.11.104/search?q=cache:sDnPKO-0kIcJ: www.icrc.org / Web / Eng / siteeng0.nsf / iwpList302 / 87DC95FCA3C3D63EC1256B660 05B3F6C+Bellagio+Task+Force+Report+on+Transplantation,+Bodily+Integrity,+an d+the+International+Traffic+in+Organs+&hl=en> at 29 June 2005.
64 Barnett II, Saliba and Walker, above n 9, 381 say this is occurring under the existing system of prohibition. The practical difficulties that can arise in such cases are illustrated by a report of the removal of a kidney from a deaf and mute Indian man who was incapable of communicating and who could not comprehend the procedure, and who was therefore not competent to give consent. His kidney was transplanted into his brother after a six week ethical debate, during which doctors evaluated the relationship between the potential donor and recipient, and took into account the family's poverty and absolute financial dependence on the transplant recipient. See Ganapati Mudur, "Doctors Take Kidney from Patient Incapable of Giving Consent" (20 March 1999) 318 *British Medical Journal* 753.
65 Ibid, 382.

about the likely and possible consequences of their decisions, and the Opponents' objection to the sale of a body part in such circumstances coincides with the principles of classical liberalism.

Opponents of a legitimate market in human body parts fear that strong coercion might become more common if body parts were freely available and/or it was harder to trace them to their sources. That strong coercion is incompatible with the fundamental tenets of liberal democratic society is indisputable, and the Opponents argue that it would surely remain unacceptable and illegal in an environment that hosted a legitimate market in human body parts. Whether it would become a more prevalent problem in such a market would be a matter for further inquiry and evidence.

2. Weak Coercion

Coercion need not be strong to deny a decision the quality of consent. It could be described as *weak coercion* if moral pressure were to be placed on a person to donate or sell a body part to help another person and if, without that pressure, the donor or vendor would not have undergone the operation to remove the body part. Another example of weak coercion would be a situation in which a person induced by poverty to sell a body part would not otherwise have done so. In each case, it is debatable how "true" the consent could be.[66]

(a) Weak Moral Coercion

Generosity towards a brother, sister or other family member might be encouraged and might even be regarded as a social duty.[67] Donations of body parts to sick relatives might be applauded. But altruistic voluntary generosity should be distinguished from coerced voluntary generosity. Regardless of whether coercion is weak or strong, the effect is similar because it detracts from the quality of the consent.[68] This is the case regardless of whether or not the decision is made to donate a body part to a relative, to sell a body part to a relative, or to sell a body part to raise money to help a relative. As the second and third of these scenarios are not legal options in most jurisdictions, opponents of the sale of human body parts fear that coercion would become more of a problem under market conditions because there would be more opportunities to engage in, and fewer penalties with which to punish, coercive behavior.[69]

---

[66] For a related discussion of the degrees of "voluntariness" among compensated and uncompensated blood donors, see Richard M Titmuss, *The Gift Relationship: From Human Blood to Social Policy* (1997) 8, 123ff.

[67] See, eg, the reasoning in *McFall v Shrimp* 10 Pa D&C (3d), (1978). See also Cara Cheyette, "Organ Harvests from the Legally Incompetent: An Argument against Compelled Altruism" (2000) 41 *Boston College Law Review* 465, 480–84.

[68] J K Mason and R A McCall Smith, *Law and Medical Ethics* (1991) 304, especially Chapter 14: "The Donation of Organs and Transplantation".

[69] This concern could also be justified in a system of "paired organ exchange", in which the relatives of two recipients donate to unrelated recipients in return for their family member receiving a compatible organ. The fear is that family members could no longer hide behind the excuse of biological incompatibility. See, eg, Cheyette, above n 67, 484, and discussion of paired organ exchanges in Michael T Morley, "Increasing the Supply of Organs for

(b) Weak Commercial Coercion

The third scenario just mentioned—moral pressure to sell a body part to raise money to support a relative—is entwined with the problem of weak commercial coercion in which the donor's motivation is dominated by the lure of financial gain.

A preliminary (and frequently unstated) assumption in discussions about commercially motivated transfers of body parts is that only those in desperate financial need would enter into a contract to sell a body part. Such commercially motivated donors are characterised by G P Smith as *forced donors*. By definition, forced donors are financially vulnerable people who are "forced as such by their own circumstances and coerced by enticement of affluent buyers" to sell or "lease" out a body part.[70] Opponents of a legal market suggest that forced donors lack reliable decision-making capability due to their social and/or economic circumstances: "It is said that they are likely to be too uneducated to understand the risks, and that this precludes informed consent. It is also claimed that, since they are coerced by their economic circumstances, their consent cannot count as genuine."[71]

While it does seem unlikely that wealthy people would offer to sell body parts as readily as those who have an urgent need for funds, the possibility that a wealthy person might wish to donate a body part in return for monetary compensation should not be ignored. Yet it is rarely (if ever) considered, and nor is the scenario of a person who is prepared to donate free of charge but who would prefer to be paid. In effect, therefore, the motivation for the donation is treated as an irrelevance when money enters the equation. When this approach is taken, all sales of human body parts are considered to be *exchanges of desperation*,[72] and the Opponents seek to block such exchanges on the basis that the lack of true consent involved in the transaction has deprived the donor of full liberal autonomy.

Arguing along similar lines, Joel Feinberg describes transactions involving forced donors as *coercive*. The donor prefers the anticipated outcome of a decision to alienate a body part in such conditions (that is, a financial benefit) over the anticipated outcome of the alternative, which is not to sell a body part.[73] Although the opportunity to enter into the contract enlarges the range of options available to the potential donor, it simultaneously places such people in a position in which the quality of their consent must be suspect. This can be more clearly illustrated by a hypothetical example. Before the offer to buy her kidney, Maria had one

---

Transplantation Through Paired Organ Exchanges" (2003) 21 *Yale Law and Policy Review* 221.
70 G P Smith, "Market and Non-Market Mechanisms for Producing Human and Cadaveric Organs: When the Price is Right" (1993) 1 *Medical Law International* 17, 25.
71 J Radcliffe-Richards, et al (For the International Forum of Transplant Ethics), "The Case for Allowing Kidney Sales" (27 June 1998) *Lancet* 351:9120, 352.
72 For an explanation of "exchanges born of desperation" see Michael Walzer, *Spheres of Justice: A Defense of Pluralism and Equality* (1983) 100. See also A Okun, *Equality and Efficiency: The Big Tradeoff* (1975) 6ff, and referred to by Walzer.
73 Joel Feinberg, *The Moral Limits of the Criminal Law: Harm to Self* (1986) 3, 23, 189ff.

option: poverty. She now perceives that she has two options: (a) poverty, or (b) poverty moderated by income from sale of the body part.[74] Where the decision-making context is desperate, the long term risks associated with donation of a body part seem low and the immediate gain seems high, it can be queried how problematic a choice this is. Is it really an exchange of desperation?

Alan Wertheimer cautions that we should not assume that "hard circumstances constitute a defect in consent."[75] Indeed, when a fully informed donor takes empirical long-term health risks into account, the strength of that donor's resolve is perhaps emphasised even when the resolve is driven by a need or desire for money. This can be illustrated by another hypothetical example. Suppose Mark is poor and unemployed, and his son needs an operation that Mark cannot afford. Without the operation, his son is expected to die; with it, the child is likely to live a healthy life. The operation and related expenses will cost $50,000, and Mark has exhausted all other legal options for raising the money. Then Mark is offered $50,000 in return for the "donation" of one of his kidneys. If he were financially comfortable, he would not accept the offer. But his choice, as he perceives it, is between his son's life and one of his two kidneys. Mark chooses to accept the offer and donate the body part. It is arguable that Mark has not been *coerced* into donating anything; it was an autonomous decision. But it was a decision that responded to a choice between two unappealing options, and one alternative was too costly to be considered seriously when there was an alternative. One option was unacceptable and the other was unfavourable, and Mark freely chose the unfavourable over the unacceptable.[76] It could be argued that his decision was informed, and rational in the circumstances. But it is nonetheless a choice that the Opponents of a market in human body parts would prefer Mark was forbidden from making. They would like to exclude the legally condoned possibility that a person is placed in a position to be able to make this choice.

---

74 Interestingly, a study into the effects of kidney sales by 305 impoverished Indian workers found that they tended to suffer financially and medically in the long-term. The interviewees were mainly labourers or vendors, 96% of whom said they had sold a kidney to pay off debts, and 3% of whom sold a kidney to provide dowries and marriage expenses for their daughters. The study found that the average payment was a third lower than the donor had been promised, and 74% (216 of 292) of those who sold a kidney to pay debts had remained in debt: Goyal Madhav, et al, "Economic and Health Consequences of Selling a Kidney in India" (2002) 288 *Journal of the American Medical Association* 1589. See also report in Deborah Josefson, "Selling a Kidney Fails to Rescue Indians from Poverty" (12 October 2002) 325 *British Medical Journal* 795.
75 Alan Wertheimer, *Exploitation* (1996).Wertheimer warns: "In particular, we should not elide the distinction between problems in one's objective circumstances or background conditions in which choices are made and problems in the quality of the choice that one is making given those background conditions." 270.
76 See, eg., Feinberg, *The Moral Limits of the Criminal Law: Harm to Self*, above n 73, 230–31. A comparison could be drawn with the situation of people who are desperate to earn a living and who therefore accept dangerous and/or demeaning jobs that they would not accept if they were in a better position to bargain or choose their work.

This opposition might be deepened by the documented experiences of numerous organ donors in countries such as India and the Philippines, where financial necessity has given rise to the remunerated donation of kidneys, corneas and other body parts.[77] The Indian experience includes stories of people selling kidneys to raise money to pay dowries for their unmarried daughters and sisters,[78] and mothers being "persuaded" to sell kidneys to repay loans they had taken to support their families.[79] Residents of Philippine shanty towns have similarly sold kidneys to raise money for the medical treatment of their children or to support their families.[80] Perhaps they submit willingly to the operations, but how real is the consent in such situations?

The Opponents must therefore address the effect that the exploitativeness of a non-coercive offer has on the voluntariness of the responsive consent.[81] In other words, can exploitation be reconciled with liberalism's fundamental principles of liberty and informed consent? Feinberg replies that the sort of offer accepted by Mark is a *freedom-enhancing coercive offer* because "one person can effectively force another person to do what he wants by manipulating his options in such a way as to render alternative choices ineligible."[82] Although he is coerced, the consent is real and the donor's choice is made autonomously. The donor's sincere preference is to alienate a body part. Regardless of the environment and social context in which the decision occurs, an ideally liberal society is bound to honour this application of self determination. But if the decision was ultimately coerced, it would remain an unacceptable and problematic scenario for the Opponents of a market in human body parts.

C. Avoid Accentuating Wealth Inequalities

Although it is probably a sub-category of the desires to avoid exploitation and coercion, the rationale of avoiding the accentuation of existing wealth

---

[77] See, eg., articles headed "Kidneys for sale" and "Losers all" on the website of the Indian Multi-Organ Harvesting Aid Network, a non-governmental organisation (NGO) seeking to encourage safe organ donation in India. It states:

> The Indian Medical Association (IMA) . . . said that it was an open secret that commercial transactions had been regularly taking place between patients suffering from chronic renal failure who needed kidney transplantation and the poor who were willing to sell their kidneys. All such transactions are illegal and punishable under the *Transplantation of Human Organs Act* (THOA) *1994*, but the buying and selling continues. In the process, the donor gets taken for a ride, gets paid a pittance and by the time he wakes up, it is too late.

<http://www.vish.com./html/body_mohan.html> at 2001.
[78] See, eg., above n 74.
[79] See *Extreme Research* website, above n 47.
[80] J Einar Sandvand, "Kidneys for Sale", AsiaObserver at <http://www.asiaobserver.com Phillippinealent to the circumstances of real-life Philippino father Satur Maico, reported in this article. It is also similar to the situation of Herbert Gibboney, who offered to sell one of his eyes for $35,000 to pay for an operation for his wife: "Man Desperate for Funds: Eye for Sale at $35,000", 1 February 1975 *LA Times* 1.
[81] See, eg., D Zimmerman, *Coercive Wage Offers* (1981) 10 *Philosophy & Public Affairs* 132 (Part II).
[82] Feinberg, *The Moral Limits of the Criminal Law: Harm to Self*, above n 73, 233.

inequalities also stands alone as an argument against the sale of human body parts. Bernard Dickens describes this as a sort of neo-Darwinian "survival of the richest"[83] in which the wealthy live healthier and longer at the expense of the poor. This claim suggests that the poor will sell their body parts to the rich and this will reinforce existing disparities. Like the Opponent's previous objections to the sale of human body parts, this assumes that impoverished people would be over-represented among organ and tissue vendors and that the state must intervene to protect the poor from selling their most personal of assets to the wealthy. Michael Walzer suggests that the reason for and/or effect of this type of state action is to "set limits on the dominance of wealth".[84]

The Opponents also fear that allowing the sale of body parts will lead to conditions in which organs such as kidneys will no longer be donated.[85] This would drive up prices so that only the wealthy would be able to afford transplantation.[86] Not only would most organ vendors be poor, but most recipients would be wealthy, and this would further accentuate social wealth inequalities.[87]

D. Avoid Commodification of the Body and Slavery

The anti-commodification argument appears frequently in the Opponents' objections to a market in human body parts.[88] Yet, as noted by H Hansmann, it "is difficult . . . to find a clear statement of precisely what is meant by commodification or why it is undesirable."[89] Stephen Wilkinson has suggested two meanings of this term,[90] and the difference between them helps to explain the uncertainty. The non-moral meaning of "commodification" offered by Wilkinson is roughly equivalent to Margaret

---

83 Bernard M Dickens, "Morals and Legal Markets in Transplantable Organs" (1994) 2 *Health Law Journal* 121, 129.
84 Walzer, above n 72, 100.
85 Edward W Nelson, et al, *Financial Incentives for Organ Donation: A Report of the United Network for Organ Sharing Ethics Committee*, 30 June 1993: <http://www.unos.org/Resources/bioethics.asp?index=3> at 29 June 2005.
86 Barnett II, Saliba and Walker, above n 9, 374
87 Ibid. But see a letter to the editor of the British Medical Journal proposing that the NHS (the UK's National Health Service) become the sole purchaser of live donated kidneys: Jeremy P Wight, "Proposal is Problematic" (12 October 2002) 325 *British Medical Journal* 835. Organs obtained in this way could then be distributed according to the same criteria as donated organs are currently allocated.
88 See, eg., comment by Rosalie Starzomski, ethics counsellor at Vancouver General Hospital and member of the Kidney Foundation of Canada's national organ donation committee, in response to a proposal to legalise kidney sales: "What this does is commodifies the body, and I think we should have some concern about that as a society . . . Once we do that—assign a price to an organ or a limb or whatever—where does that stop?" reported in C. Spencer, "Prominent Doctors Want to Legalize Kidney Sales: 'It's a . . . safe operation, it can save lives, so why not?'" *Ottawa Citizen* 4 July 1998.
89 H Hansmann, "The Economics and Ethics of Markets for Human Organs" (1989) 14 *Journal of Health Politics, Policy and Law* 57, reproduced in J H Robinson, R M Berry and K McDonnell, *A Health Law Reader: An Interdisciplinary Approach* (1999) 316ff, 324. See also discussion in Margaret Jane Radin, *Contested Commodities* (2001).
90 Stephen Wilkinson, *Bodies for Sale: Ethics and Exploitation in the Human Body Trade* (2003) 44ff.

Jane Radin's "narrow" construal of the term:[91] it refers to something that is legally permitted to be bought or sold. By contrast, the moral meaning of commodification involves objectification of the human body. It involves treating something that is not fungible (i.e., not a commodity that is interchangeable for another identical commodity, and that can therefore be replaced by an equivalent item to satisfy an obligation) as if it were fungible. This raises emotive concerns about treating humans and their body parts as acontextual objects that can be bought and sold without regard to the need for human dignity, and it invokes Immanuel Kant's principle that people are not means-to-ends and should be treated as ends-in-themselves.[92]

It seems likely that the anti-commodification view is, at least in part, a self-perpetuating product of existing social norms, including the above-given normative definitions. These norms also tend to link commodification of the human body to ownership of the body, and to link ownership of the body to notions of slavery.

This argument against slavery is deeply rooted in the history of the United States, and it is influential throughout the English-speaking world. Slaves were legally defined as property by legislatures in various American jurisdictions during the 18th century, and they could be bought, sold, taxed and inherited,[93] all of which seem incompatible with notions of liberal autonomy and the self determination of individuals. Thus, as Tony Honoré suggests "it has been thought undesirable that a person should alienate his body, skill or reputation, as this would be to interfere with human freedom. When human beings were regarded as alienable and ownable they were, of course, also regarded as being legally things."[94]

This fear of being regarded as a "thing" or "commodity"—the object rather than the subject of control over one's own body—frequently appears as an objection to "commodification" of the body.[95] This in turn serves as an objection to the sale of human body parts,[96] and it is a recurrent theme adopted by those who oppose human cloning[97] and some of the other possibilities being generated by the revolutionary breakthroughs in biotechnology and medical science.

---

91 Margaret Jane Radin, "Market-Inalienability", (1987) 100 *Harvard Law Review* 1859.
92 Immanuel Kant, *Foundations of the Metaphysics of Morals* (L Beck, trans., 1959) 47.
93 Ibid.
94 A M Honoré, "Ownership" in A G Guest (ed) *Oxford Essays in Jurisprudence* (1961) 107, 130.
95 See generally, Stephen R Munzer, *An Uneasy Case Against Property Rights in Body Parts* 259 in E Frankel Paul, F D Miller Jr and J Paul (eds) *Property Rights* (1994). This conflict is specifically addressed at 262.
96 See, eg, the arguments put by the opposition to a patent application before the European Patents Office in *Howard Florey/Relaxin* (1995) EPOR 451.
97 For a précis of the anti-commodification argument in relation to human cloning, see Wesley Chang, "Arrested Development: Patent Laws, Embryonic Stem Cell Research, and the Organ Black Market" (2004) 10 *Southwestern Journal of Law and Trade in the Americas* 407, 427–31.

E. Avoid Moral Repugnance

The related argument that it is morally repugnant to allow people to sell their body parts is another central pillar of the Opponents' case.

The Australian public was reported to express almost universal disapproval of the sale of human organs in 1977.[98] More recent surveys suggest that although more than half of the United States' population would support the notion of compensated donation of human body parts, a large proportion still disapproves. By 1993, only 12 per cent of Americans polled said they would be more likely to "donate" body parts if there were financial incentives to do so.[99] Such figures perhaps suggest that although moral repugnance is far from universal, it remains an important justification for a prohibition on the sale of human body parts.[100]

Two different objects of repugnance can be identified in the debate about whether or not to legitimise the sale of human body parts: repugnance about the sale of pieces of humans and repugnance about the circumstances of such transactions.

Repugnance about the alienation of parts of human beings is recognised as a reason why people decide not to bequeath their organs for transplant after their deaths, and why they decide not to allow the organs of deceased relatives to be harvested for donation.[101] This viewpoint is promoted by some religions,[102] and it can also occur as an emotional or religious response

---

[98] Australian Law Reform Commission, *Human Tissue Transplants*, above n 22, 85, ¶174. Though this report did not say if disapproval was moral, it can probably be assumed it was as the term *disapproval* would tend to imply moral wrongness, while the words *support/not support* would probably have been used in a carefully worded survey to suggest a more reasoned or less emotive judgment.

[99] The Gallup Organization, Inc, *The American Public's Attitudes toward Organ Donation and Transplantation*, a survey for the Partnership for Organ Donation (1993) <http://www.transweb.org/reference/articles/gallup_survey/gallup_chap7.html> at 29 June 2005.

[100] Barnett II, Saliba and Walker, above n 9, 383.

[101] This is implicitly recognised by the Australian Red Cross Blood Service's information about the donation of an organ:

> Will donation disfigure my body? Can there be an open casket funeral? Organ/tissue donation does not disfigure the body. Organ donation surgery results in an incision line and stitches just like any other operation. This is covered with a dressing. There are no other visible signs of the operation. It does not interfere with funeral plans, including open casket services.

<http://www.organ.redcross.org.au/f_faq.html> at 29 June 2005.

[102] The Australian Red Cross Blood Service co-ordinates Australian donations of human body parts and notes the religious implications of alienating a body part in its list of Frequently Asked Questions (FAQ) <http://www.organ.redcross.org.au/where.html> at 29 June 2005. It refers inquiries to an American site operated by the US Department of Health and Human Services that summarises the views of major religions towards organ/tissue donation: <http://www.organdonor.gov/denomination.html> at 7 September 2004. See also A R Gatrad, "Muslim Customs Surrounding Death, Bereavement, Postmortem Examinations, and Organ Transplants" (1994) 309 *British Medical Journal* 521; Gary Goldsand, Zahava R S Rosenberg and Michael Gorden, "Bioethics for Clinicians: 22. Jewish Bioethics" (2001) 164 *Canadian Medical Association Journal* 218; and The Bioethics Advisory Committee, The Israel Academy of Sciences and Humanities, "The Use of Embryonic Stem Cells for Therapeutic Research" (2001) <http://www.academy.ac.il/bioethics/english/report1/Report1-e.html> at 17 July 2005.

The Gallup poll of *The American Public's Attitudes toward Organ Donation and Transplantation*,

to the prospect of one's loved one being disfigured or mutilated prior to a funeral and burial.[103]

The other category of repugnance about the sale of human body parts refers to feelings of abhorrence about the circumstances in which such sales occur. These allude to the scenarios raised above in the arguments against exploitation, coercion, the accentuation of social inequalities, slavery, and the commodification of humanity. It adds a moral dimension to these arguments by suggesting that they are not only unacceptable because of the inequalities they produce or reproduce: they are also morally *wrong*.

Thus repugnance becomes an argument in itself. Regardless of whether it is the sale or the conditions of the sale that cause feelings of disgust, it is the strength of the moral judgment that counts against the sale of human body parts.[104]

Although it is generally inconsistent with the liberal principle of moral neutrality to base decisions on moral justifications, this does not undermine the practical influence of moral arguments. In 1989, one of "the most tenacious defenders of the free market, (then) Prime Minister Margaret Thatcher, declared that the sale of any organs of the human body is repugnant."[105] This statement was a reaction to reports that a Turkish peasant had sold a kidney to an Englishman for the equivalent of US$4,400. It was a moralistic response to a set of facts, and it raises further questions about the way in which the case against the sale of parts of the human body corresponds with the philosophical framework that underpins liberal democratic societies.

---

above n 99, found that 5% of Americans said they would not want to have their organs donated after their death because it was against their religions (Question 3). Further questions reveal that religious barriers to organ donation do not appear to be widespread. Black and Hispanic respondents are much more likely to report that organ donation is against their religion (14% and 13% agree, respectively) than are white respondents (4% agree). There were no substantial differences among major religious groups in the per cent agreement with this statement (Catholics 5%; Baptists 5%; "Christian" 4%; Other Protestant 4%). However, Catholics expressed significantly greater uncertainty (11% don't know) compared to the full sample (6%): <http://www.transweb.org/reference/articles/gallup_survey/gallup_chap6.html> at 29 June 2005.

103 The Gallup poll of *The American Public's Attitudes toward Organ Donation and Transplantation*, above n 99, found that 9% of Americans said they would not want to have their organs donated after their death because they did not want their bodies to be "cut up" or because they wanted to be buried "as a whole person". The pollsters noted that "Black and Hispanic respondents were also more likely than whites to indicate a desire to be buried "intact". Questions 35, 36 and 37 examined this issue further and concluded that slightly under 20 per cent of respondents were concerned about bodies being disfigured by the organ retrieval process, or being buried missing some of the their parts: <http://www.transweb.org/reference/articles/gallup_survey/gallup_chap6.html> at 29 June 2005.

104 See, eg., T O'Brien, "One-Word Solution to Organ Shortage: Cash", Editorial, *The Detroit News*, 26 January 1998: "The only real impediment here is the moral indignation of those who will find our market system inherently offensive."

105 T McConnell, *Inalienable Rights: The Limits of Consent in Medicine and the Law* (2000) 118.

IV. Liberalism and the Philosophy Underlying the Debate

It is apparent that objections to a commercial market in human body parts tend to be based on fears about the lack of self determination or liberty (coercion), the lack of fairness and equity (exploitation and wealth disparities), and the lack of morality that such a market might entail. These are the subject matter of classic liberal philosophy, but the Opponents cannot claim a monopoly over their invocation. Advocates of a commercial market in human body parts draw on many of those same principles to explain why all people could live happier, healthier lives in a society in which people are free to buy and sell bodily material as they wish. Both sides of the debate speak of autonomy, liberty, fairness, distributive justice and equity, drawing on the same classical liberal philosophical tenets in support of their respective positions. However, the conclusions of each strongly contradict the conclusions of the other. It is interesting and ironic that both the Advocates and the Opponents of a legal market in human bodily parts and products invoke many of the same central philosophical doctrines in support of contradictory arguments, and fundamental aspects of their opposing conclusions rely on differing interpretations of identical theoretical precepts.

Before proceeding to examine the reasoning of those who advocate a legal market in human body parts, this section expands on and elucidates those classical liberal ideas, assessing the Opponents' arguments against them, and thus providing a deeper philosophical background to the debate that follows.

A. The Fundamental Principles of Liberalism

The arguments for "liberty" concern the nature and limits of the power that society can legitimately exercise over the individual, and these are the principles on which liberal democratic states are broadly based. As demonstrated by John Stuart Mill's description of the Harm Principle in *On Liberty*,[106] concern for individual freedom is the central foundation of liberal discourse:

> As soon as any part of a person's conduct affects prejudicially the interests of others, society has jurisdiction over it, and the question of whether the general welfare will or will not be promoted by interfering with it, becomes open to discussion. But there is no room for entertaining any such question when a person's conduct affects the interests of no persons besides himself, or needs not affect them unless they like (all the persons concerned being of full age, and the ordinary amount of understanding). In all such cases, there should be perfect freedom, legal and social, to do the action and stand the consequences.[107]

---

[106] John Stuart Mill, *Utilitarianism, On Liberty, Considerations on Representative Government* (H.B. Acton, (ed.) 1991) 143ff.
[107] Ibid, 144.

Notions of personal autonomy and self ownership therefore reflect a sense that individuals should be free to do with their bodies as they please, and should have broad decision-making authority over their bodies. This autonomy should be limited only by the Harm Principle, which constrains an individual's decision-making authority to that which will not harm other people. People should therefore be able to do what they desire with their bodies and body parts, so long as their actions do not cause harm to other people. They should have almost unlimited decision-making authority over their bodies, and any limits on this should be strictly defined. Restrictions are imposed only to protect others and, as far as is possible, they are to be morally neutral.

B. Autonomy

Liberal autonomy similarly requires freedom from exploitation and coercion. Exploitation should be avoided because it interferes with an individual's personal autonomy; people who are exploited lose a degree of self control as their lives are partially directed by the impositions of others. Strong coercion must also be avoided. A person who is forced to alienate a body part does not display personal autonomy. Likewise, decisions about something as important as the alienation of part of one's body should only be made in circumstances of full (accurate and complete) information. Decisions made with anything less than full information are to be mistrusted because faulty information can transform apparent consent into non-consent as it denies an individual the ability to make rational, autonomous decisions. The removal of body parts without the full consent of the person from whose body they are removed obviously implies exploitation and a lack of autonomy on the part of that individual. At a fundamental level, the Opponents therefore seem persuasive in their arguments against the sale of human body parts on the grounds that it is coercive and exploitative.

However, viewed on a subjective case-by-case basis, it is perhaps questionable whether all sales of human body parts would in fact be exploitative and coercive. If not, the Opponents' case for an outright ban on the sale of body parts would be seriously undermined.

1. Presumptively Coercive and Exploitative

It is possible to envisage situations free of coercion and exploitation in which a body part could be exchanged for cash. Imagine, for example, a person who is motivated by love to give a kidney to a friend, and who is determined to do so. The only condition the donor places on the "gift" is that she be paid a large amount of money to cover expenses and to look after her children if she becomes ill and unable to work as a result of the operation.

The transaction could be regarded as uncoerced and non-exploitative, yet the laws that typically exist in liberal democratic jurisdictions would regard it as an illegal payment for a body part. It would thus seem that—at least sometimes (though perhaps only rarely)—the sale of body parts would not exploit the vendor, and in these situations the reason for interfering with the liberty of a person to make self-regarding decisions about his or her body is paternalistic.

This raises another relevant question: Is the decision to sell part of one's body self regarding? If so, it seems improbable that prohibiting such decisions does in fact uphold the liberal principle of self determination.

2. Self-Regarding Actions and Paternalism

John Stuart Mill explains the problem of paternalism for liberal societies in the following way:

> His own good, either physical or moral is not a sufficient warrant. He cannot be rightfully compelled to do or forebear because it will be better for him to do so, because it will make him happier, because in the opinion of others, to do so would be wise... These are good reasons for remonstrating with him, or reasoning with him, or persuading him, or entreating him, but not for compelling him or visiting him with any evil in case he do otherwise.[108]

A complete ban on the sale of human body parts arguably amounts to *hard paternalism*. Hard paternalism describes state action that prevents self-regarding dangerous behavior, even when the behavior is voluntary. This would encompass the voluntary donation of a body part by someone who has investigated and understood the potential medical repercussions of the operation.

In such a case, one obvious reason for preventing the person from donating the body part would be the possibility that the donor might later suffer medical difficulties as direct consequences of the donation, or difficulties whose effects were exacerbated by the donation. Even if the donor was aware of the potential health problems that could follow the operation, a state with a hard paternalistic mindset might intervene to prevent the individual from deciding to adopt this risk of suffering harm. From a liberal perspective, this is an unacceptable reason for state intervention with a person's self-regarding behavior as it abridges individual autonomy[109]

---

108 Ibid, 13. See also, generally, Feinberg, *The Moral Limits of the Criminal Law: Harm to Self*, n 73; Thaddeus Mason Pope, "Counting the Dragon's Teeth and Claws: The Definition of Hard Paternalism" (2004) 20 *Georgia State University Law Review* 659.
109 Barnett II, Saliba and Walker, above n 9, 380:

> It is quite likely that some poor people would avail themselves of an opportunity to convert some nonessential part of their least scarce and most fragile form of capital—physical human capital—into a more durable or more valuable form of wealth. However, the prohibition against the purchase and sale of kidneys forecloses that option to them . . . It effectively prevents them from making choices that they believe would increase their well-being.

See also Dickens, above n 83, 125:

> The paternalism implicit in deciding that there shall be no coercion or over-inducement of people to sell their body materials may be justified regarding young people and others in dependent circumstances. It may not be so easily justified, however, where adults are concerned who are capable of ordering their own priorities. The fear that they might act against their best interests in selling their organs is no different from the fear that they may equally reluctantly take dangerous employment, in mines, among toxic environments, or in hazardous fishery operations. It may be unjustified paternalism to

and dignity,[110] and it is not a relevant consideration to taken into account when implementing the fundamental Harm Principle that acts as a guiding test for liberal society.[111]

From the perspective of liberal philosophy, a more acceptable approach would be a *soft paternalistic* option that only temporarily prohibits a person from selling an organ or tissue. The justification for the delay would be the need to investigate and ensure that the vendor had adequate knowledge about the procedure to give his or her decision the quality of true consent, and to make sure that the sale was not occurring under circumstances of coercion. Once this has been established, liberal theory would require that the sale should be permitted.

Perhaps soft paternalism in fact provides an argument for market regulation rather than strict prohibition. It allows state interference with dangerous self-regarding behaviour if the behaviour is substantially non-voluntary or if intervention is temporarily needed in order to determine whether the behavior is voluntary or not.[112] This is justifiable state behaviour from the perspective of liberal philosophy as it seeks to protect the donor from becoming the victim of *unconsented harm*; soft paternalism would become problematic only if it was hardened by illicit judgments about moral values, such as the "wrongness" of alienating a part of the human body in the eyes of other members of society.

3. Harm to Others (Social Harm)

The soft paternalistic approach is not sufficiently restrictive for the Opponents of a market in human body parts. Joel Feinberg proposes an alternative argument that might justify prohibition: "It is always a good reason in support of penal legislation that it would be effective in preventing (eliminating reducing) harm to persons other than the actor (the one prohibited from acting) and there is no other means that is equally effective at no greater cost to other values."[113]

If it could be demonstrated that society generally—people other than those who choose to sell their body parts—would be harmed by allowing such decisions, prohibitions would not necessarily be inconsistent with the liberal harm principle.

---

impose laws against competent people's own preferences in their circumstances, for the purpose of seeking to protect them against their tendencies to make decisions that to others seem misguided.

110 David A Hyman, "Does Technology Spell Trouble with a Capital 'T'? Human Dignity and Public Policy" (2003) 27 *Harvard Journal of Law and Public Policy* 3, 10:

If we are prepared (and even enthusiastic, in some cases) to privilege third-party assessments of dignity despite the existence of crystal-clear evidence of first-party wishes, how much more likely is it that we will do so when the evidence of first-party wishes is less obvious—if it is available at all? . . . Relying primarily on third-party assessments will lead to the paradoxical effect of undermining dignity by privileging the opinions of elites instead of the autonomous choices of those most affected.

111 Joel Feinberg, *The Moral Limits of the Criminal Law: Harmless Wrongdoing*, vol 4 (1988) xix.
112 Ibid, 15.
113 Ibid.

Perhaps the fear of a growing medical welfare burden is sufficient to impose restraints on personal autonomy?[114] Particularly in places hosting a nationalised health system, society could be burdened ("harmed") by the cost of providing medical support to those who suffer ill health as a result of alienating a body part, and this might be an acceptable reason to prevent such sales. On the other hand, society might benefit from the medical costs saved by not having to supply ongoing expensive treatment (such as dialysis) to those who have benefitted from the purchase of a transplanted body part. The relative cost efficiencies would be a matter for factual evidence and, in the case of transplantation of a body part, the likelihood of any derivative harm to others is tangential and uncertain. A parent *might* be less able to take care of his or her children *if* he or she falls ill as a result of losing a body part. A donor *might* be a costly burden on the medical resources of a welfare society *if* he becomes sick as a result of the donation (however, it should be noted that the existing tendency of vendors to come from societies without strong social welfare or nationalised health systems, and of the purchasers to come from wealthier societies, means that a donor who falls ill is unlikely to be a burden on the organ recipient's health system in any event).

Other people *might* feel distressed *if* they are disturbed to see a member of their society confronted with or making such a choice. However, these considerations would apply equally if a person decides to alienate and donate a body part altruistically—a decision that many liberal societies permit and applaud—which makes the argument appear somewhat artificial and inconsistent, and it seems questionable whether this level of possibility of harm to others would be significant enough to justify state interference with the individual's self-determined actions.

Unless protection of society can be shown to be a persuasive reason to prevent the sale of human body parts by consenting adults on the grounds of protection of social autonomy, such prohibitions can be regarded as paternalistic and it is arguable that some other justification must be adopted if a genuinely liberal society is to vindicate intervention in decisions to engage in the transfer of human body parts.

C. Fairness and Equity

The Opponents of a market in human body parts implicitly invoke arguments about the liberal democratic principles of distributive justice, fairness and equality when they raise concerns about exploitation, consent and social inequity. There are various conceptions of what sorts of policies

---

114 Cf. forcing people to wear bicycle or motorbike helmets, or seatbelts in cars. See ibid, 138–139, and Joel Feinberg, *Social Philosophy* (1973) 31–32. See also J Kleinig, *Paternalism* (1984) 82; Note, (1968) 67 *Michigan Law Review* 372; K M Royalty, "Motorcycle Helmets and the Constitution of Self-Protective Legislation" (1968) 30 *Ohio State Law Journal* 371–93. Guido Calabresi and Douglas Melamed describe this in terms of "moralisms" in "Property Rules, Liability Rules, and Inalienability: One View of the Cathedral" (1972) 85 *Harvard Law Review* 1089, 1111–12.

liberalism actually demands in order to coincide with its general guiding principles of equality, freedom and moral neutrality.[115] Broadly speaking, proponents of liberalism would generally agree that wealth inequalities should be reduced through social welfare and progressive taxation systems leading to wealth redistribution. They believe that individuals should have basic freedoms and that regulations should not be based on judgements about the morality of particular forms of conduct.[116]

The Opponents might be correct. Many of the scenarios they fear as a consequence of a market in human body parts do not suggest social conditions that are consistent with these liberal democratic principles. Exploitation, coercion and social inequality are all antipathetic to liberal society. But is the case against the sale of human body parts itself consistent with liberal philosophy? Or, are the feared illiberal consequences in fact the result of deeper structural unfairness and social inequalities?

The Opponents propose prohibition, and this is arguably a paternalistic and illiberal response. As noted above, hard paternalistic policies against the sale of human body parts impose a non-consensual outcome on individuals who would like to engage in such transactions. They also reduce an individual's freedom to make choices about whether or not to sell a body part to raise money that might contribute to improving his or her financial position and immediate living conditions. Thus, instead of fortifying the social fairness and equality they seek, they perhaps undermine it. If the Opponents' position is to be grounded in liberal political philosophy, this should be noted as an inherent weakness of their case.

D. Morality

Regardless of which conception of liberalism a society adopts, a common (though not universal) principle is the moral neutrality of government.[117] Thus, a case that depends on moral arguments is perhaps not compatible with liberalism because "the traditional liberal principle [is] that government should not enforce private morality".[118] This seems to provide a fundamental problem if the Opponents' case against the sale of human body parts is to be justified on liberal grounds.

Recourse to claims about autonomy can be used to defend the liberal credentials of the Opponents' case, but autonomy claims can also be used—and perhaps more effectively—to undermine this argument. Likewise, to the extent that arguments about exploitation, consent and social

---

115 Note, however, that not all who regard themselves to be "liberals" would agree that these are the general guiding principles. See, eg., the discussion in S Mulhall and A Swift, *Liberals and Communitarians* (1992).
116 See discussion in Ronald Dworkin, *A Matter of Principle* (1985) Chapter 8 "Liberalism", 181–204.
117 This is a usual but not necessary feature of liberal thought. See, eg, work by Joseph Raz who argues that political neutrality is not possible: Joseph Raz, *The Morality of Freedom* (1986).
118 Ibid, Chapter 9, "Why Liberals Should Care about Equality", 205–13, 206. See also the definition offered by John Rawls, *Political Liberalism* (1996) 191.

inequality amount to hard paternalism, they do not accord with the liberal principles they seek to uphold. They instead seem to enforce moral judgments cloaked in liberal rhetoric.

Accepting soft paternalistic arguments would tend to support the existence of a regulated market rather than the possibility of prohibition, so the Opponents seem to retreat to arguments of morality to support their claim about the illegitimacy of the market. In doing so, they step outside the traditional liberal framework. This is problematic for a morally neutral liberal democratic society and it renders their case illiberal in nature.

This failure on the part of the Opponents provides an opportunity for the Advocates of a legal market in human body parts to strengthen the weight and persuasiveness of their case by taking a reflexive approach that succeeds on the same liberal points on which the Opponents failed. By offering a solution to the problem that is more classically liberal than the Opponents' arguments based on moral judgments, the Advocates of a legal market seek an opportunity for a victory based on reason and recourse to the fundamental normative principles of liberal democratic societies.

V. The Case for a Legal(ised) Market in Human Body Parts

Justifications for the legalisation of organ and tissue sales can be sorted into three main categories. Two of these coincide with, and simultaneously contradict, the Opponents' arguments against a market in human body parts. The first category argues that people should be free to do as they wish with their bodies. This accords with the principle of self determination in liberal theory and could be dubbed "liberty arguments". The second suggests that it is unfair to people who wish to profit by selling their body parts to prohibit them from doing so, especially when medical professionals sell their labour to make organ donations possible and commercial organisations also profit from the gifts of donors. These fall under the umbrella of "fairness" and "distributive justice" arguments.

The Advocates' third argument does not match the Opponents' final argument in its recourse to moral principles. Instead it relies on the liberal principle that markets offer the most efficient way of organising the social allocation of goods. From this the Advocates conclude that a market in body parts should be permitted, and this could be referred to as their "economic rationality" argument.

Using these main headings as a framework, the Advocates' case in favour of allowing the sale of human body parts can be shown to undermine existing norms by appealing more to the Opponents' normative philosophical foundations than the Opponents' do themselves. A fourth heading—how to establish a market—added to the schema to demonstrate how the Advocates' flexibility, indecisiveness or even internal conflict about how to structure the proposed market also helps them to meet many of the Opponents' arguments. By contrast, a rigid prohibitionist approach does not afford the Opponents the ability to adjust their arguments to meet the philosophical demands of classical liberalism.

A. Liberty Arguments
The Advocates of a legal market argue that, as a matter of autonomy and self determination, individuals who want to sell parts or products of their bodies should be able to do so.

1. Reduce Poverty
The Advocates argue that preventing such sales further diminishes the range of choices available to needy people to improve their situations, so it does not protect the poor. In 1998, representatives of the International Forum for Transplant Ethics stated: "we cannot improve matters by removing the best option that poverty has left, and making the range smaller still."[119] On this view, society should improve liberty by striving to lessen poverty and thus increase the options available to people, rather than forbidding the poor to utilise the immediate ways in which they can try to escape their plight. The less people need the money they can obtain by selling their body parts, the less attractive the option of sale will become. So global society should focus on improving the conditions of those in need rather than using laws to further limit their already limited options.

2. Reduce Hypocrisy
Furthermore, the Advocates argue, the medical risks involved in selling body parts are identical to the risks involved in donating body parts. So if people are permitted to give their body parts to others, it is inconsistent for a liberal society to forbid them from selling those same body parts that they would be allowed to give away. A prohibition on sale thus constitutes unacceptable interference with personal autonomy.

This invites further consideration about the reasons why donations of certain body parts are generally legal while sale of the same parts is not. Uncoerced donation of human body parts in return for compensation raises different concerns to those discussed earlier in the context of paternalism and coercion. In the case of uncoerced donations, free and informed consent is presumed, as is the absence of familial or financial pressures that might provide an overwhelming moral impetus to donate. Examples of uncoerced donations include blood donation in response to an announcement that a community's reserve of blood supplies is low, or an agreement to donate one's organs after one's death (eg. ticking the "I'm prepared to donate" box on one's drivers' licence). It is therefore generally considered to be donation impelled by an unselfish regard for others: "altruistic donation".

Uncompensated altruistic donation of body parts is generally lauded by society (including many of the Opponents) and supported by existing laws. It is the normative way by which human tissue and organs are made

---
119 Radcliffe-Richards, et al, above n 71.

available for transplantation. Altruistic donors tend to be treated as rescuers and "illegal" elements of their actions—such as consenting to an operation that is medically not in their own best interests—are often overlooked by the legal system. Altruistic donation is regarded as commendable.[120]

By contrast, donation for compensation is frequently condemned.[121] As noted above, the donor performs exactly the same action in each case: he or she relinquishes a body part so that it may be used to aid another person. The Advocates would suggest that the "exchange of money cannot in itself turn an acceptable risk into an unacceptable one."[122] The only material difference is that donation for compensation is accompanied by a tangible benefit to the donor rather than compensating only the recipient and others (such as doctors and administrators) who have been involved in the procedure.

From the perspective of the donor, the only other apparent difference between compensated and uncompensated altruistic donation lies in the donor's motive. Both sorts of donors might wish to contribute to society by helping a fellow human in need and both might enjoy a warm feeling of virtue that accompanies such selfless action. But the compensated donor *might* also have been prompted to act by the promise of a pecuniary reward, and the donation is thus condemned. Yet it is questionable whether this promise of reward should be accorded such significance. The fact that a donor receives monetary compensation does not indicate that his or her motives were not *altruistic* in the general sense of the word.[123] Even if the motives were less than altruistic, is that sufficient reason for society to prevent an uncoerced person from engaging in autonomous, self-regarding action? The Harm Principle does not demand altruism; it requires only that one not cause harm to others.

In the case of uncoerced donations for compensation, it is clear that the lure of reward is not the only motivation driving the donor's actions (otherwise the donation would be "coerced" and would be proscribed under a paternalistic liberally consistent state policy). Although donation for compensation may not seem as altruistic or virtuous as uncompensated donation, the basic characteristics of the two categories of bequest are alike. The Advocates therefore argue that it is problematic to suggest that the concepts of altruism and compensation are mutually exclusive.

---

120 See, eg., *McFall v Shrimp* (1978) above n 67. In that case, the Allegheny County Court declined to order that Shrimp donate bone marrow to his cousin McFall. McFall was dying of a rare disease and Shrimp was the only known compatible potential donor, but he refused to donate his bone marrow. The Court gave priority to the autonomy of the individual and the importance of the individual's actual consent. It held that the decision rested with Shrimp but—in what appeared to be a blatant attempt to shame Shrimp into changing his mind—the court described his refusal to donate the bone marrow as "morally indefensible".
121 See, eg., Australian Law Reform Commission, above n 22, 85, ¶174.
122 Spencer, above n 88.
123 M Brams, "Transplantable Human Organs: Should their Sale be Authorized by State Statutes?" (1977) 3 *American Journal of Law & Medicine* 183, 192.

3. Reduce the Black Market, Coercion and Exploitation

The Advocates propose a legitimate market in human body parts as a way of restraining the black market trade and providing conditions in which careful regulation could occur.

This argument suggests that the potential to exploit those providing body parts is reduced when the transaction occurs within a state-regulated framework rather than on a black market. Despite legal prohibitions, a black market in human body parts does exist:[124] "A black market springs up, but such a market is much more costly to operate than a free market would be (because of punishment costs, poor information, and lack of enforceable warranties), and [its prices are] higher than the free market price."[125]

Better information and safer conditions would improve the likelihood of successful transplants and reduce the risks of coercion and exploitation.[126] The Advocates therefore argue that it would be better to legitimise and regulate the market for human body parts than to drive it further underground. There is more risk of exploitation of the vulnerable when they are themselves hiding from the law due to their participation in illegal activities,[127] and more risk of profiteering by black marketeers when a market has a hidden, illegitimate nature.

---

[124] The black market is widely reported and is referred to by both the opponents and proponents of a legal market in human body parts. For contemporary examples of its operation, see the organ selling websites at: "The Life Keepers" <http://llogic.www3.50megs.com/> at 29 June 2005. One of the pages of the Life Keepers" site features a photograph of a Florida woman who identifies herself as "Vegalive" and claims to want to sell her kidney. It states:

> I am female, a member of the Caucasian race, born and raised in the United States. I am forty years old and my blood-type is A positive. I became a vegetarian at the age of sixteen, and have always embraced healthful living habits and a holistic way of life. No drugs, no alcohol, lots of fresh raw fruits and veggies and plenty of exercise. I have never had any medical problems whatsoever; that is why I do not have a medical file to share with you. Of course I realize that at some point you will want a doctor to check me out, and that is fine. I make my living as an administrative assistant within a large corporation. The reason why I need money: My fiancée is involved in a custody fight for his little girl, and we need to hire an expensive lawyer. (My fiancée is not in a position right now to "donate".)

<http://llogic.www3.50megs.com/lib/vegalive.html> at 29 June 2005. The Gallup poll of *The American Public's Attitudes toward Organ Donation and Transplantation*, above n 99, found 34% of Americans believed organs for transplant could be bought and sold on the black market in the United States; 25% said they did not know (Question 40): <http://www.transweb.org/reference/articles/gallup_survey/gallup_chap6.html> at 29 June 2005.
[125] Richard A Posner, *The Economic Analysis of Law* (1986) 140.
[126] See, eg., Richard A Epstein, *Organ Peddling* <http://slate.msn.com/id/3680/entry/24108/> at 29 June 2005: "Once transactions are legal, markets cease to be thin. As the number of choices increases, information becomes more available, and the likelihood of real exploitation is effectively curtailed . . . It is always a mistake to assume that legal markets will be just a magnification of illegal ones."
[127] See, eg., Sanjay Kumar, "Police Uncover Large Scale Organ Trafficking in Punjab" (25 January 2003) 326 *British Medical Journal* 180. This article quotes the Inspector General of Police in Jalandhar, Mr Satish Kumar Sharma: "The 'donors' were not even given proper postoperative care, and in some cases were threatened with imprisonment for the illegal act and thrown out of hospital a week after the transplant," he said. Mr Sharma confirmed the deaths of six labourers as a result.

In this sense, the Advocates undermine the Opponents' case with the Opponents' own logic. If the Opponents accept the evidence—on which they themselves rely—that exploitation occurs in black market environments, it becomes more difficult for them to reject the option of overt soft paternalistic regulation. It is harder to police paternalistic sanctions (such as criminal penalties for selling body parts or cloning humans) in a covert, illegal market. Secrecy and deception by the law breakers—vendors, brokers and purchasers alike—lead to collusion and sophisticated smuggling systems that are difficult for authorities to detect and control.[128] It would arguably be easier to monitor a legal trade with formal regulations in a controlled environment in which the state acted either as broker or as the appointer or licensor of brokers. If the supply of body parts grew in this context, demand for black market organs would be likely to fall,[129] and the effectively unregulated black market—along with its exploitative nature—would dissipate. If the implementation of the Advocates' proposal led to a market without exploitation or loss of autonomy, it would arguably be better aligned with liberal principles than is the status quo defended by the Opponents.

B. Fairness and Distributive Justice Arguments

The Advocates argue that people should be allowed to sell their body parts as this would broaden their options and increase their liberty. It would also reverse the hypocrisy of a situation in which medical personnel receive remuneration for their services and donors are the only people involved who do not materially benefit from the transaction. The Advocates say it is unfair for medical personnel and administrators to be paid for their roles in the transplantation of body parts when the donor—without whom the operation could not occur and nobody would be paid—cannot legally receive payment. This seems even more iniquitous when commercial enterprises are permitted to profit from harvested cadaveric body parts even though those parts could not legally be sold and/or donors are not informed that donated cadavers might be used in this way.[130]

The proposal that the sale of body parts be permitted raises questions about exactly what a vendor would be paid for. Options include the willingness to donate, the physical body part itself, and/or expenses arising from the operation.

---

128 The difficulty of controlling the illegal trade is alluded to by writers on both sides of the debate. See, eg, Radcliffe-Richards, et al, above n 71, who argue for a market in human body parts, and Scheper-Hughes, "Postmodern Cannibalism", above n 49, who argues against legalising the trade. See also reports of transplant tourism where poor Indian vendors travelled to the Middle East for operations to transplant their organs to wealth recipients: Mandala Project case study "India Kidney Trade", ¶2, above n 51.
129 Epstein, above n 126.
130 See, eg, L Kowalczyk and S Kelleher, "Donors Don't Realize they are Fueling a Lucrative Business" *The Orange County Register* (2000) <http://www.ocregister.com/features/body/day1.shtml> at 29 June 2005. See also related website *The Body Brokers* <http://www.ocregister.com/features/body/index.shtml> at 29 June 2005.

1. Payment for Expenses

In 1977, the Australian Law Reform Commission found that the *only* acceptable reason for allowing compensation for the transfer of body parts would be the reimbursement of expenses related to the donation operation itself.[131] The Law Reform Commission of Canada reached a similar conclusion in 1992.[132] This is an important concession as costs such as hospitalisation expenses arising from the donation might otherwise act as a *disincentive* to a potential donor. It also begs questions about the characterisation of these expenses. How proximate does the connection between the "associated costs" and the operation have to be? Is this perhaps a covert method of allowing donors to receive compensation while appearing to still condemn the sale of body parts?

Compensation or reimbursement for expenses or related costs is a matter of degree. G P Smith proposes the establishment of reimbursement policies that would cover the costs of pre-transplant evaluation, food, baby sitters, travel and housing for prospective patients, as well as economic assistance for those who are unable to work post-transplant.[133] V D Plueckhahn and S M Cordner suggest alternative choices including free medical care, life insurance and the waiving of medical bills for live donors, and the payment of funeral expenses in the case of cadaveric donations.[134] Other options might be to allow claims for wages lost while the donor takes time off work for the operation and recuperation, and a "damages" type award that would take into account the possibility of future pain and suffering or loss as a result of the operation. Damages payable for a "replenishable" body part (such as blood or bone marrow) would presumably be lower than those awarded for an irreplaceable organ (such as a kidney or cornea).

In 1999, the Organ and Tissue Donation Advisory Committee in Philadelphia (USA) proposed a scheme by which a payment of US$300 would be made to funeral homes when cadaveric organs were harvested for transplant.[135] The money was intended to contribute to funeral expenses, providing an indirect reward to beneficiaries under a will whose inheritance would probably otherwise be reduced by the cost of providing a funeral. It was intended to stimulate donation by more evenly and fairly distributing the "profits" arising from a bequest of body parts, and it was thus a first step towards allowing the sale of human body parts. However, the plan was abandoned due to Department of Health concerns that the funeral

---

131 Australian Law Reform Commission, above n 22, 87. This principle was then incorporated into Australian leglisation. See also discussion of the ALRC report in L Haberfield, "The Transplantation of Human Fetal Tissue in Australia: Abortion, Consent and Other Legal Issues" (1996) 4 *Journal of Law and Medicine* 144, 162.
132 Law Reform Commission of Canada, *Procurement and Transfer of Human Tissues and Organs*, Working Paper 66 (1992) 184, Recommendation 11.
133 Smith, above n 70, 28.
134 V D Plueckhahn and S M Cordner, *Ethics, Legal Medicine and Forensic Pathology* (1991) 130.
135 S G Stolberg, "Pennsylvania Set to Break Taboo on Reward for Organ Donations", *New York Times*, 6 May 1999.

benefit risked violating the federal law that prohibits offering valuable consideration in exchange for organs.[136] The alternative *Expense Benefit Plan for Organ Donors and their Families* was instead introduced in January 2002, giving organ donors a US$300 benefit to pay for food and accommodation costs (including those of family members) incurred due to the donation.

2. Payment for the Body Part

Payment of expenses places donors in the financial position they would have been in but for the operation. It perhaps removes the financial disincentive to donate but does not provide any positive incentive. The donor still remains the only person involved in the procedure who does not receive any tangible benefit.

Some of the Advocates therefore suggest that the expenses reimbursed for the donation of body parts should be more encompassing. Drawing a comparison with alternatives to transplantation of human body parts, Jack Kevorkian notes that the production costs of in vitro body parts include *capital expenditure* for nutrients, equipment, personnel, and facilities.[137] Laws that allowed only the reimbursement of expenses would require in vitro body parts to be "sold" at cost price, but this would nevertheless permit elements such as the growth and nurturing of the organ to be compensated. This system enables potentially infinite supplies of in vitro body parts to be sold for large sums of money to cover the presumably high costs of development and production. Why should synthetic body parts be treated differently from natural ones?

The living donor's capital expenditure covers the great expense of a lifetime of care and nurture in the "production" of body parts that are suitable for transplantation. The acts of feeding, washing, educating, exercising and just residing in a human body all contribute to the production of the body parts that can be made available for use by others. The Advocates argue that to deny remuneration to a person who has invested so much into creating a body part that can then be used by another person is unfair and inequitable, especially when medical personnel who have only limited contact with the body part are paid for their services and even private enterprise can profit from the donation.[138] Speaking of the compensation that could be given to vendors of human body parts, Kevorkian contends that: "What is glibly and mistakenly execrated as the [donor's] 'profit' is really 'at cost' reimbursement for substantial 'capital expenditure' of a uniquely biological kind over a long period of time. And that mistake is partly responsible for an unjust and harmful moral conclusion."[139]

---

136 C Snowbeck, "Organ Donor Funeral Aid Scrapped: Health Department Fears Conflict with Federal Law', *Pittsburgh Post-Gazette*, (2002): <http://www.pitt.edu/~htk/pennsylv.htm#funeral%20plan%20scrapped> at 29 June 2005.
137 Jack Kevorkian, "Marketing of Human Organs and Tissues Is Justified and Necessary" (1989) 7 *Medicine and Law* 557.
138 For a discussion of the tissue bank industry in the United States, see John J Zodrow, "The Commodification of Human Body Parts: Regulating the Tissue Bank Industry" (2003) 32 *Southwestern University Law Review* 407–49.
139 Kevorkian, above n 137, 560.

On this view the uncompensated donor is unfairly exploited. The donor makes no physical gain from his or her altruistic donation, but the recipient potentially gains a renewed opportunity to enjoy life and the medical team is paid for the technical skills they employ in making the transplant possible. While Danielle Wagner arguably exaggerates when she calls this rewarding of the medical team "unjust enrichment",[140] it does seem unjust and exploitative if only the donor, who has provided the raw materials that enabled the recipient and medical team to benefit, is left unrewarded.

Kevorkian argues that it is difficult to justify a system of uncompensated organ donation when the health care industry and professions freely pursue commercial goals,[141] and he suggests that donors should be reimbursed for both prior capital investment and current expenses: "the donor's remuneration should be very large," he says.[142] By contrast, the status quo preferred by the Opponents allows, at most, only out-of-pocket costs (current expenses) to be considered to be acceptable payments for human donors. This leads to a threshold problem: where does society draw the line between permissible compensation for expenses incurred directly from the act of donation, and impermissible broader "expenses" (such as the value of the donated body part itself)? This issue should be addressed by Opponents who wish to allow compensation for expenses on the grounds that such remuneration would fall outside the definition of "sale" of human body parts.

3. Reduce Social Inequalities by Treating the Rich and Poor Equally

As foreshadowed above, the Advocates argue that allowing the poor to sell body parts might help to alleviate social inequalities as needy people would have a new and lawful method by which to become richer. On this view, it is inequitable to reinforce social inequalities by preventing people from undertaking self-regarding activities that might improve their economic positions.

Furthermore, the Advocates point out that many body parts can be alienated with minimal risk to the donor. Bone marrow, blood and sperm are examples of body parts that many people could sell without assuming significant risks to their own health. The risk of alienating a kidney has been assessed as the same as "the risk of an average citizen of Ohio being involved in a road accident over a period of 4 years", with the risk ending four years after the operation.[143] In a society in which people are permitted

---

140 Danielle M Wagner, "Property Rights in the Human Body: The Commodification of Organ Transplantation and Biotechnology" (1995) 33 *Duquesne Law Review* 931, 955.
141 Kevorkian, above n 137, 557.
142 Kevorkian above n 137, 563.
143 This information was supplied by Swiss company Novartis Pharma AG on its transplantation website *Transplant Square*: <http://www.transplantsquare.com/public/lifestyle/livingdonors/lvpages/QA2.htm#4> in 2001. Interestingly the site did not include a percentage indication of what risk an Ohio citizen faces of being in a road accident within a four year period.

to engage in extreme and dangerous sports and work for leisure and/or employment, the Advocates suggest that it is unfair to re-enforce existing social inequalities by refusing to allow people to take steps that might give them additional income sources.[144]

C. The Economic Rationality Argument

The Advocates' third argument in favour of a market in human body parts is consistent with the tenets of classical liberalism. It is different to—and indirectly contradicts—the Opponents' case based on moral judgments. The argument of economic rationality is quintessentially liberal in nature and presents a perspective from within the liberal framework that encourages fairness derived from decision-making freedom and rational choice. This is the argument that the sale of body parts should be permitted in order to create economic efficiency, and that this would bring about justice (equality, fairness and moral neutrality).

At a generic level, the argument from economic efficiency is effectively a utilitarian claim that: "By a process of voluntary exchange, resources are shifted to those uses in which the value to consumers, as measured by their willingness to pay, is highest. When resources are being used where their value is highest, we may say that they are being employed efficiently."[145]

The most efficient way in which to organise the distribution of goods within a society is arguably through a free market. Richard Epstein argues this case in the specific context of human body parts:

> We have shortages of usable organs today, and people die as a consequence. The hope (and it is not a certainty) is that a price inducement can increase the supply of organs and counteract the shortage, as it does in other markets. Better that we have 200 people alive with one kidney each than 100 people alive with two kidneys. Better that cadaveric organs be used than be buried with the decedent. Markets could make either, or both, these things happen.[146]

In summary, this argument suggests that demand for human body parts currently exceeds supply and allowing the operation of a market for these *goods* would produce an optimal use of resources. A free market would allow prices of body parts to fall (vis-à-vis the black market) and it would make body parts more widely available. Indeed, the Advocates' economists argue that "no person who could benefit physically from a kidney transplant would need to go without one."[147] On this view, any existing injustices caused by the inability of some people—particularly those without adequate health insurance—to purchase the expensive medical care involved in organ transplants would thus be eliminated.[148]

---

144 Radcliffe-Richards, et al., above n 71.
145 Posner, above n 125, 9.
146 Epstein, above n 126.
147 Barnett II, Saliba and Walker, above n 9, 375.
148 Ibid, 378–79: "Because everyone, poor as well as rich, who needs a kidney would get one, a free market for kidneys would be more equitable than the current system."

It is nonetheless difficult to see how this would be the case in societies without strong medical welfare systems.

As it is easier to regulate a legitimate market than an underground black market, it is likely that problems such as exploitation and coercion would be more easily avoided in a market setting than under conditions of prohibition. Soft paternalistic safeguards,[149] such as compulsory counselling and education classes combined with cooling-off periods, could help to ensure that potential organ vendors were well informed about the procedures they were planning to undertake. Counselling could also help to identify reluctant vendors whose consent was uninformed, or whose consent was real but perhaps driven by circumstances making consent seem the only available option (such as cases of moral pressure on the part of family members, or pressure from a debt collector).[150]

The other aspect of the Advocates' case that coincides with the economic rationality approach is the (defeatist sounding, but perhaps realistic) suggestion that a market in body parts is operating anyway so it would be better to legitimise and regulate it than to pretend that it does not exist or that saying it is illegal will be sufficient to make it just go away by itself. By doing so, society could actively use the market to help solve the problems of exploitation and coercion that are evident in a black market environment. It could also use the market to help equalise social resources and minimise existing inequalities.

D. How to Establish a Market

The way in which a proposed market for body parts would be established is crucial to the discussion. A free market might open the door to coercion and exploitation, and it is thus condemned by the Opponents and disavowed by some Advocates.[151] A futures market might be considered to contain fewer risks. Other Advocates caution that it is a mistake to assume that a legitimate market would replicate a black market.[152] But without offering a positive statement about how an acceptable market might be organised, the Advocates' case is incomplete.

The simplicity of the Opponents' blanket prohibition contrasts with a diverse array of proposals for a market in human body parts from within the ranks of the Advocates. Within the pro-market camp, a distinction can be drawn between the free market advocates and the regulated-market advocates. Within each of these groupings, a further distinction can be drawn between advocates of a cadaveric market and advocates of a market for the body parts of live donors.

---

149 Ibid, 382.
150 Cf. cases in which forced coercion could be identified.
151 See, eg, Radcliffe-Richards, et al, above n 71: "It must be stressed that we are not arguing for the positive conclusion that organ sales must always be acceptable, let alone that there should be an unfettered market."
152 Epstein, *Organ Peddling*, above n 126: "It is always a mistake to assume that legal markets will be just a magnification of illegal ones. Their entire internal structure changes as well, and for the better."

1. A Free Market

A free market in human body parts is the basic proposal of libertarian Advocates.[153] The notion of a "free market" implies a market characterised by free competition, in which regulation is employed primarily to maintain this condition. This scenario is probably what most scares the Opponents of a market in human body parts. Such a scheme would allow living people to sell both kidneys if they wished to (even though this would condemn them to death or a lifetime of renal dialysis),[154] or to donate their hearts (even though this would cause death). Such freedom seems ghoulish to many Opponents.

Yet the reality is that very few markets are free in liberal democratic societies.[155] Liberalism generally requires governmental market intervention to alleviate inequalities and optimise trading conditions (by requiring the provision of accurate information, for example), and to prevent strong coercion. It therefore seems unlikely that a free market could meet the requirements of liberalism in a non-utopian liberal society.

2. A Regulated Market

Economic theorists are generally more interested in the efficiency of the market than its total freedom. Therefore, regulations that can make the market operate more efficiently by reducing impediments to its effectiveness are to be welcomed. These are the same regulations that some of the Advocates believe would prevent exploitation or strong coercion, and would otherwise protect the vulnerable.

A regulated market could be structured in a multitude of ways. The spectrum of options includes the ability to sell any body part (even if this would lead to the vendor's death) after receiving permission from a state regulatory or supervisory institution,[156] to the ability to sell only regenerable body parts such as blood or bone marrow, to the ability to sell

---

153 See, eg., the website *Organ Selling* written by neurobiological research scientist, Harold Kyriazi, who identifies himself as a libertarian. The site proposes a free market for cadaveric organs: <http://www.pitt.edu/~htk/> at 29 June 2005.
154 Such scenarios have also arisen under the existing donor scheme. One case came to prominence in 1998 when a Californian man offered to donate his second kidney to his 16 year old daughter after the kidney he had first donated to her started to fail. The story was more dramatic because of the facts: the father was serving a prison sentence for burglary; he had abandoned his daughter at birth; he had met her once when she was eight; he had donated a kidney to her when she was 13; and he had offered to donate his remaining kidney to her after the first started to fail when she secretly stopped taking anti-rejection drugs. The University of California's San Francisco Medical Center Ethics Committee decided to refuse the donation, and the girl later received a donation from an uncle. See: J Basu, "Removing a Person's Last Remaining Kidney Violates Physicians' Code of Ethics" *UCSF Daybreak News* (1999): <http://www.ucsf.edu/daybreak/1999/01/20_kidney.html> at 29 June 2005.
155 This is noted by Curtis E Harris and Stephen P Alcorn, "To Solve a Deadly Shortage: Economic Incentives for Human Organ Donation" (2001) 16 *Issues in Law and Medicine* 213–33, 232.
156 For a report detailing how such a policy failed to control the trade of kidneys or protect vendors in India, see: "Investigation: Kidneys Still for Sale", *Frontline*, 13–26 December 1997, vol.14, No.25. <http://www.flonnet.com/fl1425/14250640.htm> at 29 June 2005.

only cadaveric body parts, or an "organ procurement market".[157] Cadaveric body parts could be sold on a futures market or by allowing payments to relatives for permission to harvest the body parts of deceased relatives, or even to charities or other third parties.

The design of a regulated market in body parts could vary considerably from one jurisdiction to another, depending on factors such as the poverty levels and the tendency towards exploitation in the society. Normative social attitudes—including moral values and religious beliefs—could also play a role, even if that role was cloaked in liberal rhetoric.

The main issues concerning living vendor sales do not need to be revisited at this point; that would be the role of policy makers in particular jurisdictions. However, the option of selling cadaveric body parts is popular among the Advocates, and the issues it raises merit brief attention.

(a) Cadaveric Sales by Relatives
The sale of cadaveric body parts, as distinct from parts from live donors, adopts a particularly important role in jurisprudential debate about the general trade in body parts. This is arguably due to the nature of consent: consent is a right of the living. While sensitivity is displayed towards a person's wishes after his or her death (and hence the option, in many jurisdictions, of asking potential donors to mark their drivers' licenses if they wish to donate their organs after death, rather than having the state simply confiscate all suitable cadaveric organs),[158] it is clear that post-death rights are limited. This is a remnant of early common law, according to which, notes C L Levy, "the only right a live person had over his body, which would someday be a cadaver, was that he might direct the manner and place of his burial in his will. And, these wishes would be legally enforceable if they did not conflict with other prevailing standards (e.g., community religious standards)."[159]

The state is less paternalistic—or even non-paternalistic—towards the dead than the living. Its care seems to end at the point at which a person is regarded as legally dead: that is the point at which the person can no longer be harmed,[160] and his or her freedom to make autonomous decisions can no longer be infringed. Therefore the distinction seems to be driven

---

157 This is defined as a market in which the state buys organs and redistributes them according to standard transplantation criteria such as need, blood and tissue type, and potential for success. For a proposal of this type see J F Childress, "No: A Free Market Would Reduce Donations and Would Commodify the Human Body", *InsightMag.com*: <http://www.insightmag.com/news/2001/05/07/Symposium/Q.Should.Congress.Allow.The.Buying.And.Selling.Of.Human.Organs-213240.shtml> at 29 June 2005.
158 One method by which some states confiscate suitable organs is the "opt-out" system. See Marie-Andree Jacob, "On Silencing and Slicing: Presumed Consent to Post-Mortem Organ 'Donation' in Diversified Societies" (2003) 11 *Tulsa Journal of Comparative and International Law* 239.
159 C L Levy, The Human Body and the Law: Legal and Ethical Considerations in Human Experimentation (1975) 53, chapter 6, "Transplantation".
160 One anomaly is criminal legislation that, in effect, proscribes the assault of a dead body. Even this arguably aims to protect the feelings of relatives and friends, and to prevent public offence, rather than to somehow protect the deceased person.

by the lack of harm that is likely to result from donation of one's body parts after one's death.[161]

An unspoken fear is perhaps that greedy or needy beneficiaries to a will would "pull the plug" on a seriously ill relative in the hope of inheriting more (due to the payment for the body parts) and sooner. This equates with the above-noted objection that is raised in arguments against euthanasia.[162]

(b) Cadaveric Sales on a Futures Market
A futures market in body parts would allow a person to enter into a contract to donate his or her cadaveric body parts in return for compensation that could be payable at the time of entry into the contract.[163] Alternatively, the compensation could be left as a bequest to a named beneficiary. The buyer could be a governmental body or a private organisation that would contract for the right to remove the vendor's organs and/or tissue upon the latter's death. Legally, donors would enter into irrevocable trust agreements that their tissues or organs could be harvested upon their deaths.[164]

From a classically liberal perspective, the central benefit of a futures market is possibly the advancement of human autonomy that would flow from allowing people to decide irrevocably what should be done with their bodies after death. On the other hand, it is possible their autonomy could in fact be reduced if the organisations operating the futures markets were permitted to include contractual clauses restricting the lifestyles of the futures vendors (such as a clause prohibiting the vendor from drinking alcohol or smoking so as to safeguard the health of the liver, lungs and other organs). Problems of consent should also be considered and, as with all discussion about the alienation of human body parts, these remain the greatest dilemmas to be resolved.

V. Conclusions

The upshot of this debate is contradictory indeed. This article concludes, first, that the arguments in favour of a market in human body parts are probably stronger in classically liberal terms than the prohibitionist case against such a market. However the second conclusion contradicts the implications of this finding by arguing that the contemporary global society is not a liberal utopia and is unsuitable for a free market in human body parts. A regulated market would have to be very limited and tightly controlled if there is to be a prospect of meeting the goals of classical liberal theory in practice. This paradox deserves brief explanation.

---

161 Dorothy Nelkin and Lori Andrews, "Do the Dead Have Interests? Policy Interests for Research after Life" (1998) 24 *American Journal of Law and Medicine* 261.
162 See Part IIIB, above.
163 For a more detailed discussion of a futures market in human body parts, see Lloyd R Cohen, "Increasing the Supply of Transplant Organs: The Virtues of a Futures Market" (1989–1990) 58 *George Washington Law Review* 1ff.
164 See Christopher Cates, "Property in Human Tissues: History, Society and Possible Implications" (1998) 4 *Appeal* 32, 39–40.

A. Why a Legalised Market Should be Permitted (in Theory)

The Advocates arguably win the debate at a theoretical level because, in the abstract, their arguments accord better with the fundamental principles of liberal society.

If liberalism's role is to model a society in which fairness, equality and personal autonomy are the guiding principles and goals, the argument for a market in human body parts seems—in theory—to be an appropriate path towards this end.

The Advocates propose logical reasons as to why a legal market in human body parts would reduce poverty (by increasing the range of choices available to people), reduce hypocrisy (by removing the requirement of altruism that applies only to the donor), and reduce the coercion and exploitation that might thrive in a black market (by dragging the trade of body parts under the spotlights of regulators). They argue that fairness and equality would be increased as those who supply their body parts would no longer be the only people involved in the procedure who do not gain tangible rewards, and the rich and poor would be treated equally. All of these arguments seem to accord with the fundamental principles of liberalism.

They also seem to prevail over the Opponents' arguments that assume the existence of exploitation and coercion when human body parts are sold, and that offer paternalistic solutions to alleviate problems that the Opponents *assume* will occur and that they find unacceptable in a liberal society.

Another strength of the Advocates' argument is the flexibility that stems from collecting a variety of similar views together under the pro-market rubric. Not all who argue against a free market in human body parts from living vendors would object to a regulated or futures market in cadaveric parts. This creates doctrinal elasticity that can be used by those in favour of a market in human body parts to systematically meet each absolutist argument put forward by the Opponents. This is a particularly effective strategy when the Advocates counter the liberal-grounded elements of the Opponents' case. By confronting the Opponents' philosophically based anti-market arguments with pro-market arguments based on the same philosophical principles, the Advocates build a strong case. The Advocates persuasively defend a market in human body parts on the grounds of individual autonomy and liberty protected by soft paternalism.

The soft paternalistic protection offered by some of the Advocates advances the chances of a pro-market victory because it provides ways by which to limit the negative consequences of a body part market. Imposing soft paternalistic regulations on the operation of a market in human body parts in order to safeguard a degree of personal autonomy seems more in accordance with classical liberal fundamentals than does the Opponents' demand to prohibit the market altogether. Regulation of a market is not necessarily inconsistent with liberal principles. This is decision-making authority within limits that are put in place to avoid harm, and it would be misleading to argue that humans are not autonomous if their decision-making authority is limited by laws. The fact that decision-making rights are abridged and there is not absolute control over one's body is unlikely to mean that people have *no* decision-making authority over their bodies. Rather, the decision-making authority is bounded by legal limits based on socially-determined norms and, within those limits, personal decision-making authority is absolute. It follows that these limits should be set in accordance with the liberal Harm Principle.

However, it is arguably because of operation of the Harm Principle—that gives people autonomy *if* their actions will not cause harm to others—that the Advocates both win and lose their case. The problem lies in the source of the social norms that underpin autonomy-limiting laws.

B. Why a Legalised Market Should Not be Permitted (in Practice)

The source of those norms is the reality—rather than the theoretical ideal—of the social context in which the debate occurs. The inherent abstract merits of the Advocates' various arguments thus lose a degree of relevance at this stage of the discussion.

The arguments of both sides are certainly aimed at helping to make society a better place, and the arguments for a market in human body parts proposed by the Advocates would appear to be driven by intentions that are every bit as good as those of the Opponents. The aim of creating a society that better protects liberal freedoms and that simultaneously increases the supply of human tissue and organs available to those in need is far from reprehensible. The Opponents are equally well meaning. They too want liberal freedoms to be protected, but they believe the way in which this must occur is through paternalistic policies grounded in part in moral concerns. The basic difference in perspectives arises because the Advocates argue from a theoretical position while the Opponents argue from an empirical standpoint and respond to existing social norms.

The Opponents tend to explain these norms in terms of "morality" (that is, norms arising from moral objections to commodification of the body, to slavery, and to practices that are viewed as implicitly repugnant) and present them as a trump that must intrude to prevent social harm. Liberalism might ideally be morally neutral, but it is not the problems that arise from utopian liberalism that the Opponents' illiberal moral arguments are intended to combat. The Opponents instead fear the illiberal problems that, in practice, prevent nominally liberal societies from being ideally liberal. Thus the Opponents' morally driven arguments protect autonomous individuals in liberal societies from falling victim to the malfunctioning of the practical application of the dominant political ideology in those societies. They even hope to enhance the liberal pedigree of such societies by strengthening internal liberal values, albeit through non-liberal means.

This is why the Advocates ultimately fail. Although the Advocates' arguments might seem to be more rationally and philosophically persuasive than the Opponents' case, a negative moral or emotional reaction to the empirical piecemeal sale of human body parts has been sufficient to keep the market black. This reaction is arguably a response to non-liberal elements that exist within liberal societies. If liberal democratic societies were always to function along utopian lines, and if the entire world enjoyed utopian living conditions, there would be no cause for concern about exploitation, lack of consent, wealth inequalities or slavery. In a society in which no person faced financial need, there would be little reason to worry about people being unfairly influenced to sell their body parts, or being induced or blinded by poverty and the lure of a better life to make decisions with irreversible, possibly detrimental consequences. It is ironic that, although the need for body parts for transplantation and research would persist in a utopian liberal democracy, the incentive to donate (without payment) would be very similar to that in a less-than-utopian society without compensation for the donation of a body part. The norms regarding the sale of human body parts would probably remain exactly as they are at present.

The Opponents' moral arguments have an encompassing quality that loosely cloaks the objections they raise in liberal ideals; any illiberal elements are justified by the greater liberal goal of preventing coercion and unconsented harm. In the same way, the argument from the perspective of economic rationality serves to encapsulate in a liberal shell the Advocates' other (illiberal) reasons for proposing a market in human body parts. But while the economic rationality argument is consistent with pure liberalism, the arguments from a moral standpoint add a new dimension to the debate. This arguably leaves the Advocates unable to effectively quash opposition that is based on moral contentions; the Opponents move the boundaries of the debate outside the framework of liberalism in order to justify their use of arguably illiberal means to protect liberalism, and it is in this external space that they seize their victory.

Is this legitimate? If legitimacy were to be measured from a subjective liberal perspective, the answer would probably be "no", the Advocates would prevail, and some sort of market in human body parts could be established forthwith. But if legitimacy is measured from an objective external perspective, and if (liberty-promoting) paternalism is found to be just another social norm from which the legal system derives principles that it uses to order a notionally liberal society, then the resulting laws banning a market in human body parts are arguably legitimate. This requires that morality-driven paternalism is understood as a social norm that stands alongside liberalism to contribute to the social constitution, rather than requiring it to be subsumed by liberalism if it is to be legitimate.

If this conclusion is correct, it would be intellectually honest to acknowledge this at a policy level in order to avoid creating the impression that illiberal policy decisions are being unacceptably put into force by law in ostensibly liberal polities. For the Opponents to accept the Advocates' proposals and depart from the status quo, the global society would presumably have to be much fairer and safer, and more equitable and liberal, than it is today. Unless this occurs, it would be beneficial for all those concerned about the issue—the Advocates and Opponents alike, as well as potential body part donors and vendors, potential body part recipients, those involved in their counselling and medical care, and researchers seeking answers for the future—if nominally liberal societies would confront, acknowledge and explain the ostensibly contradictory nature of their anti-market policies concerning the sale of human body parts. In the absence of such intellectual candour, the dilemmas seem likely to remain intractable and impervious to the scientific and medical advances taking place despite them.

C. Remedies

What, then, should be done? How can the needs, wishes and well-being of patients, researchers, would-be body part vendors, and the poor and vulnerable members of our global society, be reconciled? The utopia that the Opponents would require as a pre-requisite to permitting a market in human body parts seems a distant, and probably impossible, dream. Meanwhile, patients die waiting for transplant organs and tissue, researchers are demanding access to human body parts to experiment on in the hope of reaching breakthroughs that will benefit millions of people, body parts continue to be traded on the black market, and the wishes of others who want to sell their body parts are being frustrated by law. The dilemma seems intractable, and that is presumably why it remains unsolved after so much discussion and debate. But ignoring the problem does not make it go away. Far from disappearing, the old debates seem to be intensifying under the pressure of new discoveries that offer innovative medical treatments and are accompanied by new perspectives on familiar medico-ethical concerns. Perhaps the biotechnological revolution needs to be accompanied by a jurisprudential revolution in this area?

An immediate step towards effectively addressing this problem might be for law makers to recognise candidly the empirical context in which the debate has been occurring: body parts continue to be sold and indigent people continue to be exploited by rapacious black market intermediaries. Prohibition is not working. Indeed, as experiences with alcohol and drug legislation have demonstrated,[165] prohibition often fails to fulfil its goals.

---

[165] At best, outlawing behaviour has a deterrent effect, but it rarely has the outcome of stopping the behaviour altogether. See, eg., Jeffrey A Miron, "An Economic Analysis of Alcohol Prohibition" (1998) 28 *Journal of Drug Issues* 741; Charles H Whitebread, "Freeing Ourselves from the Prohibition Idea in the Twenty-First Century" (2000) 33 *Suffolk University Law Review* 235; Thomas James Friedrich, "Internet Casino Gambling:

It might discourage an activity, but it will not stamp it out altogether, and some of those who engage in illegal behavior (such as taking illicit drugs or selling their body parts) will almost certainly be among the most vulnerable members of society.

There is a difference between decriminalising, de-illegalising or legalising and regulating an activity, and tacitly or actively encouraging participation in that activity. There is a difference between allowing people self determination and approving of the ways in which they choose to exercise their autonomy. Perhaps an answer lies in strictly regulating the trade in human body parts, rather than outlawing it altogether?

Perhaps the creation of an international authority to regulate the existing—mainly illegal—market in human body parts would help? Perhaps an international regulatory authority with national branches located in organ trade hotspots around the world could act as a sanctioned, official intermediary between those who wish to donate (for compensation or otherwise) and those who wish to receive body parts? Perhaps such an authority could actively discourage the sale of human body parts but nonetheless examine, on a subjective case-by-case basis, the circumstances—and alternative options—for those who remain determined to sell their body parts? Perhaps such an authority could help by offering suggestions and advice, and by providing alternative options for some of those would-be body part vendors? Perhaps such an authority could retain the right to veto body parts sales—while always offering alternative methods of obtaining income—when convinced a potential donor/vendor is being coerced? Surely such measures would go some way to remedying the illiberal, less-than-utopian situation that exists at present?

When it comes to moving beyond the present situation and determining solutions for a better future, perhaps a sea change in jurisprudential thinking needs to occur. The initial question for law makers examining the sorts of issues raised in this paper should arguably be whether individuals should be given the sort of decision-making authority over their own bodies that would allow them to trade in their body parts.[166] If law makers conclude in the affirmative, they should then consider whether such a trade should be compensable. Focusing first on these discrete questixons will hopefully help to push the debate forward towards finding workable solutions.

Once these initial questions have been answered, an appropriate legal framework through which to implement the conclusions can be chosen. It might, for example, be decided that the human body should be considered the property of its occupant,[167] and that use restrictions should attach

---

The Nightmare of Lawmaking, Jurisdiction, Enforcement and the Dangers of Prohibition" (2003) 11 *CommLaw Conspectus* 369, 382–85.
[166] See discussion in Alexandra George, "Is 'Property' Necessary? On Owning the Human Body and its Parts" (2004) 10 *Res Publica* 15.
[167] Ibid. For the question of whether or not human body parts are property, see Michell Bourianoff Bray, "Personalizing Personalty: Toward a Property Right in Human Bodies" (1990) 69 *Texas Law Review* 209–43.

to this property (just as legal use restrictions regulate how people use other pieces of their property, such as guns, cars, hammers, noisy stereos, polluting factories, and so on). Or maybe it would be decided that imposing a list of criminal sanctions is an appropriate way of regulating the ways in which people use their decision-making authority over their bodies (just as legal restrictions regulate whether people are permitted to ingest drugs, commit suicide, and so on). A number of alternatives could be considered.

Approaching the puzzle in the methodical manner just outlined should go some way to avoiding the contradictions implicit in allowing the uncompensated donation of body parts but forbidding the sale of those same parts. While remaining within the Opponents' liberal requirements, and at the same time adopting the most compelling arguments of the case offered by the Advocates, it should help to protect those who might currently fall victim to exploitation and coercion because they operate in a twilight black market, having run out of (or believing that they have exhausted) legal options. It should overcome the paternalism—and particularly paternalism towards the poor—implicit in outright prohibitionary policies. It should address the issues of fairness and distributive justice that arise when everyone involved but the donor receives a tangible benefit from the donation of a body part. Finally, and most importantly, it should help society move towards a workable solution during a period of exponential growth in scientific and medical advances that really does amount to a biotechnological revolution. And that must surely be better than throwing our hands up in frustration or clinging to the status quo as a default position because it all seems too difficult to deal with.

SOUNDS SUSPICIOUSLY LIKE PROPERTY TREATMENT:
Does Human Tissue Fit Within The Common Law Concept Of Property?

Imogen Goold*

...the legal treatment of bodies and body parts sounds suspiciously like property treatment.

Lori Andrews[1]

In Australia, human tissue use is regulated by a piecemeal, sometimes conflicting body of legislation and case law.[2] In general, these laws have been developed to deal with specific uses of tissue, such as the Human Tissue Acts,[3] and hence do not form a body of rules that can be easily extrapolated to emerging uses of tissue. The acts are limited in scope and deal only with consent to the removal of tissue, not with its subsequent use. They also cover only the removal of tissue for transplantation, medical and research purposes—which are rapidly becoming only a few of many uses to which human tissue may now be put. Beyond these acts, only for forensic purposes is the collection, use and storage of tissue samples legislatively controlled.

Ethical guidelines, particularly those released by the National Health and Medical Research Council (NHMRC), play a significant role in deterring misuse of tissue within a research context.[4] While such guidelines have been greatly influential in encouraging ethical research practice, their lack of legal force precludes them from providing enforceable resolutions to conflicts of interest. As ethical guidelines do not provide a legal cause of action, individuals may be left without a remedy against a person or institution who has misused their tissue.

---

* St Anne's College, University of Oxford.
1 L B Andrews, "My Body, My Property" (1986) 16 *Hastings Center Report* 28, 29.
2 The major cases dealing with property law and human tissue in Australia and the United Kingdom are *Dobson and Another v North Tyneside Health Authority and Another* (1996) 4 All ER 474; *Doodeward v Spence* (1908) 6 CLR 406; *R v Kelly* (1998) 3 All ER 741 and *Roche v Douglas as Administrator of the Estate of Edward Rowan (dec'd)* [2000] WASC 146.
3 *Human Tissue Act 1985* (Tas); *Human Tissue Act 1982* (Vic); *Human Tissue Act 1983* (NSW); *Transplantation and Anatomy Act 1983* (SA); *Transplantation and Anatomy Act 1979* (Qld); *Human Tissue and Transplantation Act 1982* (WA); *Transplantation and Anatomy Act 1978* (ACT) and *Human Tissue Transplant Act 1979* (NT).
4 See, eg., National Health and Medical Research Council, *National Statement on Ethical Conduct in Research Involving Humans*, NHMRC, Canberra, 1999.

Finally, the courts have developed a general rule against property in human bodies and their parts, with some exceptions. The major exception allows that human tissue may be property once it has been preserved through the application of work or skill.[5] This rule and its exception have been considered in only a few cases, mostly concerning the theft of tissue[6]; applications for access to test samples have been considered[7] and even within this class, the courts have been divided on both the law and its application.[8]

Increasingly, this situation is becoming untenable, for the uses of tissue, and the interests held in it are expanding, while the legal system fails to keep up. For one example, human tissue is now used to develop valuable therapeutic products, yet the only controls on who may buy and sell are the Human Tissue Acts' prohibitions on sale without processing.[9]

As another example, where organs and bones are retained, an individual seeking their return for burial has no legal means of compelling return and in Australia must rely on the goodwill of researchers and hospitals. Aboriginal communities that have sought the return of their ancestors' remains from museums are a particular example of the problems that can arise in this context. Despite some recent repatriation, Aboriginal groups have pointed out that most remains still rest in museums.[10] This is in part due to the fact that many museums refuse to return remains. In late 2002, a number of museums in Europe and the United States issued a declaration opposing repatriation. The signatories argue that maintaining large collections that promote culture is more important than the desire of individual countries or racial groups for the return of artefacts.[11] Without

---

5 See *Doodeward v Spence* (1908) 6 CLR 406; *R v Kelly* (1998) 3 All ER 741; *Roche v Douglas as Administrator of the Estate of Edward Rowan (dec'd)* [2000] WASC 146.
6 *R v Kelly* but compare *R v Herbert* (1961) 25 J CR L 163 and *R v Rothery* (1976) Crim LR 691, which contain no mention of either the rule or the exception.
7 *Roche v Douglas* [2000] WASC 146.
8 See *Dobson and Another v North Tyneside Health Authority and Another* (1996) 4 All ER 474 and compare *R v Kelly* (1998) 3 All ER 741.
9 *Human Tissue Act 1985* (Tas) s 27; *Human Tissue Act 1982* (Vic) ss 38, 39; *Human Tissue Act 1983* (NSW) s 32; *Transplantation and Anatomy Act 1983* (SA) s 35(1)–(6); *Transplantation and Anatomy Act 1979* (Qld) s 35(1)–(6); *Human Tissue and Transplantation Act 1982* (WA) s 29; *Transplantation and Anatomy Act 1978* (ACT) s 44 and *Human Tissue Transplant Act 1979* (NT) s 24.
10 Australian Broadcasting Commission, "Aboriginal Remains to be Returned from the UK" *ABC Radio News*, 7 June 2001.
11 P Fray and A Moses, "Top Museums Unite to Fight Aboriginal Claims", *Sydney Morning Herald*, 11 December 2002, <www.smh.com.au/articles/2002/12/10/1039379839080.html> at 1 September 2003. Among the signatories were the Guggenheim, the Hermitage, the Prado, the New York Metropolitan and the Louvre. Some British museums have, however, agreed to return remains for burial, including the Hunterian Museum of the Royal College of Surgeons, the Pitt-Rivers Museum in Oxford, the Peterborough City Museum, Bradford University and the Kelvingrove Museum in Glasgow (P Huck, "Bringing Home the Dead", *Australian Financial Review* (Sydney), 24 October 1991, 37. In Australia, museums have been required to return the collected remains of Aborigines (D G Jones, *Speaking for the Dead: Cadavers in Biology and Medicine* (2000) 120) and undertakings have also been made by the Australian government to secure the return of some remains (L Tingle, "PM Gives Word on Aboriginal Remains", *The Age* (Melbourne), 22 June 1997, 1).

a legal remedy, communities are unable to give those remains a proper burial, and to their minds the spirits of those who died cannot be laid to rest. Similarly, the law provides few answers to questions of who has rights to store and use banked cord blood; or how disputes over access to tissue samples for paternity or DNA testing are to be solved. In more general terms, the law as it now stands does not provide guidance on most of the potential future uses for tissue, on its storage, on how and when it may be removed (save in the context of research, forensics and transplantation), on the rights of the person from whom it was taken and on those of the person who gains possession of it. The specificity of the acts and the ethics guidelines in place mean that they have neither the breadth nor the flexibility to deal with new uses and problems. One response to these issues has been the view that human tissue should be deemed property, prompting a broad and complex debate on whether that would be legally workable, pragmatic or ethical.[12]

This article does enter into the general debate over whether human tissue should be dealt with through property law, which has been widely considered.[13] Instead, it seeks to add to the general debate by providing a different perspective on the central question of whether tissue can or should be property. It unpacks the notion of property and then examines how it can apply to tissue to illuminate more clearly what sort of rights and duties would be created in relation to tissue by according it property status. By analysing the concept of property in this way, the article aims to determine whether human tissue has the hallmarks of what the common law considers to be property and what this can tell us about the applicability of property law to human tissue. It is argued that this approach can be used in addition to other analyses of the property question; it is not an alternative methodology, but rather an additional way of looking at the question that can improve how we continue to consider the issue of whether tissue should be property.

All Australian museums have agreed to refrain from displaying any recent skeletal remains (R Glover and D Langsam, "Day of Reckoning for Darwin's Bodysnatchers", *Sydney Morning Herald*, 3 March 1990, 79, 80).

12 See variously L Andrews and D Nelkin, *Body Bazaar: The Market for Human Tissue in the Biotechnology Age* (2001); Nuffield Council on Bioethics, *Human Tissue: Ethical and Legal Issues* (1995); L Skene, "Arguments Against People Legally 'Owning' Their Own Bodies, Body Parts and Tissue" (2002) 2 *Macquarie Law Journal* 163; R Magnusson, "The Recognition of Proprietary Rights in Human Tissue in Common Law Jurisdictions" (1992) 18 *Melbourne University Law Review* 601.

13 L B Andrews, "My Body, My Property" (1986) 16 *Hastings Center Report* 28; T H Murray, "On the Human Body as Property: The Meaning of Embodiment, Markets, and the Meaning of Strangers" (1987) 20 *Journal of Law Reform* 1055; J W Harris, "Who Owns My Body?" (1996) 161 *Oxford Journal of Legal Studies* 55; D Mortimer, "Proprietary Rights in Body Parts: The Relevance of Moore's Case in Australia" (1993) 19 *Monash University Law Review* 217; R Magnusson, "Proprietary Rights in Tissue" in N Palmer and E McKendrick (eds), *Interests in Goods* (2nd ed, 1998) 25; R Atherton, "Who Owns Your Body?" (2003) 77 *Australian Law Journal* 178; L Skene, "Arguments against People Legally 'Owning' their Own Bodies, Body Parts and Tissue" (2002) 2 *Macquarie Law Journal* 163; J Harris and C Erin, "An Ethically Defensible Market in Organs: A Single Buyer Like the NHS is an Answer" (2002) 325 *British Medical Journal* 114.

Each incident of property will be examined in turn and with reference to some examples of tissue use, to analyse which of these incidents can be applied to tissue. Two examples of how combinations of some incidents can be observed in how tissue is used will then be examined. Some consideration of the different concerns raised by renewable and non-renewable body tissues in relation to the property question will also be examined at this stage. The paper will conclude by weighing up how well tissue has been seen to fit within the concept of property, and comment on how this affects the general debate over property law and human tissue. It should also be noted that although this paper concludes that human tissue can fit within the concept of property, and hence that it would at a basic level be possible to use property laws to regulate tissue use, this does not necessitate an argument in favour of doing so. This paper leaves the second question—the "should" question—open. There may be good reasons not to use property law to regulate tissue use. However, by taking this approach the paper marks this out as a separate issue that requires focused debate, instead of (as is sometimes the case) conflating this issue with debate about whether property law could effectively regulate the use of tissue.

The Body as Property Debate

To date, the common law approach has been to accept the general rule that bodies and their parts are not property. This rule emerged in the 18th and 19th centuries, in which a string of cases held that corpses were not property.[14] In the early 20th century, however, an exception to the rule was upheld by the Australian High Court in *Doodeward v Spence*.[15] In that case, it was held that there could be lawful, continuing possession of a corpse and that bodies and parts could become the subject of property rights "when a person has by lawful exercise of work or skill so dealt with a human body or part of a human body in his lawful possession that it has acquired some attributes differentiating it from a mere corpse awaiting burial, he acquires a right to retain possession of it, at least against any person not entitled to have it delivered to him for the purpose of burial."[16]

Subsequently, courts have applied this exception to the rule, or attempted to apply it, in a number of cases. *Dobson and Another v North Tyneside Health Authority and Another*[17] concerned the retention and treatment of stored brain tissue preserved in wax and it was held that such preservation was not sufficient for the brain to be property. By contrast, two years later in the 1998 case of *R v Kelly*,[18] the court held

---
14 *Haynes' case* (1614) 77 ER 1389; *R v Lynn* (1788) 2 TR 733; *R v Price* (1884) 12 QB 247; *Williams v Williams* (1882) 20 ChD 659.
15 *Doodeward v Spence* (1908) 6 CLR 406.
16 Ibid.
17 *Dobson and Another v North Tyneside Health Authority and Another* (1996) 4 All ER 474.
18 *R v Kelly* (1998) 3 All ER 741.

that body parts preserved and retained in the Royal College of Surgeons were property under the exception to the rule and Kelly could therefore be guilty of stealing them.

One reason the courts have begun to accept that body parts should be treated as property through exceptions to the general rule is that in many instances, the way human tissue is dealt with closely reflects the way items of property are treated, both by society and by the legal system. If they are dealt with in the same way, the argument goes, then it may be that the laws of property are a suitable means of regulating dealings with human tissue. Similarly, there has been major academic debate in this area concerned with whether excised human tissue should be accorded the status of legal property.[19]

Generally, this debate has been cast in terms of a property/no property dichotomy, and has been argued from legal and ethical perspectives (often focusing on achieving desired outcomes, rather than the strict application of principle). The debate has not, however, been characterised by a focus on whether the law can admit human tissue as an object of property, but on the pros and cons of according tissue property status in a particular setting. Debate about these pros and cons often conflates two questions—whether tissue *could* be effectively regulated through property law concepts, and whether it *should* be so regulated. This paper examines the first question, cast as whether human tissue can fit within the legal concept of property.

The Concept of Property[20]

Common law property systems are mechanisms by which access to, and control of, resources are regulated. They are both legal and social institutions, acting as an organising system where a resource is relatively scarce. As such, common law property is a system for resolving disputes between parties with different interests in an object or thing. Where more than one party wishes to use or possess an object or thing, property rules work to determine who has the better claim to it and to protect that claim, or right, from others. These rights are protected by a rules-based designation of control and the protection of that designation until it is lawfully altered.

It becomes apparent, then, why the idea of regulating human tissue through such a system has been suggested, for that tissue is increasingly a substance which different groups wish to access and control. Where a particular tissue sample is sought (either for forensic purposes or because it

---

19 Some authors have asserted that the debate as to whether human biological materials should be deemed property is a debate about the wrong issue altogether (see, eg., A George, "Property in the Human Body and its Parts: Reflections on Self-Determination in Liberal Society" (2001) *European University Institute Working Paper No. 2001/8*).

20 The author would like to acknowledge the kind help of Professors Tony Honoré and James Harris with regard to this section.

has unique uses in research), tissue also has one of the other characteristics of objects of property—relative scarcity. It is a substance in which different people have competing interests, and the most basic purpose of property systems is to determine whose interest, claim or right will prevail.

When dealing with corporeal objects, the common law does not really determine whether an object is in itself "property". Rather, it is more accurate to view the law of property as a system delineating which things may have property rights exercised over them and what may be included within those rights.[21] An object forms the centre of a web of relationships between people, each of whom has rights with regard to that object.[22] Together, these rights determine how each person may deal with the object.[23]

A particular difficulty of defining property is that the aggregate bundle of rights of which it is composed may differ in scope, in definition, in character and in effect. The bundle is not the same nor does it work in the same way in relation to every object. Rights may vary due to the character of the person who possesses them, when they are possessed and the nature of the subject of those rights. For example, the property rights which vest in a person over an intangible object such as some form of intellectual property will differ from those which vest in a tangible object like a chair. An object may be owned in a number of distinct ways and these rights are all theoretically separable from one another. Yet, it is this complexity that lends the concept of property the very flexibility that suits it to regulating the wide and varied range of relationships that individuals may have with regard to human tissue. With flexibility comes the ability to adapt to novel forms of property, of which human tissue may be one.[24] This complexity also highlights the conceptual heart of property law, namely that it aims to recognise and regulate conflicting interests and relationships.

A Bundle of Rights: The Incidents of Property

There are eleven generally accepted property rights, though they are more often referred to as the "incidents" of property as they include powers, liabilities and the like.[25] This is usually called the "bundle of rights"

---

21 See, eg., R Hardiman, "Toward the Right of Commerciality: Recognizing Property Rights in the Commercial Value of Human Tissue" (1986) 34 *University of California Los Angeles Law Review* 207, 214.
22 See S Munzer, *A Theory of Property* (1990) 16–17 on the occasional need to use also the simple conception of "property as things". It is, Munzer argues, "perfectly sound to think of property both as things (the popular conception) and as relations among persons or other entities with respect to things (the sophisticated conception)—provided that the context makes clear which conception is meant".
23 It bears noting that simply listing the rights that make up the common law concept of property does not wholly capture the concept of "ownership". Jeremy Waldron suggests that defining an owner as someone who may only use an object in accordance with their rights and the law is "vacuous" because it defines ownership only by reference to external criteria to explain ownership itself (J Waldron, "What is Private Property?" (1985) 5 *Oxford Journal of Legal Studies* 313, 316).
24 Hardiman, n 21, 215.
25 Some legal scholars reject the incident of prohibition of harmful use (for example, Jeremy Waldron).

approach, which as it is now conceived is essentially a combination of Hohfeldian rights analysis and the later work of A M Honoré.[26]

Hohfeldian rights analysis divides rights relationships into a number of specific types, conceptualising them as aspects of a relationship between individuals over an object. In this model, legal relations are organised into elements, opposites and correlatives.

The four elements of legal relations are: rights, privileges, powers and immunities.

A correlative means a duty, no-right, liability or disability that corresponds to a particular element. Where the one arises, the other arises with it, as a relationship will always involve more than one party (even if one party is "all the world"). Each element and correlative describes the position in which those parties sit—the power they may hold, the immunity they may enjoy or the right they may claim.

Opposites represent the situation that exists when the element is not held. For example, where a person does not have a power, he or she can be said to be "disabled". These elements, opposites and correlatives have been termed the "lowest common denominators of the law",[27] and are summarised in Table 1. Collectively, they will be referred to as "rights" for the purposes of this paper.

Table 1. The Hohfeldian Analytical Vocabulary

Jural Correlatives	Right	Privilege	Power	Immunity
	Duty	No-right	Liability	Disability
Jural Opposites	Right	Privilege	Power	Immunity
	No-right[28]	Duty[29]	Disability[30]	Liability[31]

These four sets of elements, correlatives and opposites are the basic structures of property rights. However, alone they say nothing of the content of those rights, but describe only the form those rights may take.

---

26 See, eg., J E Penner, "The 'Bundle of Rights' Picture of Property", (1996) 43 *University of California Los Angeles Law Review* 711.

27 W Hohfeld, "Some Fundamental Legal Conceptions as Applied in Judicial Reasoning" (1913) 26 *Yale Law Journal* 16, 64. (This notion has been criticised by Stephen Munzer, who has argued that in fact the elements as expounded by Hohfeld are reducible to two elements only: "power" and "duty", where these two elements are conceived in a slightly different manner: see Munzer, n 22, 17–22.)

28 Given that a duty is a legal obligation to do or not do something, a "right" in this context is more akin to a claim that the something in question be done or not done. A duty forms the correlative of a right as a failure to fulfil that duty will equate to a violation of the right. In the interests of clarity these rights will be referred to as "claim-rights". The opposite of a claim-right is what Hohfeld termed a "no-right", or the lack of any claim. W Hohfeld, n 27, 33.

29 A privilege allows the holder to choose not to do something. Privileges can therefore also be seen as liberties or freedoms. Where one person has the privilege to do something, another will correlatively have "no right" to prevent that person from doing so. The opposite of a privilege or freedom is a duty or obligation to do something and that one has no choice to refuse.

This content is provided by Honoré's description of property incidents that will now be examined.

Honoré outlined the eleven incidents and used Hohfeldian terms to describe them, including the notion of rights and correlatives. These incidents of property, according to Honoré, are each aggregates of various forms of "rights", such as the right to use which consists of both a claim-right to use and the privilege to exercise that claim-right over a certain object.[32] These incidents are descriptive of the rights that common law property systems allow to be held in objects to regulate allocation, and Honoré describes them as the "standard incidents of ownership"[33] common to "mature" legal systems.

If all eleven incidents are vested in one individual then that individual possesses full ownership of the object to which those incidents relate. However, property law within the common law system does not require that one individual hold all eleven incidents to have a property interest in an object. Rather, the common law as described by Honoré's concept of ownership allows for a more fragmented approach to the ownership of object, wherein a number of individuals may hold certain rights in an object and each will possess a property interest though not full ownership itself.[34] Indeed, it is rare for any one individual to hold the entire set of rights in an object. An individual will more often possess a combination of them, while another will possess some of the remaining rights.

The aim of listing these incidents is not to define any necessary conditions of a property relationship, but to illustrate certain common features which link such relationships. The incidents aim to sum up the diverse range of property rights and relationships existing at common law by creating a wide catch-all list of possible interests, rather than by providing an exclusive list of compulsory aspects. Further, the inclusion of various other liabilities and prohibitions is an attempt to shift focus from a view of property centred on rights, to clarify that the property relationship is

---

30 A legal "power" is the ability to do something, in effect to alter one's legal position (or that of another). For instance, the ability to donate an object equates to a legal power to transfer title to another, altering both one's own legal relationships and those of the donee. This donee's legal relations have been altered by the effect of the power, and the correlative therefore of a power is a liability or susceptibility to having one's legal relations changed. It follows then that the opposite of a power will be a disability, that is, the inability to alter legal relations. See further Hohfeld, n27, 44–54.
31 An immunity is the absence of susceptibility to having one's legal relations changed by another. This does not however place a duty on others to avoid altering those relations, rather others are under a correlative disability as they may not alter the legal relations of the person holding the immunity. The opposite of an immunity is a liability, or a susceptibility to having one's legal relations changed.
32 E Seeney, "Note: *Moore* 10 Years Later—Still Trying to Fill the Gap: Creating a Personal Property Right in Genetic Material", (1998) 32 *New England Law Review* 1131, n 177. See also L C Becker, *Property Rights: Philosophic Foundations* (1977) 21.
33 A M Honoré, "Ownership" in A Guest, (ed) *Oxford Essays in Jurisprudence* (1961) 113ff. For discussion of this list in other works see, eg., Becker, *Property Rights*, 18–20; Waldron, "What is Private Property?", n 23. See also S Hepburn, *Principles of Property Law* (1998) 2–3.
34 F H Lawson and B Rudden, *The Law of Property*, (2nd ed, 1982) 9.

complicated by other interests beyond those which constitute the powers held by an individual over an object. While each of these incidents or rights has particular characteristics as privileges, powers and the like, the general descriptors "incident" and "right" will be used to refer to them collectively. Honoré and others use this method, and it is grammatically less confusing.

Table 2. The Eleven Incidents of Property[35]

Right to Possess	Incident of Transmissibility
Right to Use	Incident of Absence of Term
Right to Manage	Prohibition on Harmful Use
Right to the Income	Liability to Execution
Right to the Capital	Residuary Character
Right to Security	

Can Human Tissue Fit Within the Concept of Property?

Having begun to analyse what property is, it now becomes possible to consider whether human tissue does bear its hallmarks. To determine whether human tissue can fit within the concept of property, three further questions will be posed in the context of each of the eleven property incidents. First, can the incident be applied to human tissue, meaning is it possible to do so effectively and without producing absurdity? Second, is this incident already reflected in the way human tissue is dealt with? Third, does the legal system uphold or recognise this incident in relation to human tissue? The answers to these questions will show not only how far tissue could be fitted into a property system, but perhaps how far it already has been.

1. Right to Possess

The right to possess is a claim-right to exclusive physical control of an object, and with this comes the complementary claim-right to exclude others from controlling the object.[36] If the object cannot be physically possessed, that is, where the object is intangible or immovable, this right may be regarded as a right to exclude others from use or from benefit derivable from the object. Others are under a correlative duty not to take exclusive control, which is reflected in laws prohibiting theft.[37]

---

35 As stated in Honoré, "Ownership", 113–28.
36 In some instances it could also be regarded as a privilege. For example, a transplant surgeon may possess an organ to place into the body of her patient, but it is unlikely that the law would accord the same right to someone who was not qualified to do so.
37 Yet if this right to possession was merely a right to have present possession protected, possession itself would not be well protected. Instead, it is necessary to add another dimension to the right to possess—a claim-right to be put in control. The need for this is illustrated simply by considering what would happen if only present possession were protected. If A has possession of an object, and that possession is taken over by B, A no

This right to possess is, according to Honoré, "the foundation on which the whole superstructure of ownership rests".[38] Property systems often focus on protecting possessory rights to enable protection of other property rights. For instance, in many cases it would be nearly impossible for a legal system to protect the rights to use and manage if anyone was free to take possession of the object of those rights. For example, a person may have the right to drive his car as and when that person wishes. However, without a right to possession which is upheld against others, anyone may rightfully sit in the car, take control of it or exclude the individual from entering it.[39] For this reason, the right to possess is a right in rem, that is one which can be held out against all other people, aside from those who fall within certain exceptions.[40]

Could a right of possession be exercised over human tissue? Tissue is a tangible, visible object, whether in the liquid form of blood or as a solid organ or piece of skin. As such, clearly it can be physically held, and thus it is possible for tissue to be held in an individual's physical control. It is also possible to exclude others from it either by placing it inside a safe or securing it in some other form of container which is protected from removal, as even an entire body is small enough and sufficiently containable to be kept in a secure container. Tissue, in fact, is more amenable to being the object of a possessory right than many other objects which one may already legally possess, land being a prime example.

Is something akin to a right of possession already asserted over human tissue? In newborn screening programs, newborn screening cards are securely stored in hospitals, and others are prevented from using them without permission. The same can be said of tissue held for pathology or testing purposes which are retained by laboratories and are generally not released under any circumstances, even to the person from whom they were originally taken. Similarly, scientists possess tissue samples used in research and exercise control over who may access them, as do museums that hold physical remains. Reports of tissue retention in Australia and

---

longer has present possession. If the right to possession was protected only by prohibiting others from taking possession, once dispossessed A would have no right to regain possession of what was hers. Protection of that original right to possess is properly upheld against all persons only where it remains in effect after unlawful dispossession, giving A the ability to have her possession of the object restored. That is, A is no longer in exclusive control of the object, but she has not lost her right to be in control. She has the right to have that exclusive control still and hence may claim against B that the object be handed back. Honoré has expressed this as a distinction between "having" an object and "having a right to" an object, or the distinction between "rules allocating things to people as opposed to rules merely forbidding forcible taking". See Honoré, "Ownership", 115.
38 Ibid, 113.
39 It is in this sense, as discussed above, that while each property interest is separable in theory, in practice in many cases such a separation would be unworkable (although this will be dependent on the type of object in which rights are held and how those rights are divided).
40 For example, government officials and police often have the right to enter onto land owned by an individual in certain exceptional circumstances laid down by the law.

the United Kingdom over the past five years have also demonstrated how widespread tissue possession has been.[41]

The law has upheld these and other possessions, and in some cases made it an offence to interfere with possession. Theft prosecutions in the cases of *R v Rothery*,[42] *R v Welsh*[43] and most recently *R v Kelly*[44] are instances where the legal system has upheld a right to possession. In *Kelly*, the Royal College's right to possess was tacitly recognised by the finding that Kelly had stolen preserved body parts from its museum, while in *Rothery* and *Welsh*, the police having possession of blood and urine samples were able to defend that right against interference even from the source of the tissue. Both Rothery and Welsh were effectively regarded as under a duty not to interfere with the samples taken from them. Human tissue both lends itself to being possessed and is in fact often already possessed, both in a real and in a legal sense.

2. Right to Use

Taking a narrow view of "use", the right to use does not include the rights to manage and to reap the income of an object. It is a claim-right to the personal enjoyment of an object, or in some cases a privilege to use it. The list of uses to which an object may be put is open-ended, but its scope may be limited by rule of law. Where a person has a right or privilege to use an object, others will either be under a duty not to use it, or have no right to do so.

Whether it is possible to uphold a right or privilege to use human tissue is perhaps best answered simply by pointing to the vast array of uses to which it is already is put. Human tissue has acquired a myriad of uses in recent times, but even before the advent of scientific and medical developments it has long had a place as a valuable resource. Tissue is clearly used in testing and pathological examinations; for treatment (namely donated organs and tissue); for medical research; in forensic procedures; and even as artwork and educational displays, as the work of Mark Quinn and Gunther von Hagens demonstrates.[45] It is in fact almost unnecessary to ask if tissue is used, as it has been for centuries.

Many of these uses are sanctioned by the legal system, though often as privileges rather than as rights to use. The Human Tissue Acts are explicitly designed to legalise certain uses, though as noted in Chapter Four, they do not entirely achieve this. Use of organs for transplantation is legal, and

---

[41] See, eg., Department of Health, Department of Education and Employment and the Home Office, *Report of a Census of Organs and Tissues Retained by Pathology Services in England: Conducted in 2000 by the Chief Medical Officer* (2001); Crown Solicitor for Western Australia and Commissioner for Health for Western Australia, *Final Report: Removal and Retention of Organs and Tissue Following Post-mortem Examinations* (2001); South Australia Solicitor-General, *Report into the Retention of Body Parts after Post-Mortems* (2001).
[42] *R v Rothery* (1976) Crim LR 691.
[43] *R v Welsh* (1974) RTR 478.
[44] *R v Kelly* (1998) 3 All ER 741.
[45] Quinn created *Self,* a model of his head, using his own, congealed blood as a work of art.

can be regarded as giving surgeons a privilege to use organs for treatment. Similarly, the NHMRC *National Statement on Ethical Conduct in Research Involving Humans* (National Statement) in conjunction with the Human Tissue Acts condone the use of tissue for research. The police can seek to take blood samples and swabs for forensic purposes in accordance with the *Crimes Act 1914* (Cth) and state legislation,[46] and individuals are under a correlative duty to supply samples where the law requires.[47] Tissue use is both possible, and legally sanctioned.

3. Right to Manage

The right to manage is a combination of a power to determine who may use an object and how they may do so, and a claim-right that the object is dealt with as directed.[48] Others are under a correlative liability to having their relationship to the object altered, perhaps by having been given a right to possession and a duty to use it only as authorised. Management power allows a person to enable others to deal with the object in a manner which would otherwise be prohibited. For instance, the owner of a car may allow a person who has no right to use the car to do so—perhaps through a licensing agreement, as is the case in car rental operations.

There is little legal difficulty with according a power of management over human tissue. The person holding that power could use it to allow others to perform research on a sample, to test it, to store it as part of a research database or to dispose of it after removing it during surgery. In fact, human tissue is well suited to being subject to a management power. Such a power could be given to a person who has a strong interest in tissue, most likely the person from whom it was taken. That person would then be able to empower a pathology laboratory to perform a genetic test on it, but would still be able to prohibit them from using the sample in research.

Management power works well in the context of tissue as it allows for more than one person who has an interest in a portion of tissue to pursue that interest, while giving overarching control to a person who will be the most detrimentally affected if it is dealt with in a way that conflicts with his or her interests.

Examples of management powers and rights being asserted over tissue can be readily found. It could be said that a person who supplies tissue to a testing laboratory is authorising that laboratory to perform tests on it. The laboratory would not perform tests that were not authorised, and in effect would be acting as if under a duty to deal with the sample provided

---

46 See, eg, *Crimes Act 1914* (Cth), Pt 1D; *Crimes (Forensic Procedures) Act 2000* (NSW), Pts 3–8.
47 On situations where supply of blood samples is required by the law, see generally Australian Law Reform Commission and Australian Health Ethics Committee, *Essentially Yours*, ch 39.
48 Some legal writers have held that the power to alienate comes within the aggregate of powers that make up the management power. See, eg, Lawson and Rudden, *The Law of Property*, 8–9. However, following the Honoré model, this power will be examined within the context of rights to the capital of an object.

only as requested. For example, a pathology laboratory is not permitted later to sell tissue or test it for other conditions. This kind of restriction could be constructed as a management power, although the legal and ethical regulations that cover pathology laboratory use of tissue do not legally construct it in this way.

Where tissue samples are stored, the organisation that stores them exercises management powers by determining who may have access to them. For example, hospitals and testing laboratories restrict access to newborn screening cards, allowing researchers to use de-identified cards[49] and the police to use them in accordance with relevant memoranda of understanding.[50]

The laws and ethical guidelines regulating to the use of tissue can be viewed as protections of management rights and powers, as they are in some ways mirrored in requirements of consent. Tissue cannot be removed without consent, according to the Human Tissue Acts, and those acts aim to restrict use of removed tissue to certain purposes, such as transplantation, as determined by the source. The NHMRC *National Statement* is a better example, however, as it explicitly requires that tissue samples be used only in accordance with the terms of consent given by the person from whom the sample was taken.

Effectively, the *National Statement* recognises a power or right of the source of the sample to direct what sort of research may be performed on it, and by whom and whether it may be stored. The researcher is placed under a correlative duty by the *National Statement* only to use the sample in accordance with those terms, and incurs sanctions for transgressions.

4. Right to the Income

The right to the income partially overlaps with the right to use. The right to the income allows owners to benefit from any profits that may be generated by the object, either through using it themselves or allowing its use by others. Income may be derived simply by using something, such as by living in a house.[51] Income might also be generated by using the object to produce a valuable product or service; through exploitation of the object by working on or with it, or by allowing others to use the object in return for something else, such as money.

One example of this occurring (and being sanctioned by the law and ethics guidelines) is that researchers using tissue are not precluded from profiting from the developments achieved through their research,

---

49 See, eg., NSW Health Department, *Test to Protect Your Baby* (2000); South Australian Neonatal Screening Centre, *Screening Tests for Your New Baby* (2002); Australian Law Reform Commission and Australian Health Ethics Committee, *Essentially Yours: The Protection of Human Genetic Information in Australia* (2003) ALRC 96, 19.3.
50 See, eg., Victoria Police and Genetics Health Services Victoria, *Memorandum of Understanding*, 23 January 2003; New South Wales Commissioner of Police and New South Wales Health Department, *Memorandum of Understanding*, 17 April 2002.
51 Honoré points out that under English tax law, rent-free use or occupation of a house is regarded as a form of income. See Honoré, "Ownership", 117.

particularly pharmaceutical companies developing drugs for sale. Tissue can be used to test pharmaceuticals which are sold for profit. It can also be used to cultivate cell lines that can then be maintained for varying lengths of time and profitable uses made from them, such as in research or in producing therapeutic substances. The case of John Moore in the United States, where a highly lucrative cell line was developed, is a famous instance of the income that can be generated using tissue in research.[52]

This is one of the most difficult issues in the debate about applying property rights to tissue. Generating income from tissue could be criticised. But showing that such a right already exists does not suggest either that it is right or wrong for this to be so. Nor does it mean that allowing tissue to be property is inherently problematic—each of the incidents of property is separable, and the right to the income can be excluded as a right in tissue. What this section shows, though, is that that right is already being exercised in accordance with the law and hence that tissue has the capacity to be subject to a right to income.

5. Right to the Capital

The right to the capital of an object is an aggregate of a power to alienate it, and privileges to consume it or to waste it. It is a right to access the value held in the object itself, rather than the value it may generate without being diminished. The power of alienation accorded by a right to the capital of an object allows the owner to alienate it during life or after death, and this may be done via sale, gift or other means.[53] This power will pass to others when the owners have passed title to them. The privilege to destroy enables the holder of the right to use it as a resource that will be consumed by that use, while the privilege to waste allows the holder to let it degenerate.[54] This right may, like others, have restrictions upon it, perhaps where it is in the public interest for an object not to be destroyed, though that approach is somewhat at odds with a liberal conception of ownership.

It is certainly possible that tissue may be wholly transferred by gift or by sale (where the capital value is obtained by the source). For example, it would be possible to sell blood, hair, and tissue samples, particularly given the value of some of these tissues to research and other profit-making activities which could create a demand market. It should be highlighted, however, that the power to alienate under this incident does not have to equate to a power to alienate within the market. It can mean simply gifting or transferring tissue permanently, such as by donating blood or giving tissue samples for research.

---

52 *John Moore v The Regents of the University of California*, 51 Cal. 3d 120, 793 P.2d 479, 271 Cal. Rptr. 146 (1990).
53 Honoré said of this incident "Most people do not wilfully destroy permanent assets; hence the power of alienation is the more important aspect of the owner's right to the capital of the thing owned". See Ibid, 107.
54 See further E J McCaffrey, "Must We Have the Right to Waste?" *University of Southern California Olin Research Paper* No. 00–16.

The right to the capital value of tissue, and gifted transfers of tissue without compensation, *are* both legally possible in Australia, although most types of such transfers are legally prohibited. The sale of human tissue is largely prohibited in Australia, however all states and territories allow for the exception of "processed" tissue for therapeutic, scientific and medical purposes.[55] This would seem to allow commercial sale of preserved tissue for these purposes. Generally, the legislation has been interpreted as prohibiting sale, particularly of entire organs for transplant. There is no legislative definition of the scope of the processing exception, nor has it been judicially considered. However, it is most likely to apply only to researchers and perhaps hospitals that have stored tissue rather than individuals who seek to sell their own body parts, as the exception extends only to processing where "the sale or supply is made for the purpose of enabling the tissue to be used for therapeutic purposes, medical purposes or scientific purposes".[56]

Donation of tissue is also a form of transference, and one which is not only possible under current laws regulating tissue, but one which is actively encouraged at many levels. For example, research participants give portions of their tissue to researchers who may then possess and use them as part of their study. They gain full control over the samples, subject of course to ethical requirements. The same applies to tissue provided for testing, in that it is transferred and the receiving party gains the capacity to use it in a particular way subject to some restrictions, and does not return that tissue and is not required to. The reality is that a relationship of transfer surrounds tissue in all facets of its use once excised. Indeed the very reason for excision, especially after death, is to transfer that tissue permanently to others, and this reason is not only sanctioned, but promoted through organ donor programs and the Human Tissue Acts.

6. Right to Security

Security in the context of property means an immunity from expropriation of the object. Owners may control and possess objects for as long as they choose, provided there is no rule of law that allows circumvention of this right. In general, this immunity will exist until the owner becomes bankrupt or the property is liable to execution for a debt. State authorities may also retain powers to expropriate property in some limited, legally permitted circumstances, in which case appropriate compensation must be paid. It could be argued that, if a general power to expropriate made the taking of property legitimate as long as reasonable compensation was given, a system

---

[55] *Human Tissue Act 1985* (Tas) s 27; *Human Tissue Act 1982* (Vic) ss 38, 39; *Human Tissue Act 1983* (NSW) s 32; *Transplantation and Anatomy Act* 1983 (SA) s 35; *Transplantation and Anatomy Act 1979* (Qld) s 35; *Human Tissue and Transplantation Act 1982* (WA) s 29; *Transplantation and Anatomy Act 1978* (ACT) s 44 and *Human Tissue Transplant Act 1979* (NT) s 24.
[56] See, eg., *Human Tissue Act 1983* (NSW) s 32(2). There are no examples of the exception being interpreted more broadly than this.

of property would again be incapable of functioning.[57] For example, if A cannot be sure that he will have possession of his land, he will have little incentive to plant crops on it or improve it if it could be arbitrarily taken away from him at any time. Therefore, it would be irrational to improve or use property in any but a very short-term sense, which would prevent production and hence the functioning of the economy.

It would generally be possible to make tissue immune from expropriation in the same way other items of property are immune. This may, however, interfere with the accepted practice of taking organs from the deceased where no dissent has been expressed and also with the accepted ethical practice of using anonymised tissue samples for research. In these cases, however, it is of course possible to make exceptions to the immunity if these practices are to continue. Similarly, police could be given powers to appropriate tissue samples found at crime scenes or taken from suspects, where the exception is in the public interest.

There appears to be an expectation that excised human tissue will be immune from arbitrary expropriation. In many of the interviews conducted by the author, pathology laboratory technicians, hospital staff and medical researchers spoke of tissue as something they were able to use without fear of its being claimed by others. Conversely, the incidences of organ and tissue retention uncovered over the past six years have demonstrated that people are incensed when body parts are taken without consent.[58]

A general immunity from expropriation also appears to be protected by the law in some situations. In *Roche v Douglas as Administrator of the Estate of Edward Rowan (dec'd)*[59] the Supreme Court of Western Australia did appropriate a tissue sample from the Western Diagnostic Pathology, but this can be regarded as a legal limitation on the immunity, and it is not unique in law for there to be such limitations where it is necessary for the courts or the government to acquire property which it requires.[60] The case of *R v Kelly*[61] is another example of the law preventing expropriation, with the court upholding the security of the preserved body parts held by the Royal College. Further, having once obtained possession for an authorised use, there are as yet few, if any, rules enabling others to reclaim tissue. The best that can be said is that tissue samples used in research that the

---

57 Honoré, "Ownership", 119.
58 The distress people experienced following the revelations of organ retention appears to have been considerable and widespread (Interview with Mary Dorcan, Retained Organs Office, Oxford Radcliffe Hospital, (Personal interview, Oxford Radcliffe Hospital, 25 September 2001)). This is also demonstrated in government inquiries on the organ retention. See, eg, Witness statement of Paul Bradley, WIT02290001, *Bristol Royal Infirmary Inquiry*, <www.bristol-inquiry.org.uk/evidence/wit/WitSMent/witPBradley.htm> at 25 October 2005.
59 [2000] WASC 146.
60 For example, the Constitution of Australia gives the Federal Government power for "[t]he acquisition of property on just terms from any State or person for any purpose in respect of which the Parliament has power to make laws". See *Commonwealth of Australia Constitution* s 51(xxxi).
61 *R v Kelly* (1998) 3 All ER 741.

individual later objects to may see researchers required to cease that use in accordance with ethical guidelines. Similarly, while genetic profiles must in some cases later be destroyed by police after use in forensic investigations, the police have a right to continued possession of the actual sample which is secured by the legislative provisions and the common law.[62]

7. Incident of Transmissibility

The power of transmissibility gives the owner the ability to devise or bequeath the object. Hence, upon death the object will be transmissible by will, or otherwise in accordance with the rules of succession, to the owner's successors.[63] The owner's interest is indefinitely transmissible—there being no limit on the number of transmissions which may be made.

Allowing people to devise excised portions of tissue and organs upon death would not produce absurdity *per se*. Organs and tissues are already taken from dead bodies and given to others, the only difference would be that the person from whom they are taken would previously have chosen the recipient. For example, one could choose to bequeath one's kidneys to a relative who needs a transplant. While this is not absurd, it would disrupt the present methods of organ allocation which is determined according to the need and health of the potential recipient. Allowing people to donate their organs to family members who may not be yet in grave need would exclude others who need the organs more, and hence may not be ethically defensible (although these persons may only be prepared to donate to family members at all). On this basis, if donation of non-essential organs by living donors is already lawful, expanding this to donation after death may not be too problematic. Tissue donations also occur every day, with many people transferring organs, corneas, bone and skin for transplantation and to benefit scientific research.

The law does currently allow for bodies and their parts to be donated upon death in some contexts—one may donate one's body for scientific or anatomical use and of course, donate all one's organs for transplantation—however a donor cannot legally direct to whom these will be transferred (and not by will). The testator may make directions in his or her will as to the disposition of the body in general, but these will have no legal force.[64] It appears, then, that the law does not presently allow transmissibility of tissue by will or after death to a great extent. This might, however, be partially attributed to the limited uses after death that are currently condoned by the law, rather than a principled objection to directing how tissue should be dealt with through succession laws. Also, for the policy

---

62 *Crimes Act 1914* (Cth) ss 3ZK, 23WA(5). Destruction of "forensic material" under the Act merely requires destroying any identifiers. See also *R v Rothery* (1976) RTR 550; *R v Welsh* (1974) RTR 478.
63 The incident of transmissibility differs from the right to alienate found in the right to the capital as it deals specifically with transmission upon death.
64 General authority for this principle is the English case of *Williams v Williams* (1882) 20 ChD 659. See further Griggs and Mackie, "Burial Rights" (2000) 7 *Journal of Law and Medicine* 404–414.

reasons noted above, it has not been considered acceptable to donate organs directly, as they can be better distributed through central processes. That may also explain the lack of legal capacity to donate them to a particular person on death.

8. Incident of Absence of Term

The incident of absence of term is related to transmissibility as both affect the duration of ownership. Absence of term refers to the indeterminate length of one's ownership rights. This differs from other legal situations, such as a lease which has a definite and determined time limit placed upon it (as has patent law). Ownership, thus, would continue indefinitely unless terminated by the owner, but for the fact that at some point the owner will die. It is for this reason that an indeterminate interest must be linked to a power of transmissibility to deal with the fate of the object upon the owner's death.[65] An interest for life differs slightly, as it is determinate, ceasing at death.

It would be possible to allow for absence of term in relation to human tissue. This would mean that an individual with rights over the tissue would hold those rights indefinitely. In itself, there is no absurdity in this as for the most part individuals using tissue would wish to be able to do so as long as they chose. However, there may be problems with determining who is the owner with an indefinite interest. Consider a situation where a woman transfers her tissue sample to a hospital when she allows them to take a biopsy of a suspected tumour. The hospital now has a right to possess the sample to test it, but of the two of them who will have an indefinite interest? It may be that both have indefinite but specific interests, for instance the hospital may possess the sample indefinitely but the woman will always hold the power to manage the tissue. These complexities do not preclude the incident of absence of term existing in relation to tissue, but they do require consideration.

At present, neither the Human Tissue Acts nor the few common law cases deal with absence of term in relation to tissue. As the legislation works on a consent model, and defines only the uses to which tissue may be put, it does not make any determination on what happens to that tissue once the specified use has been made. The legislation does not, however, contain any suggestion that once it has been used the right to use it ceases, or that possessory rights cease either. In the absence of such provision, it seems that most researchers, hospitals and tissue banks have simply continued to hold tissue indefinitely. For example, newborn screening cards are created initially for screening purposes, but are held indefinitely after that and there is no legal requirement that prevents this.

In some instances, however, there is a definite term of ownership. Pathology samples collected for the purpose of testing are to be held for

---

65 Although there would still be some value in an indeterminate interest as no fixed date would be set for its end. See Honoré, "Ownership", 122.

up to 50 years for quality assurance and future testing purposes. Once that time has expired, they must be destroyed. Despite this particular case, in most situations no limits have been put on how long tissue may be retained. For the most part ownership rights end when there is a specified legal direction that they must be destroyed, but in the majority of instances such as forensics, tissue banks and the like, there is no legal direction either way. Ethical guidelines also do not require use and possession to cease—often it is only required that a piece of tissue be de-identified. At that point, most uses are permitted indefinitely.

9. Prohibition against Harmful Use

This duty, imposed on the person who holds property rights in an object, is subject to debate. Some commentators, such as Jeremy Waldron[66] and Alan Carter,[67] have argued that it does not form one of the standard incidents of property at all. If it exists, this prohibition acts to place a duty on owners not to put their property to harmful uses. What constitutes harm and how far this prohibition extends is arguable also, but is best viewed in a very broad sense including invasions of privacy and physical harm.

It would certainly be possible to limit the uses to which tissue is put because they may cause harm. There are many harmful ways tissue can be used, such as unwanted testing for a genetic condition which will invade the privacy of the person from whom it was taken; or planting a sample at a crime scene to falsely incriminate someone; or injecting someone with blood carrying a virus without their consent. Prohibitions on these actions would, in part, equate to this incident of property, if it were one.

Prohibitions on harmful use of tissue are already in place. If harm is conceived as doing something with tissue that would offend or distress the person from whom it was taken, then the NHMRC *National Statement* is a good example of such prohibitions, despite the fact that it does not have the same force as legislative measures.[68] It provides that researchers should not use tissue except in accordance with the wishes of the person from whom it was taken. Generally, however, it is more likely that legal prohibitions are directed at the harm done, not at who owns the tissue. Hence, injecting someone with infected blood without his or her consent would be treated as a battery under common law, and the person who injected the blood, regardless of whether he or she "owned" the blood, would be criminally liable.[69]

---

66 See, eg., Waldron, "What is Private Property?", n 23, 320–21.
67 A Carter, *Philosophical Foundations of Property Rights* (1989) 5.
68 See further on the legal force or otherwise of the National Health and Medical Research Council, *National Statement on Ethical Conduct in Research Involving Humans* and other ethical guidelines, I Goold, "Tissue Donation: When Does Ethical Guidance Become Legal Enforceability?" (2000) 3 *Centre for Law and Genetics Occasional Paper Series* 92.
69 A battery is any intended application of force, regardless of how slight, to the person of another without consent. On the common law definition of a battery see *Jones v Sherwood* (1942) 1 KB 127; see also *Sidaway v Board of Governors of the Bethlem Royal Hospital and the Maudsley Hospital* (1985) 2 WLR 480.

10. Liability to Execution

Liability to execution is a liability on the owner, with a correlative right vesting in others against the owner, allowing the object to be taken from the owner in lieu of payment of debts. Honoré argues that such a liability is an incident of property as without it the growth of credit would be hampered and property rights would be a means for the owner to defraud creditors.[70]

Once human tissue has been excised from the body, it is separate from the person. This paper deals only with tissue already excised, so liability to execution in this context would not mean forcing a person to remove part of his or her body, such as a kidney. Instead, it would mean allowing creditors to take sections of tissue already removed in payment of a debt. It is easy to imagine this being possible in the case of a valuable cell line, made from a sample taken from someone. A company which has developed the cell line makes profits from its exclusive control of the cell line and its power to grant others access to sections of it. Rights to manage and derive income from this cell line are lucrative, and there is no reason why it would not be possible to transfer them to another company, with the value of the line being taken in lieu of a debt.[71] At present, however, tissue does not appear to be liable to such execution and there are no specific laws in relation to expropriation of tissues to pay debts.

11. Residuary Character

This area of property rights covers rules governing the reversion of lapsed rights. In accordance with the rules of a particular legal system, when an owner's property rights in an object lapse, corresponding rights will vest in another.[72] Honoré uses the example of an easement, where for instance the easement holder has a right to exclude the owner, but upon the lapse of this right the owner gains the right to exclude the previous easement holder. These rights are corresponding but not identical.

Rights that lapse may not always pass to another in a corresponding form. It is possible for rights to lapse and vest in no-one, the object becoming ownerless or *res derelicta*. Conversely, the right may lapse and vest in the state. Generally, however, rights lapse and it is the individual who has a residuary right in the object who will regain these rights. This is often

---

[70] Honoré, "Ownership", 123 and see 123–24 for discussion of Honoré's speculation on whether any other limitations on ownership (such as a liability to tax or expropriability by the State) could be regarded as standard incidents of property.

[71] Generally, however, tissue on its own has not been regarded as valuable. There are some exceptions, for example when the tissue is useful, as in the case of hair used for wigs. For the most part, though, it has been seen as valuable once worked on (as in a cell line). Therefore, it is unlikely that the law has had to deal with this aspect of dealings with tissue, and that anyone would have sought access to tissue in lieu of a debt. This is particularly the case as tissue usually does not have a clear market value, as for the most part it has not been treated as a commodity like other products—that is, there is no defined market value for my finger if I cut it off to pay a debt, even though in some cases tissue is sold once processed.

[72] Meaning rights which are similar, but cannot be precisely the same rights as they are exercised by another person.

the owner and this may occur, say, upon the cessation of an easement or bailment. In other situations, such as a sub-lease, it will be the lessee who regains the rights which correspond with those of the sub-lessee when the sub-lease terminates, rather than the owner. That is, the rights will return to the previous and still legitimate right holder, namely in this case the lessee who is still acting within some agreement with the owner allowing him or her to exercise these particular rights.

Whether it would be possible for human tissue to have residuary character is perhaps not too difficult a question to answer. If rights in that tissue lapse, and the material is still identified, it will always be possible to find at least one party who may have some claim to the rights as residuary—the person from whom it was first taken (or his or her family, if deceased). It will almost always contain his or her DNA, and hence have an intrinsic link to him or her on which to base residuary status. Where the sample is no longer identified, the research and forensic value of tissue may mean that the state has a good claim as residuary, as it can put the tissue to some use that is of general benefit to the community.

For the present, this incident does not seem to have arisen in the context of biological materials. However, it could be argued in relation to attempts by Aboriginal communities to have the remains of their ancestors returned by the museums currently holding them,[73] that the remains have residuary character. Their claim to the remains is based on their place as descendants of the people whose remains are held, and if the residuary nature of tissue is linked to its place as part of a person, then those people with the closest link as relations may be the proper residuaries.

At present, there do not appear to be any legal provisions in relation to tissue that deem it to have residuary character. On the contrary, in some cases where there is no apparent residuary to determine what will be done with tissue, then without his or her consent, nothing can be done with the tissue. The Human Tissue Acts provide that the hospital holding a body may only use its organs for transplantation with the consent of the deceased or of a next of kin. To some extent, the next of kin could be regarded as a form of residuary, but beyond this, it appears none is identified by the legislation and hence nothing can be done with the body.

However, where tissue is de-identified, ethical guidelines take a different view, and tissue may then be used in research without consent. It appears that the ethical guidelines ignore the possibility of residuary rights, or regard them as extinguished if tissue is de-identified. For the most part, though, it does not appear that tissue has been treated by the law as though it has any character, residuary or otherwise.

---

[73] For more information on the retention of Aboriginal remains in museums around the world, and attempts to retrieve them, see, eg, various reports contained at Working Group on Human Remains Report, Department for Culture, Media and Sport (UK), *The Working Group on Human Remains Report* <www.culture.gov.uk/cultural_property/hr_uk_institutions/default.htm> accessed at 20 April 2005.

Bringing the Incidents Together: Two Possible Scenarios

Although the preceding discussion has dealt with each incident separately, it is rare that only one incident will be held in relation to an object. Far more commonly, a combination of a number of incidents will vest in one or more people in relation to the object. This section considers two possible instances where a range of incidents might be held and demonstrates how tissue dealt with in this way does fit within the common law notion of property.

Example 1: Research use of heart valves

Body tissue removed during surgery is often used in research. In this example, a surgically removed diseased heart valve is donated by the patient to the hospital for research in accordance with the Human Tissue Acts consent provisions. The researcher takes possession of the tissue once donated, uses it in research and determines how that tissue will be used in the research. If we cast this example in terms of property incidents, what kinds of incidents might vest in the researcher? Clearly, the right to use, as the researcher will be working on the tissue. The researcher will also act as though he or she has a right to possess the tissue to undertake this work, and, we might also say a management right, as the researcher is legally allowed to direct what happens to the tissue, albeit constrained by the terms of the consent. From this perspective, it is clear that the legislation allows the researcher to act in a manner very similar to that which could be provided by vesting in him or her these proprietary rights in relation to the tissue.

There are some distinctions to be made, however, between the legislative approach and the property approach that are salient to the "should" question—should we deal with tissue in this way. The legislative approach lays down clear limits on what may be done with the tissue—it may only be used for the purpose for which consent has been given and in specific contexts. Arguably, on the property approach, once the rights have vested in the researcher, these limitations would need to be established in a different manner. This could be achieved by the donor retaining some management rights, or the rights being limited by time and purpose.

Additionally, if only the rights in accord with the legislative approach vest in the property approach, some concerns arise. Who has the right to determine what may be done with the tissue in the future? Can it be stored? Can it be transferred and if so, what rights does the recipient gain? Is the donor the original residuary and does he retain any rights in relation to the tissue? I argue that although these are challenges for fitting tissue with the concept of property, they are not fatal—the tissue can be dealt with like property and achieve the same approach as the legislation, albeit with some difficulties. Rather, applying the property approach highlights limitations of the current, legislative approach, as the legislation does not deal with these issues. They are dealt with through some ethical guidelines, but these leave both the individual and any future possessors with few if any clear rights. This suggests that tissue in this case could be regulated via property law, but just as the legislative approach has flaws, the property approach would have the same flaws. They would need to be addressed just as those in the legislative framework should be.

Example 2: Orlan's reliquary

In this second example, a more unusual use of tissue is given, although the example is taken from actual event. Orlan is an artist famed for her work in undergoing plastic surgery as a form of conceptual performance art. Following her cosmetic operations, she retains portions of the excised skin. From these, she creates what she terms "reliquaries", skin and gauze containing images of her face, which are subsequently sold as artworks.[74]

Under the Human Tissue Acts, this artistic enterprise would be unlawful, as the sale of tissue is prohibited.[75] Two exceptions apply—tissue may be sold with Ministerial approval;[76] or where it has been processed and is sold for therapeutic, medical or scientific purposes in accordance with the directions of a medical practitioner.[77] Yet, there are good social policy reasons why this consensual use and sale of her own tissue should be lawful. Artistic expression is culturally valuable, as is freedom of expression, particularly in this case where there is no clear harm to others resulting from the use and sale of the tissue.

The tissue used and traded in this context could fit within a property model, however. In this scenario, Orlan's dealings with the tissue could be conceived of as an exercise of the rights to possession, use, management, transfer and income of the tissue. Current restrictions on these rights in the context of sale could be applied, including to meet public health concerns. In this scenario, Orlan is trading an artwork that simply happens to be human tissue—setting aside ethical issues that might arise, this kind

---

[74] L Andrews and D Nelkin, *Body Bazaar: The Market for Human Tissue in the Biotechnology Age* (2001) 136.

[75] *Human Tissue Act 1985* (Tas) s 27; *Human Tissue Act 1982* (Vic) ss 38, 39; *Human Tissue Act 1983* (NSW) s 32; *Transplantation and Anatomy Act 1983* (SA) s 35(1)–(6); *Transplantation and Anatomy Act 1979* (Qld) s 35(1)–(6); *Human Tissue and Transplantation Act 1982* (WA) s 29; *Transplantation and Anatomy Act 1978* (ACT) s 44 and *Human Tissue Transplant Act 1979* (NT) s 24.

[76] *Human Tissue Act 1985* (Tas) s 27(4); *Human Tissue Act 1983* (NSW) s 32(4); *Transplantation and Anatomy Act 1979* (Qld) s 35(6); *Transplantation and Anatomy Act 1983* (SA) s 35(6); *Human Tissue Act 1982* (Vic) s 39(2); *Transplantation and Anatomy Act 1978* (ACT) s 44(4); *Human Tissue Transplant Act 1979* (NT) s 24(3).

[77] *Human Tissue Act 1985* (Tas) s 27(2); *Human Tissue Act 1983* (NSW) s 32(2); *Transplantation and Anatomy Act 1979* (Qld) s 35(3); *Transplantation and Anatomy Act 1983* (SA) s 35(3); *Human Tissue and Transplantation Act 1982* (WA) s 29(4); *Transplantation and Anatomy Act 1978* (ACT) s 44(2); *Human Tissue Transplant Act 1979* (NT) s 24(4). In Victoria, the same provisions apply but Ministerial approval is also required. See *Human Tissue Act 1982* (Vic) ss 38(2), 39(2).

of instance is again one where a combination of property incidents could workably be applied to tissue.

While the example is unusual, the principle remains the same for other forms of tissue trade. For example, renewable tissue such as blood could be sold in this way, with individuals holding rights to the income of their tissue. This right could be restricted in the same way as other rights to sell (and constraints on what may be sold, where and of what quality would also apply). The point here is that other things, such as selling blood for transfusion or tissue for commercial research and product development, do not differ in their fundamentals from other property transactions and could be conceived of as such. They do have similar features to other items of property that are sold and, where it is acceptable to the individual from whom they are taken and they are fit for sale in the sense that they are not dangerous and their quality is sufficient, then as a general principle they can be treated in the same way as other properties.

There are, of course, other issues involved, such as concerns about commodification of persons and their parts; about the effects on the cost of treatment and therapeutic productions; and about the effects on the community of allowing people to trade their own bodies. These, however, are separate issues to the one under consideration here. What this example does, as the previous example also does, is demonstrate that we can successfully conceive of transactions in tissue in terms of property incidents. Tissue, in these contexts at least, does fit within the common law concept of property.

Conclusion

Common law legal systems have long regarded human tissue as a substance somehow deserving rarefied, special status. There is good reason for this, because tissue is unique and does hold special significance within Western societies. Genetic science has also allowed us to uncover intimate information about individuals from their tissue, creating an ongoing link (and attendant privacy issues) that differentiate tissue from other objects. However, as tissue has come to take on other statuses—as commercial resource, as donation, as research subject, as evidence, as art—a need to recognise this legally has developed.

Property law has gradually begun to emerge as a possible legal mechanism for dealing with tissue. This paper has attempted to demonstrate that there are rather fewer practical legal problems with using property law to regulate human tissue than has perhaps been generally considered. The analysis of the concept of property has demonstrated that human tissue is aptly suited to having property status, and that the various property rights, such as rights to use, to possess, to manage and to the income can almost all be applied to tissue without legal absurdity.

More generally, this analysis has shown that at the conceptual level, there are few legal difficulties with viewing human tissue as property.

Finally, it has also been demonstrated that in many cases rights akin to these property rights are effectively already exercised over tissue, even if they are not called "property rights". People, and the law, do already deal with tissue like they deal with property in many instances, and hence conceptually it is certainly possible to deem tissue property.

There may be other barriers to admitting human tissue as property (including legal barriers). Applying property law may produce adverse legal results, or work in opposition to some of the social goals we seek to achieve through our use of tissue. Hence, there may be a need to adapt the particular rights that may be exercised over human tissue to promote social goals and prevent unjust legal results. However, this paper demonstrates that the initial question of whether tissue could fit within the classes of things our legal system is capable of treating as property is answered in the affirmative. The further investigation of other aspects of applying property law to tissue, such as more specific legal concerns as well as the moral, social or practical reasons why human tissue should not be subject to property rights, should be considered in light of this affirmative answer. In doing so, it should be borne in mind that this affirmative answer shows that it would be possible to adapt property law concepts and rules to cover tissue, just as property law has previously been adapted to other novel forms of property, like intellectual property.

REGULATING HUMAN BIOLOGICAL ENHANCEMENTS:
Questionable Justifications and International Complications

Henry T. Greely*

Enhance: 3. To make greater, as in value or desirability.
Webster's Unabridged Dictionary (2d. ed. 1934).

From the definition, it seems that to enhance something would be a good thing. But when humanity is at issue, enhancement is controversial even though human beings historically have struggled to enhance themselves. Humans used stone tools, fire, clothing, and domesticated plants and animals for enhanced safety, health, nourishment, and power—making ourselves "greater". The difference today is our growing knowledge of biology.

Human power over living things is not new. Our agricultural ancestors effectively created all of our crops and our domestic animals; selecting, culling, and crossing individual plants to create wheat, corn, and rice and to turn wolves into everything from great danes to chihuahuas. The biological revolution of the last 50 years has brought a level of control that, although not unlimited, is certainly unprecedented. Science can now form creatures by mixing genes, cells, and tissues not just among near relatives, but across biological orders, classes, and kingdoms. We can make genetically identical copies of many mammals. And, if we chose, we could begin a project that could be described as building biological super-humans. The controversy today centers on the use of new, technical methods to change the structure or function of the human body, typically through drugs or drug-like substances or through surgical interventions.

Some view the prospect of "enhancing" humanity as liberating, and exciting;[1] for others it seems to be disturbing, even frightening. The vast literature on enhancement is rapidly increasing, exploring many aspects of a wide variety of enhancements.[2] This article tries to add two things

---

* Stanford University. The author would like to thank the many audiences on whom these ideas have been tried out, an anonymous peer reviewer, and his very diligent research assistant, Jason Tarricone.
1 The World Transhumanist Association is a group that supports human biological enhancement. *See* World Transhumanist Ass'n Home Page, http://www.transhumanism.org (last visited Oct. 8, 2005).
2 *See* ALLEN BUCHANAN ET AL., FROM CHANCE TO CHOICE: GENETICS AND JUSTICE (Cambridge

to that literature: an analysis of whether human biological enhancement is meaningfully different from other forms of human enhancement and a discussion of some of the implications of international realities for the regulation of enhancement.

The article begins with examples of controversial human *biological* enhancements and a review of the arguments against such enhancements. Next, it intensively examines whether human biological enhancements are meaningfully different from other kinds of human enhancement. Then it analyzes ways in which human cultural diversity and splintered political sovereignty cut against effective curbs on such enhancements. The article concludes that human biological enhancements are not inherently different from other forms of enhancing technologies and regulation of enhancement technologies remains a challenge.

I. Human Biological Enhancements: Examples and Objections

The story of humanity is the history of enhancement. Stone tools, control of fire, and clothing all enhanced the success of hunter gatherers. Agriculture enhanced food supply and population size and made possible the specialization of labor. Writing systems enhanced our ability to communicate, among people and across time, and strengthened our memories; printing reduced the costs of mass distribution of information. Metallurgy and engineering, electricity and computers have all increased what humans can do and what we can be. These enhancements came with their social costs, including toil, war, and stress. The legend of the Golden Age is a legend of life before the enhancements called civilization. Although the legend is deeply attractive, it is unimaginable that anyone would seriously consider a return to the hunter gatherer existence of our ancestors, even with their enhancing stone, wood, and bone tools.

Controversy today focuses on enhancements that seem different because they increase our abilities by enhancing our biological selves through new technical inventions. This article will discuss five examples—cosmetic surgery, personality improvement, sports performance enhancing drugs, genetic enhancements, and cognitive enhancements—but only after making one very important distinction.

Univ. Press 2001); Carl Elliott, Better Than Well: American Medicine Meets the American Dream (W. W. Norton & Co. 2003); Frances M. Kamm, *Is There a Problem with Enhancement?*, Am. J. Bioethics, May-June 2005, at 5; Maxwell J. Mehlman, Wondergenes: Genetic Enhancement and the Future of Society (Univ. of Ind. Press 2003); Enhancing Human Traits: Ethical and Social Implications (Erik Parens ed., Georgetown Univ. Press 1998); President's Council on Bioethics, Beyond Therapy: Biotechnology and the Pursuit of Happiness (Regan Books 2003); Sheila Rothman & David Rothman, The Pursuit of Perfection: The Promise and Perils of Medical Enhancement (Pantheon 2003); Michael J. Sandel, *The Case Against Perfection*, Atlantic Monthly, Apr. 2004, at 50.

A. Enhancement Uses versus Medical Uses

Technologies that are controversial as enhancements are largely viewed as mundane when used "medically".[3] These medical uses either restore normal function to someone who has lost it through injury or disease or confer normal function on someone who, generally because of birth defects, never had it. Precisely the same surgical technique is encouraged, covered by public and private health plans, when it restores a nose damaged in an accident but is somewhat controversial; and *not* covered by health plans when it improves the aesthetics of a nose to be within the normal range of attractiveness. When cosmetic surgery is performed to treat psychological disorders, such as shyness or low self esteem, it is unclear as to whether it is a medical treatment or an enhancement. (Vaccinations may also be viewed as intermediate between medical and enhancing technology; they are not usually used to treat disease but to prevent it by enhancing the subject's immune system.)

The use of otherwise enhancing technologies to help someone with a disease or defect is rarely controversial because of its "enhancing" characteristics; the focus is on its restoration of normal function. There are, however, at least two examples of disputes about those kinds of uses. One involves professional sports, when the Professional Golf Association (PGA) denied Casey Martin the use of a golf cart during tournaments, because it was an "enhancing technology", even though he had a circulatory disorder that made walking extremely painful.[4] The United States Supreme Court held that the PGA's policy violated the Federal *Americans with Disabilities Act*. As the Court noted, there was no evidence that the combination of his disability and the golf cart gave him an advantage over a golfer with healthy legs. The second concerns a technology called a cochlear implant that can alleviate some forms of deafness. Some members of the deaf community initially opposed the use of cochlear implants in deaf children because the implants had the potential greatly to reduce, or even eliminate deafness, and thus to eradicate deaf culture.[5]

This distinction between applauded medical uses and controversial enhancement uses of biological technologies is important for two reasons: First, it demonstrates that it is the *purpose* for which the technology is used,

---

3 See the discussion of this distinction in Eric Juengst, *What Does* Enhancement *Mean?*, in ENHANCING HUMAN TRAITS: ETHICAL AND SOCIAL IMPLICATIONS, *supra* note 2, at 29.
4 PGA Tour, Inc. v. Martin, 532 U.S. 661 (2001); Henry T. Greely, *Disabilities, Enhancements and the Meanings of Sport*, 15 STAN. L. & POL'Y REV. 99, 103-12 (2004).
5 Shortly after the Food and Drug Administration approved cochlear implants for children in 1990, the National Association of the Deaf (NAD) opposed their use. See John Barry, *Silence Is Golden?*, MIAMI HERALD, Sept. 22, 1991, at 8; Gene Warner, *Girl, 5, Makes Medical History with Ear Implant*, BUFFALO NEWS, June 23, 1991. In October 2000, however, NAD's Board of Directors expressed cautionary approval of the implants. COCHLEAR IMPLANT COMM., NAT'L ASS'N OF THE DEAF, NAD POSITION STATEMENT ON COCHLEAR IMPLANTS 1 (2000), http://www.nad.org/site/pp.asp?c=foINKQMBF&b=138140. *See* MICHAEL CHOROST, REBUILT: HOW BECOMING PART COMPUTER MADE ME MORE HUMAN 130-35 (Houghton Mifflin 2005).

not the technology itself, which makes some enhancements controversial. Second, it explains the increasing flow of human biological enhancements. These technologies are almost always sought and developed to cure disease or disability. Health care systems provide large, well organized, and lucrative markets for expensive new technologies. The medical, restorative powers of plastic surgery, anabolic steroids, human growth hormone, Ritalin, and cochlear implants also bear extensive enhancement side effects. To borrow a term from arms control, these are "dual use" technologies, with substantial public, political, and financial support for their development for medical uses. The enhancing uses are usually an unintended, but controversial, consequence.

B. Controversial Human Biological Enhancements

Some of the discussion that follows is methodologically suspect: the discussion regarding which enhancements are controversial and why people find them controversial is based on subjective impressions. This personal introspection is surely not strong evidence of a culture's beliefs, but, without the time or funds to commission massive surveys or multiple focus groups, I can hope that it offers a perspective that may provoke interest in this type of analysis. Furthermore, even if there is some validity in that analysis, it is only an analysis of the culture in which I live, a mainstream version of the culture of the United States.

Egyptian burials provide evidence that people enhanced their attractiveness from at least the dawn of civilization, while cosmetic surgery has existed since the early 20th century.[6] Cosmetic surgery does not have a stigma when used to repair the ravages of injury or disease or birth defects. When used for these ends, cosmetic surgery is both socially approved and generally covered in health care costs. When the same techniques are used to reshape roughly normal noses, breasts or penises, or to remove fat, the surgeries become controversial and are not generally covered by health insurance. On the other hand, enhancing one's appearance through diet and exercise is normally approved; as, to a lesser extent, is the use of cosmetics, hair dye, skin creams, and other beauty aids.

The rise of neuropharmacology, from early sedatives to current antidepressants, has been accompanied by concern about the use of such drugs by people who are not "sick". *Prozac Nation*, *Listening to Prozac*, and similar works have talked about the use of these drugs for "personality enhancement".[7] Improving one's personality by anger management, will power, religious conversion, meditation, stress reduction, and similar methods seems unobjectionable. During the 20th century, psychotherapy and counseling also became acceptable. The history of social responses to intoxicants, including alcohol, as "personality" or "mood" enhancers is mixed.

---

6   *See* ENHANCING HUMAN TRAITS: ETHICAL AND SOCIAL IMPLICATIONS, *supra* note 2.
7   *See* ELIZABETH WURTZEL, PROZAC NATION: YOUNG AND DEPRESSED IN AMERICA (Riverhead Books 1997); PETER D. KRAMER, LISTENING TO PROZAC: THE LANDMARK BOOK ABOUT ANTIDEPRESSANTS AND REMAKING THE SELF (Penguin Books 1997); ELLIOTT, *supra* note 2.

Perhaps the form of human biological enhancement most recently discussed in the press is the use of performance enhancing drugs in sports.[8] "Doping" stories have made headlines—from erythropoietin for endurance, to steroids and human growth hormone for strength and injury recovery, and to stimulants for concentration. At the same time, enhancing performance through better nutrition, conditioning, techniques, equipment, and even mental preparation through sports psychology, has remained uncontroversial. As with cosmetic surgery and neuropharmacology, the interventions used were developed for treatment of various pathologic conditions, but proved to be useful for enhancing healthy people.

While public discussion of enhancement has focused on sports, much of the academic discussion in recent years has focused on genetics.[9] Some discussion has concerned parents (or states) enhancing the next generation through selection of particular genetic variations for children, either through selective abortion or through selection of genetically "better" embryos through pre-implantation genetic diagnosis. In many countries, this technology has been accessible to parents for several years. Other discussions have examined more direct interventions through gene transfer (often referred to inaccurately, or at least, to date, too optimistically, as gene "therapy"), either into existing humans or in germ line transfers to eggs, sperm, or zygotes.[10] These methods are being developed to treat disease, but thus far those efforts have had very limited success.

Cognition provides a final example of enhancement.[11] At this point, biological technologies for improving a healthy person's cognitive abilities are quite limited. A few pharmaceuticals, such as Adderall, Ritalin, and Modafinil, show some ability to improve concentration or alertness in healthy people. Intense efforts at finding drugs to improve memory in those with dementia may well lead to another category of enhancing interventions. There are also non-pharmaceutical possibilities, notably through neuro-electronic interfaces. These methods of directly connecting the human nervous system to electronic devices are aimed at restoring the function of inputs to the brain (the way cochlear implants can restore hearing to some deaf persons) or the functioning of body parts that need outputs from the brain (as through research aimed at bridging spinal cord injuries). Much older forms of cognitive enhancement, such as education, are not controversial; the prospect of students using "memory pills" is.

---

8 Greely, *supra* note 4, at 112-25, 128-32.
9 *See* BUCHANAN ET AL., *supra* note 2; MEHLMAN, *supra* note 2.
10 *See* DESIGNING OUR DESCENDANTS: THE PROMISES AND PERILS OF GENETIC MODIFICATIONS (Audrey R. Chapman & Mark S. Frankel eds., Johns Hopkins Univ. Press 2003); SUSANNAH BARUCH ET AL., GENETICS & PUB. POLICY CTR., HUMAN GERMLINE GENETIC MODIFICATION: ISSUES AND OPTIONS FOR POLICYMAKERS (2005), *available at* http://www.dnapolicy.org/content.labvelocity/pdfs/6/68176.pdf.
11 Henry T. Greely, *The Social Consequences of Advances in Neuroethics: Legal Problems; Legal Perspectives*, in NEUROETHICS (Judy Illes ed., forthcoming 2005).

C. Five Objections

I have addressed objections to enhancement in several earlier works.[12] I believe those objections fall into five categories: safety, coercion, fairness, integrity, and naturalness.

Safety objections focus on the risks that enhancement technology holds for its recipient. Thus, the bad health effects of anabolic steroids are an argument against their use. This argument must consider the risks that societies already allow their members to take.

Coercion is a more complicated objection. In its most direct form, the argument about frank coercion worries about people being ordered to use enhancements against their will, perhaps by governments or employers. Parental coercion deals with children who cannot give informed consent to risks imposed on them by others, including parents who may have a strong interest in their enhancement. A third argument concerns implicit coercion, when people, in a particular context, feel they have no real choice but to use an enhancement. Weight lifters or bodybuilders, for example, may currently feel that if they want to compete successfully, they must use performance-enhancing drugs. It is possible that in the future, mental enhancements will make aspiring pre-medical students feel compelled to use a memory pill for help with organic chemistry.

Fairness objections focus in two ways on the advantages that the enhanced person will have over those who are not enhanced. One set of concerns centers on particular competition, athletic or otherwise, in which the enhanced person will have an advantage, or can look more broadly at the enhanced person's whole life. The second set focuses on the overall social unfairness of allowing optional and *costly* enhancements—if enhancements are expensive, only the rich and their children will be enhanced. At the extreme, these fears include the possibility of an enhanced and self-perpetuating "nobility", possibly evolving themselves through genetic interventions into a superior species.[13]

Integrity is an issue in two different ways. In an obvious way, if particular enhancements are illegal or against the rules in some competitions, the integrity of the enhancement users and of the competition will be undermined. The more interesting question about integrity, though, asks whether enhancements that are not prohibited undermine the integrity of an activity. Some argue, for example, that biological enhancements contravene the ideal of sports. Although that ideal may rarely or never be fully met, enhancement nonetheless should be banned in order to preserve

---

12 Henry T. Greely, *Human Genetic Enhancement: A Lawyer's View, Review of Wondergenes: Genetic Enhancement and the Future of Society by Maxwell J. Mehlman*, MED. HUMAN. REV., Fall 2003, at 42 (book review); Greely, *supra* note 4; Henry T. Greely, *Seeking More Goodly Creatures*, CEREBRUM, Fall 2004, at 49; Greely, *supra* note 11.

13 Mehlman talks of our need to take action to avoid a "genobility" composed of the rich who genetically enhance their children, generation after generation, possibly ultimately becoming a new species. *See* MEHLMAN, *supra* note 2, at 120.

the value competitors and fans take from sports.[14] Those who believe in meritocracy might make similar arguments against the use of cognitive enhancements by students.

The last objection to enhancement may well be the most powerful component in the popular concern about them: human biological enhancements are objectionable because they are unnatural. This may come from a religious view (they change humans from what God intended), from a view derived from evolution (they change humans from what natural selection, or evolution, or nature "intended"), or just from a more visceral reaction (the "yuck factor").

Enhancement has a bad reputation in Western cultures, which likely stems from religion. These concerns appear in Genesis:

> And the LORD God said, Behold, the man is become as one of us, to know good and evil: and now, lest he put forth his hand, and take also of the tree of life, and eat, and live for ever: Therefore the LORD God sent him forth from the garden of Eden, to till the ground from whence he was taken.
> So he drove out the man; and he placed at the east of the garden of Eden Cherubims, and a flaming sword which turned every way, to keep the way of the tree of life.[15]

Parallel to the Hebrews, the Greeks told of Prometheus, enhancing mankind with the gift of fire, but suffering an eternity of torment as a result; and of Icarus, who used his father's invention to fly too high and so fell to his death. Modern literature has seen Faust, Frankenstein, The Island of Dr. Moreau, and, most interestingly, Brave New World. In each case the attempt of mankind to rival the gods ends in disaster, or, at least, dystopia. (Fictional accounts of successful enhancement are far rarer, whether because they go against our cultural grain or whether they just lack dramatic tension. Arthur C. Clarke's Childhood's End is one interesting example of this approach.[16]) This deep cultural archetype of the dangers of men attempting to "become too much" can certainly affect reactions to bioscience[17] and to human biological enhancement.

II. Are Human Biological Enhancements Meaningfully Different from Other Forms of Human Enhancement?

Human enhancement is everywhere, from clothing to the Internet, from jet planes to cosmetic surgery, and from education to anabolic steroids. "Enhancement," as a controversial issue, seems to be limited to

---

14 Thomas Murray, Director of the Hastings Center, has made this argument. *See* Michael Dobie, *Of Might Mice & Super Men*, NEWSDAY, March 19, 2005, at B10; Mark Sappenfield, *Pervasiveness of Pills Dulls Outrage Against Steroid-Using Stars*, CHRISTIAN SCI. MONITOR, Dec. 10, 2004, at 1.
15 *Genesis* 3:22-24 (King James). The story of the Tower of Babel is another example of mankind being punished for overreaching. *Genesis* 11:1-9 (King James).
16 ARTHUR C. CLARKE, CHILDHOOD'S END (Ballantine 1953).
17 *See generally*, JON TURNEY, FRANKENSTEIN'S FOOTSTEPS: SCIENCE, GENETICS AND POPULAR CULTURE (Yale Univ. Press 2000).

new technical interventions that change the human body's structure or functioning, typically through "medicine-like" interventions: drugs or genes, surgical removals or implants. But are those enhancements really different in ways that have meaning, for either ethical or policy analysis?

This section of the article explores that question. It starts by discussing the weak foundations for an important and generally assumed distinction between tools and changes to the human body that enhance our abilities. It then looks at the distinctiveness of human biological enhancements with respect to the five general objections to enhancement discussed above. It follows with a discussion of five other factors that may affect our views of human biological enhancement. It concludes that human biological enhancements for the most part are not meaningfully different from other kinds of human enhancement and that they should not be treated differently just because they are *biological* enhancements.

A. Tools versus Selves

Reports of tool use by non-human primates, porpoises, and even birds make it increasingly clear that *Homo sapiens* is not the *only* tool-using animal, but our tools are clearly central to our existence. Thomas Carlyle wrote "Man is a Tool-using Animal . . . . Nowhere do you find him without Tools; without Tools he is nothing, with Tools he is all."[18] Over its history, *Homo sapiens* has enhanced the quality and quantity of its lives mainly through the use of tools. Our species' hominid ancestors used stone tools for pounding, cutting, and other purposes; our species' innovations range from clothing and controlled fire to personal computers and nuclear weapons.

Tools, defined broadly, enormously enhance our abilities over those of humans in a "state of nature". They allow us to eat better, be stronger, move faster, communicate over greater distances, and generally to do more. Yet, with the exception of a few religious sects, such as the Old Order Amish, few people feel qualms about using modern tools. And even the Old Order Amish allow the use of some tools, those similar to the tools used by their ancestors when the sect was founded.

Helping a man change himself so he can throw a discus a foot farther is controversial; letting men build tools to shoot bullets thousands of feet, and shoot rockets thousands or millions of miles, is not. It would be controversial to engineer humans who were capable of even slow and limited flight, yet we do not think twice about crossing the Pacific at enormous speeds and heights. Why?

I think most of us would react that the tool is not the self, or, at least, is not so perceived. Tools are not part of our biological organisms. They can be added or subtracted. They are (usually) inanimate, lifeless objects (although some working animals, such as sheep dogs, are effectively "tools"). Using tools does not change "us."

---

[18] Thomas Carlyle, Sartor Resartus 31 (Univ. of Cal. Press 2000) (1831).

But is that really true? Eyeglasses have been part of my life for over forty years. Although I do take them off to sleep, to shower, or to swim, they seem more a part of me than, say, my useless smallest toe. They seem more a part of me than various internal, unperceived and largely unknown organs, such as my appendix or my spleen. Eyeglasses are a medical intervention, not an enhancement, but the point here is that they are "tools" that can *feel* like part of oneself. And other tools, not used as medical interventions, can produce the same reaction. Athletes in some sports talk of feeling that the bat, the glove, and the racquet are extensions of their arms. In some moods, a personal computer connected to the Internet can feel like another, vastly powerful, organ. Cars, cell phones, and iPods similarly take on deeply personal meanings for people, complete with their own "personalizing" touches, marking the tool as distinctively belonging to the owner— or, perhaps, distinctly *part* of the owner.

Even apart from tools that blur the distinction between our things and ourselves, why, after all, should we make such a distinction? If we focus on the action performed, the end accomplished, is there a difference between a person using binoculars and a person engineered to have spectacular distance vision? The objection *must* be to the means, not to the end, which in both cases is better distance vision, but what is the meaningful difference? The next sections of this paper will consider, and dismiss, several ways in which one might argue that tools are inherently different from human biological enhancements. I am not confident that this effort clearly demonstrates that they are not different; I do believe it shows that the argument for a moral distinction between the two is not an easy one.

One other aspect of the tool/self distinction should be noted. There are some interesting things that exist somewhere in the middle of this apparently sharp distinction, tools that are implanted into the body and become "part" of it—heart pacemakers, cochlear implants, and, to some extent, prosthetic limbs. Thus far, these exist for medical reasons, to restore or preserve "normal" functioning. Rapidly improving technologies for connecting neural systems directly with electronic systems hold out the prospect of direct mental control of "tools"[19] or of direct inputs into the brain from artificial sensory organs, implanted or distant.[20] This could be used for restoration, as in restoring lower body motion and sensation to those with spinal cord injuries. It could also be used for enhancement,

---

19 *See e.g.*, Jose M. Carmena et al., *Learning to Control a Brain-Machine Interface for Reaching and Grasping by Primates*, 1 PUB. LIBR. SCI. BIOLOGY 193 (2003); Jonathan R. Wolpaw & Dennis J. McFarland, *Control of a Two-Dimensional Movement Signal by a Noninvasive Brain-Computer Interface in Humans*, 101 PROC. NAT'L ACAD. SCI. U.S. 17849 (2004).
20 CHOROST, *supra* note 5 (cochlear implants); Mark C. Peterman et al., *Localized Chemical Release from an Artificial Synapse Chip*, 101 PROC. NAT'L ACAD. SCI. U.S. 9951 (2004) (artificial retina); A. Asohan, *Leading Humanity Forward*, STAR (Malay.), October 14, 2003 (discussing Prof. Kevin Warwick giving himself a new sense, sonar-based distance finding, through a neuro-electronic interface).

bringing closer to reality the possibility of "bionic" people or cyborgs, who seem problematic because they are cases where tools have become major components of selves.[21]

On the other hand, fantasies of a rapid spread of cyborgs need to be tempered by an appreciation of the power of tools. If a person can use binoculars, why run the expense, the risk, and, for the near future at least, the lower quality, of an implanted distance vision system? It may be that the first cases of enhancement through implanted tools will occur in injured or disabled people who will need a cochlear implant or artificial retina—with its attendant costs, risks, and quality issues—to restore their abilities, but decide they should try one that enhances their capabilities beyond the normal human range.[22]

B. The Five Objections to Enhancement

Four of the five objections to human biological enhancement face the problem that they also apply both to non-biological enhancements and to human biological enhancement when used in medicine. This lack of distinctiveness is not necessarily a fatal blow to these objections. It might make sense, for example, to use a technology to treat deadly pancreatic cancer while banning its use to sculpt more sharply chiseled biceps for a bodybuilder. One could further argue that it may be preferable to prevent the spread of new bad practices even if their existing uses are too firmly planted to uproot. Nevertheless, the fact that those four objections are not specific to human biological enhancement significantly affects the arguments.

1. Safety

Human biological enhancements certainly may be unsafe. Even those that are approved for medical uses may be unsafe for enhancement uses. First, the medical clinical trials may not have examined their safety in healthy people at the doses used for enhancement. This seems to be the case for anabolic steroids, which athletes use very differently from the way doctors prescribe them. Second, safety is a relative term. A drug or a surgical procedure may be safe enough to use when weighed against the risks of some diseases, but not in the context of another disease, or of the enhancement of a healthy person. Previous medical approvals of

---

21 Gregory Stock discusses the difference between capabilities derived from tools and those from tools embedded within us. A person with a cochlear implant is a cyborg; a person with a hearing aid is a "fyborg" – a functional cyborg. GREGORY STOCK, REDESIGNING HUMANS: CHOOSING OUR GENES, CHANGING OUR FUTURE (Mariner Books 2003).
22 The character Geordi La Forge from *Star Trek: The Next Generation* provides a fictional example. Blind from birth, his artificial vision implant allows him to "see" the entire electromagnetic spectrum, an ability that, in his role as chief engineer, comes in handy from time to time. Non-fictional examples are provided by people who, when they get laser eye surgery to improve below normal distance vision, ask the surgeon to try to give them better than normal distance vision. William Saletan, *The Beam in Your Eye*, SLATE, April 17, 2005, http://www.slate.com/id/2116858/.

enhancing technologies as safe may provide some useful evidence of the enhancement's safety, but they cannot be conclusive.

The safety objection is, at most, an argument for regulating the safety of human biological enhancements in ways akin to the regulation of the safety of medical interventions. One should note that, even with medical interventions, states generally regulate the safety of drugs and medical devices by requiring pre-market approval, but do not apply such prior safety regulation to medical *procedures* such as new surgical techniques. But *non*-biological human enhancements are not subject to any general pre-market safety approval. Nor, for that matter, are most other human activities, from skydiving to playing rugby to watching television. Societies regulate the safety of things for a variety of historical, legal, political, and cultural reasons, usually, but not always, related to the degree of danger they present. There seems to be little reason to treat human biological enhancements differently, but instead safety regulations should be imposed on those enhancements where and how it seems appropriate.

2. Coercion

Coercive enhancement, in all three of its forms (frank, parental, and implicit) does pose distinctive questions because of the nature of the intrusion they involve. Human biological enhancements will almost always involve physical intrusions into a person's body, either through surgical procedures or biochemical interventions. Such intrusions are not suspect if they are the result of a genuinely voluntary decision, but the law has long provided special protections for a person's body, ranging from the common law action for battery to the decision by the United States Supreme Court that forcible bodily intrusions by the police could violate the Fifth Amendment's guarantee of due process of law when they "shocked the conscience".[23]

Other forms of enhancement will generally not involve this kind of physical intrusion; an employer might, for example, require employees to attend training sessions to enhance their performance without raising substantial concerns. And although medical practice often requires this precise kind of invasion of a person's body, competent adults have an almost absolute right to refuse medical treatment. The major exception concerns infectious epidemic diseases where one person's lack of treatment may endanger many others; even in this context, American court decisions upholding mandatory treatment are generally old and may be questioned in light of the growth of civil rights over the past century.[24] Mandatory treatment for mental illness has a more complicated history, but coerced treatment, though not eliminated, has been increasingly limited over the last several decades.[25]

---

23   Rochin v. California, 342 U.S. 165 (1952).
24   MARK A. HALL ET AL., HEALTH LAW 783-805 (6th ed. 2004); *but cf.* LAWRENCE O. GOSTIN, PUBLIC HEALTH LAW: POWER, DUTY, RESTRAINT 204-24 (Univ. of Cal. Press 2001).
25   GEORGE J. ALEXANDER & ALAN W. SCHEFLIN, LAW AND MENTAL DISORDER (1998).

Coercive enhancements will need to be regulated. Frank coercion needs to be limited as appropriate; this may well vary with employers, for example, being more constrained in what they can order employees to do than the military is with respect to soldiers, sailors, and airmen.

Coercion of children is more complicated. The government requires certain enhancements for children, notably education and vaccinations. And we not only allow but encourage and even require parents to coerce their children into other enhancements, like nutrition, study habits, and braces to improve a child's teeth and smile. In the United States parental discretion in parenting even has some, admittedly poorly defined, constitutional protection.[26] At the same time, we put some, admittedly loose, limits on parental discretion when parents are clearly acting against their children's best interests. The unusually stringent limitations on children's participation in risky medical research as to whether or not the parents consent provide one example.[27] Some specific forms of enhancement that are particularly risky might need to be regulated to prevent their use on children. In some cases that will mean that the children can make their own competent decisions when they become adults; this position is widely recommended for genetic tests where the results do not lead to interventions during childhood.[28] The harder questions will revolve around enhancements that are effective only during (or, in the case of embryonic or fetal interventions, before) childhood. Some regulatory scheme, either governmental or professional, may be necessary to limit the use of risky or unproven enhancements in embryos, fetuses, or young children.

Implicit coercion poses the hardest questions. It is said that most television news presenters in the United States have had cosmetic surgery by the time they are 40 years old. That may be the result of implicit coercion; the need to look youthful in order to be competitive in a difficult business. Yet if everyone can be enhanced to the same extent, to retain their own optimal 30 year old appearance, no one's competitive position is changed. But even though the eventual result is the same, people take the risks of surgery, spend money, and perhaps feel coerced. Similarly, an athlete may not want to take a performance-enhancing drug, but may feel compelled to do so either to protect his or her livelihood or merely to be competitive. In these cases, where everyone engages in the costly

---

26   Meyer v. Nebraska, 262 U.S. 390 (1923) (the state cannot prevent parents from having children learn a foreign language); Pierce v. Soc'y of Sisters, 268 U.S. 510 (1925) (the state cannot prevent parents from sending children to private schools).
27   Additional Protections for Children Involved as Subjects in Research, 45 C.F.R. §§ 46.401-.409 (2005).
28   The Am. Soc'y of Human Genetics Bd. of Dirs. & The Am. Coll. of Med. Genetics Bd. of Dirs., *Points to Consider: Ethical, Legal, and Psychosocial Implications of Genetic Testing in Children and Adolescents*, 57 AM. J. HUM. GENET. 1233 (1995), *available at* http://genetics.faseb.org/genetics/ashg/pubs/policy/pol-13.htm (stating that "*If the medical or psychosocial benefits of a genetic test will not accrue until adulthood, as in the case of carrier status or adult-onset diseases, genetic testing generally should be deferred*") (emphasis in original).

behavior (enhancement) to no one's ultimate benefit, a successful ban on all performance enhancing drugs might improve everyone's situation.

This may be true if we assume that only the quality of the performance relative to that of the other competitors is important, which might be the case, for example, with many sports. If, on the other hand, the quality of the performance has both a relative value to the actor and an absolute value to others, the situation is more complicated. The quality of medical research might be such an example, where using a cognitive enhancement to become a better researcher both helps one's own competitive position among researchers and, presumably, helps society by producing better treatments. Each form of biological enhancement may have to be analyzed separately in light of implicit coercion; in some cases, particularly those where the benefits would be only relative, it is likely that either enhancements should be generally banned (if an effective ban is feasible) or people who choose not to be enhanced should be protected from the negative consequences of their choices.

Of course, whether an enhancement only has value relative to the performance of other people or has a more absolute value may not be easy to answer. Is a particular gymnastics routine made possible by an enhancing technology only valuable to the performers whom it makes better than others or does the resulting novelty or beauty have its own value? And, of course, any regulation is likely both to have some costs and to be imperfect. As a practical matter, regulating enhancements in order to avoid implicit coercion may often prove extremely difficult.

3. Fairness

The fairness objection, on the other hand, seems less troublesome. The fairness problems of enhancements are not unique to human biological enhancements, nor are they without plausible regulatory solutions. As President Kennedy said, in a very different context, "Life is unfair".[29] It is hard to imagine any competition, athletic or otherwise, to which the contestants bring exactly the same physical, mental, and emotional capabilities. Many of those capabilities will be the result of genetic variation, early environment, and chance, none of which the contestant "deserved". It is not clear why biological cognitive enhancements should be any more, or any less, unfair than the cognitive enhancements that come from good nutrition, family encouragement, good schools, or a preparatory course for college entrance examinations. Nor is it clear that the use of a performance-

---

[29] President John F. Kennedy, News Conference at the State Department Auditorium (March 21, 1962) (transcript available in the John F. Kennedy Library and Museum), *available at* http://www.jfklibrary.org/jfk_press_conference_620321.html. The full quotation is "There is always inequity in life. Some men are killed in a war, and some men are wounded, and some men never leave the country, and some men are stationed in the Antarctic, and some are stationed in San Francisco. It's very hard in military or personal life to assure complete equality. Life is unfair." Kennedy was responding to a question about the unfairness of recalling National Guard forces that had earlier seen hard service to active duty.

enhancing drug by an athlete is any more, or less, unfair than having a great coach, excellent equipment, the services of a sports psychologist, or good genes. (Some of these various enhancements, biological or otherwise, may require more or less "work" by the enhanced person than others; that issue is discussed below.) The use of any enhancement that is available only to some may be unfair to those who do not have access to it, whether or not it is a human biological enhancement. One could even imagine a case where biological enhancements were only permitted to make competitions "more fair", by providing compensating abilities to those who lost out in the genetic, parental, or early life environment lotteries.

It might be argued that in some competitions—athletic, intellectual, occupational, or other—biological enhancements would be too valuable and would be unfair because they would overwhelm all other factors. Professor Max Mehlman makes such an argument about the power of inherited genetic enhancement to make success in life unfair, both within one generation and across succeeding generations. As a result, he calls for banning such enhancements. Alternatively, though, one could solve the fairness problem in that situation by making the enhancement available to all, a strategy already used in some contexts. If we accept primary and secondary education as an "enhancement," as surely we must, the common response to the fear of unequal access has not been to ban education but to make it a universal entitlement. Although this may be an area where it is harder to dislodge existing practices than to prevent new ones, those worried about the long term unfairness of self-reinforcing inequality may prefer to fight for inheritance taxes and excellent universal education rather than try to regulate still speculative human biological enhancement technologies.

There remains a fairness question of what to do about people who have access to an enhancement, but voluntarily choose not to use it. This issue is, in part, discussed above with regard to implicit coercion. If the costs of foregoing an enhancement are sufficiently dire, one might want to protect people against the coercion implicit in such a choice, as a matter of avoiding coercion more than as a matter of fairness.

But even if the situation is not effectively coercive, we might still feel that fairness requires us to protect some people from the effects of their decision not to enhance. For example, one might (or might not) want to protect people's choices that are influenced by religion. American employment discrimination law not only bans overt discrimination based on religion, but affirmatively requires employers to make reasonable accommodations to an applicant's or employee's religious beliefs, which might involve, for example, special work schedules or exemptions from some clothing rules.[30] Presumably, a religiously motivated choice not to use a human biological enhancement would be covered by the same

---

30 Title VII of the Civil Rights Act of 1964 § 701(j), 42 U.S.C. § 2000e(j) (2005).

provision. In other situations we usually allow (or force) people to accept the consequences of their decisions not to choose an enhancing technology, just as we let people live with the results of their educational or investment choices. One might argue that fairness would require the protection of someone who does not want to use a human biological enhancement for principled, but not religious, reasons, only if we concluded that the question of enhancement should be viewed as important or as special as questions of religious observance.

4. Integrity

The integrity objection also applies more broadly than to human biological enhancements. Parallel to the argument about fairness, other kinds of enhancement might undercut "the essence" of the activity. Special equipment or treatment by a sports psychologist may be as inconsistent with "the spirit" of sport as performance-enhancing drugs; test preparation or cram courses may be as inconsistent with meritocracy as cognitive-enhancing pharmaceuticals. Whether human biological enhancements are inconsistent with the integrity of an activity depends on the definition of the "essence" of the activity, which will often be difficult to determine.[31] That, in turn, requires some way of determining whether any one group's definition of the essential aspects of the activity should be allowed to bind other people with other views. Thus, if some people believe performance-enhancing drugs ruin the meaning of sports, but others, whether they approve of the use of such drugs or not, do not believe their use undermines the value of sports, whose view should control?

Pluralism is one response. One could let those who want "pure" sports have "drug-free leagues" and let others have "open" leagues, just as some

---

[31] Justice Scalia made this argument in the Casey Martin case, as he castigated the Court for trying to define, or to divine, the "essence" of golf:

If one assumes, however, that the PGA Tour has some legal obligation to play classic, Platonic golf—and if one assumes the correctness of all the other wrong turns the Court has made to get to this point—then we Justices must confront what is indeed an awesome responsibility. It has been rendered the solemn duty of the Supreme Court of the United States, laid upon it by Congress in pursuance of the Federal Government's power "to regulate Commerce with foreign Nations, and among the several States," U.S. Const., Art. I, § 8, cl. 3, to decide What Is Golf. I am sure that the Framers of the Constitution, aware of the 1457 edict of King James II of Scotland prohibiting golf because it interfered with the practice of archery, fully expected that sooner or later the paths of golf and government, the law and the links, would once again cross, and that the judges of this august Court would some day have to wrestle with that age-old jurisprudential question, for which their years of study in the law have so well prepared them: Is someone riding around a golf course from shot to shot *really* a golfer? The answer, we learn, is yes. The Court ultimately concludes, and it will henceforth be the Law of the Land, that walking is not a "fundamental" aspect of golf. Either out of humility or out of self-respect (one or the other) the Court should decline to answer this incredibly difficult and incredibly silly question. To say that something is "essential" is ordinarily to say that it is necessary to the achievement of a certain object. But since it is the very nature of a game to have no object except amusement (that is what distinguishes games from productive activity), it is quite impossible to say that any of a game's arbitrary rules is "essential."

PGA Tour, Inc. v. Martin, 532 U.S. 661, 670-71 (2001) (Scalia, J., dissenting).

people abide by rules governing amateurs and others prefer professional status. To do so would be to consider enhancement a matter of taste, a preference as to which reasonable people might differ. It might (or might not) be appropriate for a government to help leagues enforce their rules, but there seems to be little reason, under the claim of integrity, for a government to ban enhancement for everyone.

5. Naturalness

The final objection, naturalness, is akin to integrity but instead of focusing on the activity affected by the enhancement, it concerns the integrity of the species whose member is enhanced. Like the integrity argument, it requires an agreement on the essence of humanity itself. For some, that definition may be religious. Jewish and Christian scripture holds that God created man in his own image; presumably, changing man from that image would be sinful.[32] For those without a religious basis for their definition, humans in a state of nature might be a plausible measure of appropriate humanity (although there are serious logical problems with the idea that what is "natural" necessarily has normative force, often referred to as "the naturalistic fallacy"[33]).

Both ways of defining "appropriate humanity" face the problem that little about today's humans resembles those at the time the religious definitions were created, resembling even less humans in a "state of nature". What we eat, what we wear, how we live, travel, and communicate have all changed markedly as a result of human enhancements. Even our physical beings are longer lived, larger, and generally healthier than in the past. It is not clear why some changes are natural, or religiously licit, and others are unnatural or sinful. And in heterogeneous societies, a group that does come up with a thorough description of religiously or naturally appropriate humanity has the further problem of convincing others that its definition is correct. The feeling that human biological enhancements, at least in more extreme cases, are "wrong" has great emotional appeal and, I suspect, broad popular support, akin to that of the so-called "yuck factor." Whether this feeling can be justified is less clear.

C. Other Factors

Some other factors seem to be at work in causing controversy about human biological enhancements. They are not strong or self contained enough to constitute independent arguments against enhancements, but are rather

---

[32] It appears that Islam does not hold that Allah created man in his own image. Instead, "Allah is unique, unimaginable and highly exalted above his creation. He can never and in no way be compared with mankind, who are his creatures and servants." Christine Schirrmacher, The Fall of Man and the Redemption of Mankind (unpublished essay, on file with author), (June 11, 1997), *available at* http://contra-mundum.org/schirrmacher/fall.html.
[33] For a brief discussion of the naturalistic fallacy, *see* Owen D. Jones & Timothy H. Goldsmith, *Law and Behavioral Biology*, 105 COLUM. L. REV. 405, 484-85 (2005); Owen D. Jones, *On the Nature of Norms: Biology, Morality, and the Disruption of Order*, 98 MICH. L. REV. 2072, 2087-88 (2000).

perceived distinctions between biological and other enhancements or other concerns that feed public discomfort about biological enhancements. This section discusses five such factors: the physical nature of biological enhancements; their perceived permanence; their unearned nature; their novelty; and, lastly, concern that human biological enhancements are examples of human hubris.

1. Physical?

Some of the feeling that biological enhancements are different may come from the sense that they make physical or, in some cases, biochemical changes in the body when tools or other enhancements do not. It is not clear why physical changes should be crucial, but, in any event, other enhancements do change our bodies. Weight training and good diet change the shapes of our bodies; conditioning and practice change our physical capabilities. Our tools give us calluses and change our muscles and joints (sometimes for the worse). Our clothing changes the texture and color of our skin.

Perhaps most powerfully, though least visibly, enhancement through learning *physically* changes our brains. Memories and mental skills are embodied in physical changes in how our brains operate. Synapses, the connections between neurons in the brain, get stronger or weaker, are destroyed or are created. Anything that one learns from reading this article exists in the mind because of those *physical* changes in the brain. Learning to read, learning to type, and learning to play the guitar both cause and are caused by these physical changes to the brain. These changes are as real and physical as, though possibly less tangible than, the changes caused by cosmetic surgery, gene transfer, or cognition enhancing pills.

2. Permanent?

Another factor may be the feeling that biological enhancements are more permanent than using tools or other forms of enhancement. But this distinction also fails. Some biological enhancements may be easy to stop, such as memory-enhancing pills or anabolic steroids. Others may be hard but possible to undo, such as cosmetic surgery. Even gene transfer, when and if it ever becomes feasible, should probably be reversible through counteracting gene transfer. Some biological enhancements might be effectively irreversible, such as those that affect childhood development—drugs that increase a child's growth might be an example—but most will not be.

In another sense, however, many of these enhancements will be irreversible. An athlete who has steroid enhanced muscles is always different from one who has not, even after the muscles have reverted to normal. But this is true of all human enhancements, and indeed of all human experience. Learning to read has irreversible effects, as does going to law school or falling in love. Biological enhancements seem likely, in general, to be no more and no less irreversible than other enhancements or experiences.

3. Unearned?

The first two factors, physical change and perceived permanence, seem related to the (weak) distinction between tools and selves. The third factor, the unearned nature of biological enhancements, seems related to both fairness and integrity. People may believe that muscles from weight training and good grades from diligent study are earned and therefore good; muscles from anabolic steroids and good grades from cognitive-enhancing pills are unearned and are therefore bad. This assumes first that the enhancement does not require any ethically significant effort. Anabolic steroids do not build muscles in people who do not exercise; they can improve the muscle-building results of exercise. Pills that improve attention would not replace studying but would make it more efficient. Even cosmetic surgery is arguably "earned," if not by cash payments, then by the pain of the recovery period.

The bigger problem with this idea is that we rarely reward pure effort. Competitions are not judged based on who tries the hardest or prepares most diligently. Those factors are often important, but the performance is determinative, not the effort. The Nobel Prize is not awarded to the hardest working scientist; athletic fame and fortune come from successful results, not mere effort. Many factors other than hard work affect success in most endeavors, including inherited traits, good training, and luck. We may not like this; we may prefer to believe that our successes are completely the result of our own efforts and, hence, "earned" by those efforts. But it takes very little reflection to recognize that many "unearned" factors affect success; it is not clear why biological enhancements should be viewed as peculiarly inappropriate unearned factors.

4. Novel?

A cynic might note one generally applicable distinction between controversial and non-controversial enhancements: the controversial enhancements are newer. Cosmetic surgery, the oldest of the biological enhancements discussed in this article, is also the least controversial and seems to have grown less controversial with time. In vitro fertilization and recombinant genetic engineering were both extremely controversial when invented in the 1970s; both are today routine, at least in most circumstances. Novelty raises some legitimate concerns, primarily safety concerns from the limited extent of our knowledge of the long term effects of an innovation. Novelty, however, does not seem to have any independent ethical significance—at least not in Western culture, which has been changing at a dizzying rate for the last several hundred years.

5. Hubris?

Hubris is the last of these other factors. The Greeks originally used the term to mean presumption toward the gods; it now means overbearing pride, presumption, or arrogance. Adam and Eve, the Tower of Babel, Icarus,

Dr. Frankenstein—they all are stories of people who attempted to do what humans should not do. Are we really foolish enough, many ask, to believe that we are wise enough to change ourselves? It is a fair question. There seems little reason to believe that we can successfully plan changes in our species. Our knowledge—our ability to predict the actual consequences of the changes we effect—is certainly limited; our wisdom—our ability to make the ethically or morally appropriate choice even if we could accurately predict the future—is at least equally suspect.

But this question is moot. We are constantly changing our species. Agriculture, writing, and printing vastly changed human life. The revolutions of the last two centuries have made life in the industrial or post-industrial world more distant from the lives of modern subsistence farmers. Based on our history, one powerful way to describe *Homo sapiens* might be as a species that is constantly reinventing itself. Human biological enhancements may be a new method of reinvention, but they are surely not uniquely, or even particularly, susceptible to the charge of hubris.

D. Concluding Thoughts on whether Human Biological Enhancement Is Different

The general approach of this section has been to compare new human biological enhancements with existing forms of enhancement and to show that, in many ways, they are not very different. One could argue, as an anonymous peer reviewer has suggested, that even if any enhancement differs in any particular way only slightly from existing, well accepted approaches, the combination of a number of small differences may be important. That may be true, but I would require an argument about *why* that combination made an ethically significant difference.

One might say that if people react viscerally against a particular enhancement, that reaction itself is evidence that such a culmination of small differences has become significant. I see no reason to believe, as a factual matter, that popular repugnance is necessarily a consequence of such a summation of small differences. It seems more likely to be a negative reaction to some part of the enhancement. Neither am I willing to accept repugnance as an independent ethical argument. One's sense of repugnance to something—whether an unusual sexual activity or an odd-smelling food—may be a good reason not to indulge it oneself. On its own, it is not a good argument for prohibiting interested people from trying it.

III. International Implications

This article was written by a middle-aged, white, male, American law professor. That is not an apology, but it is a limitation. The culture from which I have tried to draw insights and conclusions is not the culture of all 300 million residents of the United States and certainly not that of our entire species. But the fact that the roughly 6.4 billion members of Homo sapiens form thousands of different cultures, organized into hundreds of different sovereignties, has crucial implications for the future of human biological enhancement.

A. Cultural Diversity

Different cultures react differently to various human biological enhancements. The wealth of a culture will affect what enhancements are available, as will its scientific and medical infrastructure. The economic and social conditions may make some enhancements more, and others less, interesting. A culture where memorized texts are important might be especially interested in memory-enhancing drugs. A culture that does not participate in the Olympics may well not be very interested in performance-enhancing drugs for Olympic athletes.

Particular enhancements might be unacceptable in some cultures for specific reasons, as, for example, a pig-based implant might be unacceptable in Jewish or Muslim cultures.[34] Some cultures might find the whole idea of human biological enhancement uninteresting if what their culture values most cannot be affected by these kinds of enhancements. Thus, a culture with a strong religious orientation, away from a worldly life, might find most enhancements irrelevant, distasteful, or possibly irreligious. It would, however, be rash to generalize too strongly about how certain kinds of cultures would react to some kinds of enhancement. A wonderful fictional example of a religious use of a modern technology comes from an Arthur C. Clarke short story where Tibetan Buddhists install a computer to complete a prayer cycle, with surprising consequences.[35]

But cultural variation is interesting and important in another sense. One way to determine what is "natural" is to follow an Aristotelian definition of natural law—natural law comprises those rules that all humans (or all human cultures) accept. The existence of some positive views of particular human biological enhancements would be evidence that there is no universally acknowledged natural law against them.

B. International Rivalry

The billions of living humans are not only members of thousands of different cultures, but are governed by several hundred sovereign national governments. The existence of different sovereignties adds further complications to the questions of human biological enhancement—some of those sovereignties may see human biological enhancement as a competitive advantage. We know the former East Germany used performance-enhancing drugs to improve its competitiveness in the Olympic Games

---

[34] Although at least Jewish religious leaders do accept the transplantation of pig heart valves in humans when medically necessary. See Fred Rosner, *Pig Organs for Transplantation into Humans: A Jewish View*, 66 Mount Sinai J. Med. 314 (1999), *available at* http://www.mssm.edu/msjournal/66/PAGE314_319.PDF. *See also* Jules Crittenden, *Advance Seen on Pig-to-Human Transplants*, Boston Herald, Sept. 18, 1998, at 26.
[35] Arthur C. Clarke, The Nine Billion Names of God (reissue ed., New Am. Library 1987).

and other international sports competitions.[36] It seems unlikely that a government will care enough about its population's beauty to encourage enhancing cosmetic surgery, but other uses are more plausible.

Military applications are the most obvious. Human biological enhancements might yield better soldiers, for offensive or defensive purposes. Already, the United States Defense Department is spending many millions of dollars on research projects in cognitive enhancement.[37] These range from research on maintaining alertness and normal cognitive function in the face of limited sleep to efforts to use direct neuro-electronic connections for direct mental control of weapons. Although long term genetic intervention—the creation of armies of cloned warriors—seems unlikely, somatic cell gene transfer to improve soldiers' physical abilities, for either the short or the long term, seems plausible. So do performance-enhancing drugs.

But not all competition is military. Some countries already see advantages in competing in the global economy with an educated workforce. Biological enhancements might prove useful in improving the education of a country's population. Nations seem to compete in scientific research for short term economic benefits, but also for prestige, military spin offs, and sheer pride. Such countries might well encourage human biological enhancements that improved their researchers—and their researchers' results. Even personality or mood enhancers could be of great interest to a national government, perhaps not as much for international competition as for avoiding domestic disaffection and possibly for improving economic outcomes. National governments might encourage, or compel, the use of human biological enhancements for reasons we see as good (public health), bad (political control), or relatively unimportant (Olympic medal counts). But, if important enhancements are available, governments that have the means to use them will not ignore them.

C. Transnational Regulation

The existence of different sovereignties complicates regulation of enhancement. If certain kinds of enhancement are felt to be so bad, for whatever reason, that they must be banned, to be effective, all of the world's states would have to enact—and to enforce— the ban. More subtly, the competitive incentives discussed above mean that a ban even in one country might be undercut by the use of the enhancement in competing countries. Without such an international ban, countries that would like to ban an enhancement may not feel able to do so for competitive reasons. Even if they do ban the enhancements, they will then have the problem of preventing their nationals from becoming "enhancement tourists" who go outside the country to get the enhancements they want. But universal

---

36 Steven Ungerleider, Faust's Gold: Inside the East German Doping Machine (2001).
37 *See* Jonathan D. Moreno, *DARPA On Your Mind*, Cerebrum, Fall 2004, at 91.

bans on forms of human biological enhancement will be difficult to create and probably impossible to enforce.

Unless they embody, or become, "customary" international law, international treaties or conventions are enforceable only in countries that ratify them. It may well prove impossible to convince every country to ratify a treaty banning some or all human biological enhancements, particularly if the objections are based on cultural responses that are not universally shared. Even if most countries are willing to sign, the remaining countries might see an opportunity to build a lucrative specialty as an "enhancement haven". And, of course, even if a convention were adopted universally, it might not be enforced. At least six international conventions ban slavery and various forms of forced labor,[38] yet it is estimated that millions of people remain slaves.[39]

The Treaty on the Non-Proliferation of Nuclear Weapons provides another useful example; 187 countries have ratified this treaty.[40] At least three of those that have not ratified the treaty have produced, or are widely believed to have produced, nuclear weapons: India, Pakistan, and Israel. North Korea, which is believed to be producing nuclear weapons, had probably been violating the Treaty for several years before it formally withdrew in 2003. Some countries that have ratified and that have not withdrawn from the Treaty are believed to have violated, or to be violating, its provisions by seeking to develop nuclear weapons, including Iran, currently, and Iraq, in the past. Developing nuclear weapons is an enormous scientific and industrial endeavor, requiring large, difficult-to-conceal facilities and costing billions of dollars.

Human biological enhancements are likely to be much easier and less expensive to develop and produce. They will usually flow from medical developments that will involve publicly available drugs and devices and openly described procedures. These "dual use" technologies should make it easy for a country to secretly enhance at least some of its citizens. A successful universal prohibition of an attractive enhancement seems impossible.

---

38 Universal Declaration of Human Rights, G.A. Res. 217A, at art. 4, U.N. GAOR, 3d Sess., 1st plen. mtg., U.N. Doc. A/810 (Dec. 10, 1948), *available at* http://daccessdds.un.org/doc/RESOLUTION/GEN/NR0/043/88/IMG/NR004388.pdf?OpenElement; United Nations, International Covenant on Civil and Political Rights art. 8, *opened for signature* Dec. 16, 1966, 999 U.N.T.S. 171, *available at* http://www.unhchr.ch/html/menu3/b/a_ccpr.htm; League of Nations, Slavery Convention, Sept. 25, 1926, 60 L.N.T.S. 253, *available at* http://www.unhchr.ch/html/menu3/b/f2sc.htm; International Labour Organization, Forced Labour Convention, June 28, 1930, 39 U.N.T.S. 55, *available at* http://www.unhchr.ch/html/menu3/b/31.htm; International Labour Organization, Abolition of Forced Labour Convention, June 25, 1957, 320 U.N.T.S. 291, *available at* http://www.unhchr.ch/html/menu3/b/32.htm; United Nations Convention for the Suppression of the Traffic in Persons and of the Exploitation of the Prostitution of Others, Dec. 2, 1949, 96 U.N.T.S. 271, *available at* http://www.unhchr.ch/html/menu3/b/33.htm.
39 *See, e.g.*, Pius Kamau, *Slavery a Reality Even Here*, Denver Post, June 23, 2005, at B7; Nicholas D. Kristof, *After the Brothel*, N.Y. Times, Jan. 26, 2005, at A17.
40 Treaty on the Non-Proliferation of Nuclear Weapons, *opened for signature* July 1, 1968, 21 U.S.T. 483, 729 U.N.T.S. 161, *available at* http://www.state.gov/t/np/trty/16281.htm.

Professor Mehlman has discussed the problems of international bans on enhancement in detail with regard to inherited human genetic enhancements. Although he strongly supports such bans, his analysis is not encouraging. He calls, ultimately, for the use of American economic and political pressure to "encourage" other countries to adopt and enforce such bans and, at the extreme, American military intervention to compel their enforcement.[41] The feasibility of such a policy is questionable; recent events in the Middle East make its attractiveness – inside and outside the United States – minimal. Any policy on the regulation of human biological enhancements will have to confront the reality that attractive enhancements almost certainly cannot be universally and enforceably forbidden.

Conclusion

> Explanations exist; they have existed for all time; there is always a well-known solution to every human problem—neat, plausible, and wrong.
>
> H.L. Mencken[42]

This is the fifth time that I have written about human biological enhancement. It will not be the last. Each time I write about this question, I see new issues and new arguments; each time I believe I am approaching nearer to the core of the problem, but I am still not close to being comfortable, either viscerally or intellectually, with a set of final conclusions about human biological enhancement.

I do believe, though, that the area of enhancement will have no good easy answers. Many of the broad ethical concerns about human biological enhancement seem to me unfounded. In most respects these technologies are not ethically different from other enhancing technologies we have long used and accepted.

At the same time, this article is not intended as an argument that biological enhancement should exist in an unregulated, laissez faire status.

---

41 MEHLMAN, *supra* note 2, at 152-54.
42 H. L. Mencken, *The Divine Afflatus*, N.Y. EVENING MAIL, Nov. 16, 1917, *reprinted in* PREJUDICES: SECOND SERIES 158 (Octagon Books 1977). An interesting side note about this quotation is that it is widely reported on the Internet as "For every complex problem there is an answer that is clear, simple, and wrong." It is possible, of course, that Mencken paraphrased his own quotation at some point after its initial publication in 1917, but it is equally possible that the many Internet sites have fed off of one another, with one misquote spiraling into dozens more. Interestingly, and somewhat disturbingly, even purported quotation websites, such as BrainyQuote, have gotten this quotation wrong. BrainyQuote.com, H. L. Mencken Quotes, http://www.brainyquote.com/quotes/authors/h/h_l_mencken.html (last visited Oct. 8, 2005). They seem not to have bothered to look up the quotations they share with the world. Even odder is the fact that two different collections of Mencken's writings have different versions of the quotation contained in the same essay, "The Divine Afflatus." A MENCKEN CHRESTOMATHY published the quotation as follows: "Explanations exist; they have existed for all *times, for* there is always *an easy* solution to every human problem – neat, plausible, and wrong." H. L. Mencken, *The Divine Afflatus, in* A MENCKEN CHRESTOMATHY 443 (Alfred A. Knopf 1949) (emphasis added). If any reader of this article can provide more information about this Mencken quotation, the author (and his research assistant) would be very interested in learning it.

Each kind of enhancement will need to be treated on its own, weighing the benefits of the technology against the costs it may impose, as well as the costs of regulation. There will be what I would consider good reasons to restrict or even ban some human biological enhancements. And societies may choose to act for reasons I would consider irrational; for the most part, at least where human rights are not involved, people, individually and collectively, are entitled to act on their tastes, preferences, and biases. California bans human consumption of horse meat; Singapore severely restricts the use of chewing gum. Neither action seems to me "rational", but neither seems improper. Societies may well choose to limit or ban some enhancements for similar reasons, although, as noted above, international pressures may limit the effectiveness of those efforts.

The "right answer" about human biological enhancement will surely vary from technology to technology, from culture to culture, and from time to time. We will not be helped to the right answer by viewing human biological enhancements as qualitatively different from other human endeavors. Instead, like all new technologies, we will need to ask whether and how these technologies can be used "to make greater, as in value or desirability" our lives, our societies, and our world.

SURROGACY IN ISRAEL:
A Model of Comprehensive Regulation of New Technologies

Jacqueline Hand[*]

Fifteen percent of the population of the United States (and of Israel) are infertile. Unlike earlier generations who had little choice but to live with this limitation, the accelerating development of new reproductive technologies has provided an ever increasing number of options for these couples, options unthinkable even two decades ago. (Baby Louise, the first test tube baby has just turned 27.[1]) These new technologies came onto the scene precisely as traditional principles of family law have been transformed by the women's movement (enhanced by another technological fix—contraception) and the gay rights movement. The result is a high level of uncertainty as to the legal status of the various parties to the new arrangements, particularly those who have moved ahead of the law by participating in a surrogate mother arrangement.

The institutional response to this situation varies widely from essentially no regulation (California) to complete prohibition to partial or piecemeal regulation. The only jurisdiction that has legalized surrogacy, while regulating it under a complex and comprehensive regulatory scheme, is Israel. The genesis of this scheme, in the experiences and ideologies of the individuals responsible for this Surrogate Motherhood Agreements Law[2], is the subject of Professor D. Kelly Weisberg's new book, *The Birth of Surrogacy in Israel*.[3]

This chronicle is valuable on several levels. First it provided a sort of pilot program of how a complex regulatory scheme can be effective at managing this controversial, but often deeply desired practice. Secondly, it illustrated the impacts of technology on the core structures of society. Finally, and perhaps most significantly, it exemplifies a deep legal history of how individuals have lasting effects on legal development.

The book, which was researched while Professor Weisberg was a Visiting Professor of Law at Hebrew University, begins with an in-depth description of the first two cases of surrogacy which occurred immediately after the

---

[*] Professor of Law, University of Detroit, Mercy School of Law.
[1] *Test Tube Baby Comes of Age*, BBC News, July 25, 1999, http://news.bbc.co.uk/2/hi/uk_news/403116.stm.
[2] Surrogate Motherhood Agreements (Approval of Agreement and Status of Newborn) Law 5756-1996, 1996, S.H. 1577, 176 (unofficial English translation available from Aryeh Greenfield Publications, P.O. Box 7422, Haifa, Israel 31070).
[3] D. Kelly Weisberg, The Birth of Surrogacy in Israel (2005).

passage of the law. In each case Weisberg provided a vivid journalistic portrait of the parties, both the intended parents and the surrogates and their partners. The contrasting experiences of these two sets of participants led to several changes in the regulations under the statute. The first contract between the infertile couple,[4] Rachel and Ben and Sara, their surrogate, resulted in healthy twins for the intended parents and a looming feeling of exploitation on the part of the surrogate. The surrogate's perception of being ill-used was a result of the intended parents' efforts to control all aspects of her life during the pregnancy and left her to feel as if her role was that of "a paid domestic".[5]

By contrast, in the second case 40 year old surrogate Hanna sustained a warm relationship with the intended parents, Naomi and Dan, which continued long after the birth. In fact, she indicated a willingness to carry a second child for them. The very particular experiences of these two families acted as a sort of pilot for implementing regulations under Israel's newly passed statutes. After these two cases the regulations were fine tuned to standardize the contract (but not the level of compensation), to provide additional personal privacy for the parties and to limit both the age of the surrogate (between ages 22 and 40)[6] and the number of times she can be a surrogate (no more than twice, both for the same family).

Having illustrated the real world impact of the legislation, Weisberg then explores its genesis. In many ways, the legal treatment of surrogacy throughout the world developed in reaction to the notorious case of *In re Baby M.*[7] In that case, the surrogate mother (who was the source of the ovum as well as the carrier of the baby), refused to fulfill her contract with the intended father (source of the sperm) by refusing to relinquish the baby to him. His wife, having no genetic relationship to the child, had no legal connection to the transaction. Ultimately the intended father sued for custody of the child; after months of unrelenting publicity the New Jersey Supreme Court ruled that the surrogacy contract, arranged by a commercial surrogacy center, was invalid because its enforcement constituted "baby selling". The Court granted the father custody based on the same standards as any other custody dispute—the best interests of the child. This spectacle, together with the public reaction to baby selling, generated an immediate response worldwide.[8] Australia, Britain, France, Germany *and* Israel banned commercial surrogacy.[9]

---

[4] The names of individuals who were not part of publicized legal cases were changed to preserve their privacy.
[5] WEISBERG, *supra* note 3, at 29.
[6] Ultimately, in the interests of the child, the ages of the intended parents were limited as well, in that the intended father could be no older than 59 and the intended mother no older than 48.
[7] *In re* Baby M, 537 A.2d 1227 (N.J. 1988).
[8] Immediately thereafter, 27 state legislatures considered bills to restrict or outlaw surrogacy. These were often prefaced by comments that one of the purposes of the legislation was to "avoid a Baby M case". WEISBERG, *supra* note 3, at 38.
[9] Britain has since recognized private surrogacy arrangements but still bans payment

In Israel the ban was accomplished by a series of three regulations issued by the Health Ministry, which, without ever mentioning the term "surrogacy", had the practical effect of banning it. In short order, many of the numerous infertile couples in Israel began circumventing the law by traveling to the United States (particularly California), where surrogacy centers operated. While effective, these pilgrimages were not without problems. The most obvious is the expense of travel, as well as of the surrogacy arrangements themselves, limiting the procedure to wealthier couples. The second, which continues to complicate the practice, is that Jewish law provides that the religion of a child is that of the birth mother. Thus, if the surrogate is not Jewish, the child potentially loses his or her Jewish identity.[10]

The unsatisfactory nature of this state of affairs was dramatically brought to the attention of Israeli politicians and public by another high profile case, that of Ruti and Danny Nachmani. Ruti was unable to carry a child, having lost her uterus to cervical cancer, but since her ovaries were not damaged she was able to have her egg fertilized with her husband's sperm to produce an embryo, which was genetically connected to both herself and her husband. After numerous requests to the Health Ministry to allow the first portion of the process (in vitro fertilization of her eggs) to take place in Israel (which would save the Nachmanis substantial money and time), they sued the Ministry, asserting that the Ministry[11] rules were promulgated without proper authority and that the rules lacked a "reasonable basis."

Fearing the results of a judicial decision, the Ministry settled the case, allowing the egg to be fertilized in Israel so long as the implantation in the surrogate took place abroad. This waiver of the rules was granted solely to the Nachmanis.[12] In addition, the Ministry agreed to set up an expert committee to investigate the whole practice of surrogacy.

This committee, named the Aloni Commission after its chair, laid the groundwork for the legislation that was ultimately passed. Weisberg's detailed description of the parties who were appointed again highlights the impact that individual personalities make in the development of the law. The key example of this is Ministry of Justice Attorney Carmel Shalev, who after graduating from Hebrew University in Jerusalem, acquired a postgraduate degree from Yale University. Her doctoral dissertation examined

---

of compensation to the surrogate for her services. It is allowed in parts of Australia, but continues to be banned in France as well as *inter alia* China, Italy and Vietnam. *Id.* at 203-04.
10   *Id.* at 56.
11   *Id.* at 74.
12   *Id.* at 91-92. This victory turned out to be a pyrrhic one for Ruti Nachmani because after the embryos were created and frozen, but before they could be implanted, the marriage broke up and Danny refused to allow the embryos to be implanted. Ruti initiated a second high profile lawsuit that she ultimately won, but attempts at implantation were not successful. (This is often the case when frozen embryos have been stored for a lengthy period.)

surrogate motherhood from a feminist perspective, concluding that by recognizing a woman's right to contract, including the right to receive economic compensation for supply of reproductive services, surrogacy empowered rather than enslaved women.[13] Not only was Shalev appointed to the commission herself, but her boss, the Minister of Justice, accepted many of her recommendations for other appointees. These included, in addition to two physicians appointed by the Health ministry, professors of psychology, sociology and medical ethics. Three of the members were women and as the sociologist member, Lela Amis commented, "This was the first committee in the history of Israel, to study issues that were related to women that actually was composed of half women members."[14] Even more startling, three of the four were self proclaimed feminists. Their influence was further enhanced by the fact that one of the two rabbis appointed resigned after being named one of Israel's two chief rabbis.

The resulting 135 page report dealt broadly with fertility issues, including right of access to fertility treatments, definitions of parenthood and information and privacy concerns on the part of both parents and of children. The committee recommended that surrogacy be permitted, then proposed a structure under which it should be regulated. This included setting up a government committee providing for psychological examination and counseling for all parties, and setting the amount of payment allowed to surrogates by government regulation. If the surrogate revoked her consent, the contract would not be enforceable, and if the couple refused custody, the surrogate should have first right of refusal. Two minority reports also supported surrogacy, but disagreed on the details, particularly on issues such as who should be allowed to serve as a surrogate. This report was expected by most parties to languish on bureaucratic desks because of its controversial nature and the expected opposition of religious parties.

The fact that the exact opposite result occurred is directly attributable to another strong woman, Michal Zabaro. Michal, who was born without a uterus, filed suit against the Health Ministry challenging the validity of its regulations. After the suit was made public, 49 other couples joined as plaintiffs in the case. After several months of legal maneuvering the Supreme Court ordered the regulations cancelled in five and one half months (the interim allocated to allow the government time to enact new legislation).[15] Acting with amazing speed, particularly given the deeply controversial nature of the matter, the Knesset enacted the legislation within eight months of the Court's ruling. This is particularly remarkable because of the strong beliefs of the various constituencies. The religious parties were deeply suspicious of surrogacy because of concerns about incest and adultery.[16]

---

13 CARMEL SHALEV, BIRTH POWER: THE CASE FOR SURROGACY (1989).
14 WEISBERG, *supra* note 3, at 99.
15 *Id.* at 127.
16 Under the interpretations of Jewish law by some rabbis, artificial insemination of a

Feminist organizations also had strong, but sometimes contradictory, views on whether surrogacy protects or exploits women. The "liberal feminists" (like Carmel Shalev) were in favor of believing that by affirming women's ability to contract they are empowered and recognized as autonomous persons. By contrast the "radical feminists" took the position that in a paternalistic society, women's freedom to contract is an illusion and that surrogacy is simply another opportunity for men to take control of women's bodies.[17] As a result of this split, they had less influence on the final shape of the law than in the Aloni Commission recommendations.

The *Surrogacy Law* that finally passed reflected (as might be expected) both the general concerns that have been raised about surrogacy, particularly by the Aloni Commission, and Israel's unique status as a Jewish state. Weisberg does an excellent job of explaining how the final law emerged. At the same time as both traditional Jewish culture and Israel's political situation militate toward laws that encourage reproduction, the inclination of the religious parties is profoundly conservative. As a result, the legislation reflects many of the Aloni Commission recommendations, such as an approvals committee made up equally of men and women, also requiring that a surrogate be unrelated to either of the intended parents and of the same religion. Similarly it only allows gestational surrogacy and prohibits the use of sperm other than that of the intended father. These requirements reflect the Rabbinates extreme concern about the possibility of incest and illegitimacy.

Weisberg concludes that generally surrogacy itself is a positive development and that the Israeli law has been a success. She points out that under the law 78 children have been born and that there has been no instance where the surrogate has attempted to breach the agreement.[18] In her concluding chapter she provides a very interesting and useful discussion of the current practice of surrogacy worldwide, noting that the growth of the Internet has facilitated the matching of infertile couples with potential surrogates.

The Birth of Surrogacy in Israel is a valuable resource not only for family and contract lawyers, but is useful for attorneys and legal scholars with broader concerns than the practice of surrogacy itself. At the most basic level it provides a template of a comprehensive system regulating the sensitive area of reproductive technology. While it exemplifies many useful ideas, it also has peculiarities generally not likely to be compatible which other jurisdictions. For example, the requirement that the surrogate be unmarried and that the sperm must come from the intended father reflects a religious concern related to a technical definition of adultery not shared

---

married surrogate with a fertilized egg from an intended couple would constitute adultery because the sperm was from a man not her husband. *Id.* at 192-93 (for the basis of the concern regarding sex with a genetic relative).
17 *Id.* at 147-48.
18 *Id.* at 202. The Approvals Committee has approved 169 of 191 applications.

in much of the world. On the other hand, aspects of surrogacy that have troubled many scholars and legislators were relatively uncontroversial in Israel, particularly those revolving around payment to the surrogate beyond expenses and her right to change her mind after the baby is born (the Israeli law allows reneging only under very limited circumstances)

On a broader level, the book provides a comprehensive study of the impact of technological change on the core structures of society. As we follow the historic progression from artificial insemination, to in vitro fertilization, to surrogacy, first with the birth mother's ovum, then to gestational surrogacy, we see the definition of family transforming. The social aspects of parenthood have been gradually uncoupled not only from sexual intercourse, but from childbearing and the genetic raw materials. The resulting possibilities have not only allowed couples with reproductive limitations to have genetically connected children, but also enabled male gay couples to form families with genetic links.[19]

By presenting the personal history that shaped the personalities of the key players throughout the process that ultimately resulted in the *Surrogacy Law*, Weisberg illuminated the importance of individuals in legal development. In effect, it suggests that Thomas Carlyle's "Hero Theory" of history is at least as applicable to legal events as to military ones. While this law is the culmination of social forces from feminism to the profound importance Judaism places on family, both its enactment and its particulars are the product of a complexity of forces not usually available in the legislative history of even the most well documented legislation.

---

[19] Ginta Bellafante, *Surrogate Mothers' New Niche: Bearing Babies for Gay Couples*, N.Y. Times, May 27, 2005, at A1. The surrogates interviewed in the article suggest that working with gay couples is particularly satisfying because it does not require dealing with the emotional needs of the intended mother, who may have struggled, often for a number of years, to bear a child.

PROPHECY WITH NUMBERS:
Prospective Punishment for Predictable Human Behaviour?

Brad Johnson[*]

A discussion about the way in which people reason about events in the physical world will prove to be beneficial before considering the provisions of Queensland's *Dangerous Prisoners (Sexual Offenders) Act 2003* and is necessary in order to identify and deconstruct the process by which psychiatrists evaluate dangerousness. In the physical world it is both possible and useful to identify relationships or connections between events where one event or constellation of events immediately precedes the occurrence of another. In such circumstances two possibilities may arise:

(i) it may be observed that the presence of one event or constellation of events always precedes the occurrence of another; or
(ii) it may be observed that the presence of one event or constellation of events sometimes precedes the occurrence of another.

The difference between the two possibilities which lies in the use of the words "always" and "sometimes"[1] can be illustrated by considering contrasting examples. If the element potassium is combined with water a violent reaction will result, producing potassium hydroxide and hydrogen gas which combusts spontaneously at room temperature. A chemist would not expect the reaction to produce any exceptions, but would expect them to obey a well observed rule that the combination of potassium and water is always followed by the production of potassium hydroxide gas. Such an expectation reveals an underlying and unprovable belief that future observations will conform to past observations so that certainty in the past will endure in the future. By contrast some associations between events admit random exceptions with the consequence that the past cannot serve as a perfect guide to the future. Habitual smoking is an event, repetitive in nature, which sometimes precedes the development of lung cancer. Some, rather than all, habitual smokers develop lung cancer and as a result for a given population of smokers it is impossible to distinguish between those who will develop the disease and those who will not.

---

[*] Part time lecturer in legal philosophy, Southern Cross University.
[1] See Rudolf Carnap: *An Introduction to the Philosophy of Science* (1995). Carnap makes a similar distinction between universal laws and statistical laws.

Expectations or Uncertainty

Our attitude towards, and beliefs about, future events in the physical world depend upon our memory of past experiences. Without any past experiences or memory of those experiences it would be difficult to develop any expectations about events in the physical world. For example, in the absence of any past experiences it would be difficult to predict that the setting sun will return; that the incoming high tide will recede or that the snow of winter will melt in the summer. For the observer without any past experiences, the physical world offers many objects never before seen in the context of a dynamic environment of change. Amongst the many things that can be observed, the bright object of the sun changes its position with the passage of time and continues to do so until it sets behind the horizon. For someone who has never before seen a sunrise there is no past experience or memory of a past experience that would suggest that the setting sun will ever return. If it returns, then the observer will recognise the object based on memory of the experiences from the previous day and notice that it behaves in a similar manner as it sets again. After observing two sunsets a pattern may not be obvious. How many sunsets and sunrises however would a person need to observe before developing the expectation that the sun will always rise and set? Although only an arbitrary answer can be offered to such a question, most people believe that the sun will rise and set tomorrow given their experiences and the experiences of countless generations of past observers who have watched the sun behave without exception. The expectations of people with respect to the rising and setting sun may be contrasted with the uncertainty of the weather. Not many people would expect rain every day or every second day or third day since the number of days between rain and sunshine according to our experiences is not periodic, but variable and therefore uncertain. Given the presence of something that always occurs, it is common for people to develop expectations. The presence of something that sometimes occurs will usually give rise to uncertainty.

Which category does human behaviour belong to? Unlike chemical elements and compounds such as potassium and water, human beings display comparatively complex behaviour and interactions between each other and with their environment. Chemical compounds don't parent children, enter into romantic relationships, go to war, struggle to improve their standard of living, laugh politely at an attempted joke or commit crimes against other chemical compounds. Humans, who appear to possess some freedom of will or volition, are complex, as are their relationships and behaviour with respect to others. Whether or not human behaviour can be accurately predicted depends upon the existence of patterns that always occur as opposed to patterns that sometimes occur. In the context of the *Dangerous Prisoners Act* it is necessary to recognise that although people exercising their free will can behave in many ways, some behaviour has been labelled criminal and as a result it would be useful to know if it is possible to predict whether a particular individual will commit a crime. If you can identify individual offenders before they have opportunities to execute their crimes then actual victims can be replaced with potential victims who need not learn to live with the trauma of violation.

For reasons that will become apparent, the main obstacle to achieving accurate predictions with respect to human behaviour is the presence of uncertainty. The response to this uncertainty has been systematic since the gradual development and advent of science through which we have sought to replace "sometimes" with "always" in a quest to eliminate uncertainty and establish order with respect to the behaviour of objects and forces in the universe. Some investigations have witnessed spectacular success, whilst others have left our desires unfulfilled. Where uncertainty has not been eliminated, the methods of statistics and probability theory have emerged as tools for understanding and minimising the risks often associated with it. Essential to these methods—as they are applied to most types of human behaviour—is the process of comparing relative frequencies and the identification of sample populations each based on a specific group of attributes. Here the term "population" can refer to any collection of objects or events, not just people. Either way it is a simple concept that can be understood easily without a background in mathematics.

The goal of such analysis is to predict what outcomes will follow given the presence of certain attributes or behaviours in a population of individuals who all possess the same attributes or display the same behaviour. Smoking and lung cancer offer an illustration. In this case the sample population being studied comprises individuals who display the same behaviour: habitual smoking. The outcome observed is whether or not the individual develops lung cancer. The sample population is divided into two groups, those who develop lung cancer and those who don't. Two relative frequencies can then be calculated:

(i) the ratio of the number of individuals who develop lung cancer to the total number of individuals in the sample population.
(ii) the ratio of the number of individuals who do not develop lung cancer to the total number of individuals in the sample population.

Example: a given population of habitual smokers might include 1,000 individuals. If 800 develop lung cancer and 200 do not then the following relative frequencies will be obtained:
i) lung cancer present: 800/1,000 or 80%
ii) lung cancer absent: 200/1,000 or 20%

Relative frequencies for certain outcomes where the future conforms to the past present quite a different picture. For example, the sample population might consist of an experiment repeated 1,000 times in which potassium is combined with water. The outcome of interest is whether or not potassium hydroxide is produced. Again, the sample population can be divided into experiments that produce potassium hydroxide and

experiments that do not. We should expect to see the following relative frequencies:
Potassium hydroxide present: 1,000/1,000 or 100%
Potassium hydroxide absent: 0/1,000 or 0%.

It can be seen that the data from the sample populations reveal that habitual smoking is only sometimes associated with lung cancer rather than always, whilst the presence of potassium hydroxide is always associated with an experiment in which water and potassium are combined. The distinction between sometimes and always in this case means the difference between accurate predictions and inaccurate predictions. Before an experiment is conducted we should expect to be correct if we predict that the outcome will produce potassium hydroxide. If we predict that a given habitual smoker will develop lung cancer however, then it is possible, given the relative frequencies of the sample population, that we will be surprised by contradiction. In this case the relative frequencies of the sample population also specify the margin of error for any prediction inferred from them. There is an 80% chance that our prediction will be correct and a 20% chance that our prediction will be incorrect for any given habitual smoker predicted to develop lung cancer.

The relative frequencies for a given sample population with respect to a particular outcome can be further analysed by comparing them to the relative frequencies of a second population, defined according to different attributes. For instance the relationship between lung cancer and smoking can be further analysed by comparing the relative frequencies for the same outcome of two or more sample populations defined according to different attributes. Typically, the relative frequencies for a sample population of smokers are compared to the relative frequencies for a sample population of non-smokers.

Example: for a sample population of 1,000 smokers where 800 develop lung cancer and a sample population of 1,000 non-smokers where 100 develop lung cancer the following relative frequencies can be determined and compared:
i)   smokers with lung cancer: 800/1,000 or 80%
ii) non-smokers with lung cancer: 100/1,000 or 10%.

The comparison of the sample populations reveals that the chance of developing lung cancer is greater for smokers than non-smokers. In neither case can accurate predictions be made from the relative frequencies of either sample population, however, it is possible to infer that there is an increased risk of developing lung cancer for smokers. As a result predictions that a smoker will develop lung cancer should be more accurate than predictions that a non-smoker will develop lung cancer.

In all of the above examples the relevant data satisfy some of the basic postulates of the probability calculus and demonstrate that there is an intimate relationship between relative frequencies and probability theory. The basic postulates include the following:

(i) the probability of an event must be a rational number that is greater than or equal to 0 and less than or equal to 1,
(ii) the complement probability of an event, that is the probability that it will not occur, can be represented as follows $P(!E) = 1 - P(E)$ where $P(!E)$ represents the probability that the event will not occur and $P(E)$ represents the probability that it will occur,
(iii) the probability of an event that is certain to occur is equal to 1 whilst the probability of an event that is certain not to occur is equal to 0.

For all other events it follows that the likelihood of the event occurring increases as the value approaches 1, and decreases as it approaches 0. Having considered some of the basic principles employed in analysing uncertain events in the physical world, it is necessary to examine their application to the specific example of predicting the occurrence of future sexual offences for convicted sexual offenders as required by the *Dangerous Prisoners (Sexual Offenders) Act* 2003.

Cogent Evidence to a High Degree of Probability

Before deciding whether to make an order to continue the detention of a convicted sexual offender, the court may only make the decision if it is satisfied by acceptable cogent evidence—and to a high degree of probability—that the evidence is of sufficient weight to support the decision[2], and that the submitted evidence demonstrates that the offender represents a serious danger to the community. In this case the nature of the evidence and its reliability require careful consideration. The evidence that is of primary importance is that offered by the court-appointed psychiatrists who may be commissioned to prepare a report for the purposes of executing a risk assessment order.[3] The risk assessment order requires the preparation of reports by two psychiatrists with each report indicating the level of risk that the prisoner will commit another serious sexual offence if released and the reasons for the psychiatrist's assessment.[4]

What is risk, and how do psychiatrists determine a convicted sexual offender's level of risk? It is important for the court to consider these questions and evaluate the experts' psychiatric evidence critically in order to assess the reliability of their research methods and conclusions. In reaching a conclusion about an offender's chance of re-offending, the court should be supplied with the facts and assumptions upon which the expert opinion is based, the process of inference which reveals the relationship between the facts or assumptions and the conclusions reached by the expert so that the court can scrutinise the conclusions and their reliability.[5]

Risk cannot be measured in the same manner as physical dimensions such as length, mass and time. For each physical dimension there exists

---

2 See *Dangerous Prisoners (Sexual Offenders) Act 2003*, ss13(1), (3)
3 Ibid ss 8(2)(a), 9.
4 Ibid s11(2).
5 *Makita v Sprowles*, (2001) 52 NSWLR 705, Heydon JA (as he then was) at [81].

an experimentally defined standard unit to measure it. For length it's the metre, for mass it's the kilogram and for time it's the second. For risk however, no standard unit has been experimentally defined. Rather than being measured experimentally with standard units, risk is typically associated with the concept of probability, so that the risk of something occurring increases as its relative frequency approaches 1 and decreases as it approaches 0. Risk, however, need not be defined exclusively in terms of a rational number between 1 and 0, but may also be defined qualitatively in terms of risk levels such as low, medium or high. For either method the data or facts that influence the risk determination are critical, as are the limitations that affect the process of making inferences from the data.

Psychiatrists and psychologists have employed a number of methods for determining risk with respect to human behaviour, which include the following: clinical assessment, actuarial risk assessment and actuarially informed clinical assessment which combines elements from each. The difference between clinical and actuarial assessment is reflected in the type of data relied on in order to determine the level of risk—clinical assessment relying primarily on data about the person being assessed and actuarial assessment relying on data from a population of individuals who share a number of attributes in common with the person being assessed, thus allowing statistical comparative judgements.

Clinical Assessment

In a clinical assessment, information about the client or patient is collected through an interview process during the course of which the client will be confronted with a series of questions, his or her responses and demeanour being carefully scrutinised by the psychiatrists. In addition to an interview, the client may be required to complete a self report questionnaire and the psychiatrist may also interview individuals who may offer observations about the client that can be compared to the responses of the client. The psychiatrist must carefully consider the information from the interviews and questionnaires before forming a clinical judgement about the risk of the client re-offending, the client's state of mind or a disorder diagnosis.

Some general reservations that should be identified with respect to clinical research methodology in psychiatry and psychology include the following:
(i) presence of hypothetical constructs
(ii) unreliable diagnostic methods
(iii) absence of experimentally defined standard units of measurement.

Hypothetical Constructs

Scientific research involves the collection of data that correspond to observations or measurements of perceivable entities in the physical world, and the forces that may influence their behaviour.[6] A hypothetical construct however is an idea rather than an object or entity that can be perceived as sensory information, for which data that correspond to an observation or measurement can not be collected. Human emotions offer a useful example of a hypothetical construct. Many people believe that they experience emotional states despite the absence of empirical evidence to support their existence. For example, my wife is a perceivable object in the physical world, and I believe that I love my wife. I can see my wife, a physical object, and my wife is the object of my love, however, I can not see the love that I believe I feel for her. Love can not be seen, touched, measured or weighed as it does not possess any of the properties of matter. Research methods in psychology have embraced emotional states such as love, depression, anxiety, happiness and many others. Disorders such as those defined in the DSM IV[7] are themselves hypothetical constructs. In an attempt to avoid the absence of perceivable data about such constructs, some research methodologists have assumed the existence of a connection between human behaviour and human emotions. It is believed that certain emotional states to some degree correspond to a constellation of observable behaviours. Anger, an emotional state, might be thought to correspond to the following behaviours: raised voice or shouting, physical assault, threatening gestures etc. Researchers have also attempted to identify associations between chemicals and emotional states or disorders. In addition to observable behaviour that is thought to correspond to particular emotional states, the client offers an introspective opinion about his or her emotions during the interview process. This however requires the co-operation of the client being interviewed, as well as honest responses and an ability to describe emotional states accurately, since the person being interviewed may lie about emotional states or be mistaken. The psychiatrist or psychologist is dependent upon the honest and accurate testimony of the client being interviewed and the honest and accurate testimony of other individuals who have observed and interacted with the client. Dishonest or inaccurate information will ultimately affect the reliability of a diagnosis or assessment of risk.

Diagnostic Methods

Information collected from a clinical assessment may be used to diagnose the interviewed client with a recognised disorder as well as for determining the risk of self harm or harm to others. If disorders, however, are hypothetical

---

[6] Research may also accommodate theoretical explanations as well as experimental observations. The observation that the combination of zinc and copper in the presence of an electrolytic solution, such as salt water, will produce a measurable voltage or potential difference, may be distinguished from the theoretical explanation based upon the unequal distribution of electrons between the zinc and copper electrodes. One is observable through measurement, the other currently is not.

[7] The DSM IV (*Diagnostic and Statistical Manual of Mental Disorders* Version IV) lists the currently accepted disorders and the criteria by which they are diagnosed.

constructs defined in terms of certain behaviours and emotional states then a reliable diagnosis is dependent upon a number of factors.

Before considering diagnostic methods in psychiatry it will be helpful to briefly discuss an example of a well defined condition in medicine that corresponds to an observable or measurable physiological condition in the human body, in order to make comparative judgements. To diagnose whether or not a patient has a simple bone fracture, a radiologist can perform an x-ray on the suspect bone, in which case a visual inspection of the x-ray will reveal whether the bone is fractured or not. In this case there is a direct relationship between an observable physiological state in the body and the condition that is diagnosed. Different doctors who examine the same x-ray of a simple bone fracture are unlikely to reach different diagnoses.

By contrast, disorders in psychiatry and psychology are operationally defined. Operational definitions attempt to define disorders which are unobservable hypothetical constructs in terms of observable behaviours and the self report testimony of the client. As a result, psychiatrists do not directly observe the disorder but rather the behaviour and subjective mental states of the client that are believed to indicate the presence of the disorder. This is somewhat like diagnosing a simple bone fracture based on certain patient symptoms without taking an x-ray of the bone. Consider the diagnostic criteria for the DSM-IV-TR[8] defined disorder, "paranoid personality":

A. A pervasive distrust and suspiciousness of others such that their motives are interpreted as malevolent, beginning by early adulthood and present in a variety of contexts, as indicated by four or more of the following:

(1) suspects, without sufficient basis, that others are exploiting, harming, or deceiving him or her
(2) is preoccupied with unjustified doubts about the loyalty or trustworthiness of friends or associates
(3) is reluctant to confide in others because of unwarranted fear that the information will be used maliciously against him or her
(4) reads hidden or demeaning or threatening meanings into benign remarks or events
(5) persistently bears grudges, i.e. is unforgiving of insults, injuries or slights
(6) perceives attacks on his or her character or reputation that are not apparentto others and is quick to react angrily or to counter-attack
(7) has recurrent suspicions, without justification, regarding fidelity of spouse or sexual partner.

The criterion serves as an operational definition for the disorder "paranoid personality" and guides the interview process by classifying a constellation of behaviours and mental states into a specific disorder

---

8 The DSM-IV-TR is the text revision (TR) of the fourth edition of the *Diagnostic and Statistical Manual of Mental Disorders* of the American Psychiatric Association, published in 2000.

which can hopefully be distinguished from other disorders that are also operationally defined. As the interview process proceeds, the psychiatrist attempts to find a correspondence between the defined criterion and the information collected about the client, so that a diagnosis can be reached. The criterion that operationally defines paranoid personality disorder however can not be directly observed. For example, suspiciousness is an attribute or trait of a person that can only be inferred from someone's behaviour and communication over a period of time. Information about the client must be collected and interpreted in order to determine which disorder their behaviour and mental state most closely corresponds to. This process however is imperfect as the different disorders do not enjoy discrete boundaries but rather overlap in terms of the criterion which defines them. As a result it is possible that two psychiatrists who examine the same patient will arrive at a different diagnosis despite the application of the same diagnostic criteria. In addition, mental states such as suspiciousness are not well defined, so different psychiatrists may examine the same information about a client and arrive at different conclusions with respect to whether the clients behaviour reveals an overly suspicious state of mind. Finally, incomplete information about the client will ultimately affect the reliability of the diagnosis. You must have enough information that allows you to identify the presence or absence of a disorder. Since the failure of the psychiatrist to obtain relevant information or to consider relevant information can affect the outcome of the interview, there is a much greater emphasis on the interviewing skills of the psychiatrist or psychologist and their experience with clinical assessments. Despite these limitations in clinical research methods, psychiatrists and psychologists attempt to diagnose mental disorders in a climate that lends itself to conflicting conclusions. Given that the presence or absence of a mental diagnosis can affect the outcome of a clinical risk assessment, unreliable methods of diagnosis are unacceptable.

Standard Units of Measurement

There are no standard units that have been experimentally defined in psychiatry or psychology. In order to understand the significance of standard units consider the following question: how long is a metre? Many people would find such a question confusing, offering the answer "100cm". This however does not answer the original question but rather a second question: "How many centimetres are there in a metre?" In physics the question is resolved by identifying an experimentally defined standard unit of measurement. The metre is a standard unit of measurement and the experiment that defines its length is the distance travelled by light in a vacuum during 1/299,792,458 of a second. Other units include the second, kilogram and coulomb each of which, including the metre, attempts to measure one of the four fundamental dimensions in physics: length, mass, time and electrical charge. By contrast, experimentally defined standard units of measurement are noticeably absent and infrequently used in either psychology or psychiatry, a state of affairs that can best be explained by the presence of hypothetical constructs. Given that hypothetical constructs are concepts rather than perceivable objects in the physical world, it follows that it is not possible to measure them directly, and without a system of measurement it is not possible to make comparative judgements. For example, it is not possible to measure someone's level of clinical depression and compare it to another person's level of depression, but only to make a judgement about its presence or absence. In contrast, a person's height is a dimension that can be measured in centimetres. It is possible to measure the heights of two different people in order to determine whether one is taller than the other and by how much. Of the standard units that currently exist, as maintained by the International Standards Organisation, it is difficult to see what assistance any would be in a clinical setting. For example, a psychiatrist could measure a client's height in centimetres, but it seems unlikely that there would be any relationship between a client's height and risk of re-offending or mental health.

Clinical risk assessment suffers from the same defects that affect clinical diagnosis of mental disorders. They are often intimately related. The question that needs to be considered is whether or not the presence of a diagnosed mental disorder will increase the risk of a person committing an offence. Alternatively, how is risk to be assessed if no disorder is diagnosed? Although it is beyond the scope of the present article to address these issues, statistical studies and their use as criteria in actuarial instruments suggest that certain disorders, which are not well defined and are difficult to diagnose with reliability, are associated with an increase in incidence of certain offences. Where the person being assessed is not diagnosed with any disorder, then clinical assessment may rely on methods that don't require expert training. The main issue however, with respect to clinical assessment methods, is the issue of reliability. Reliability which should not be confused with accuracy, concerns consistency with respect to clinical diagnosis or risk assessment as conducted by independent psychiatrists. Reliable diagnostic criteria of assessment procedures should produce similar or identical assessments for independent observers. However different psychiatrists frequently arrive at different conclusions with respect to diagnosis or risk.

Actuarial Risk Assessment

Actuarial risk assessment departs from clinical assessment methods by examining populations of released offenders in order to identify attributes that are associated with an increased risk of recidivism. The data with respect to recidivism rates collected from multiple sample populations of released offenders can be used to make some simple inferences. The relative frequency of recidivism for a particular sample may be used to make a probability statement about the chance of an individual, who shares the attributes that define the population, committing a future offence. Alternatively the relative frequencies for various populations may be compared to determine which samples display a higher level recidivism, which in turn is believed to indicate a greater risk of recidivism. The process of establishing relative frequencies with respect to recidivism begins by examining an initial population of released offenders for a specific period of time which yields relative frequencies for those who re-offend and those who do not. The sample population being investigated also allows researchers to look for attributes that are associated with recidivism. The initial population can then be analysed by specifying further attributes that break the population down into more clearly defined demographic groups in the hope of identifying greater recidivism rates for specific populations. Example: for a given population of 1,000 released offenders where 600 re-offend within a seven year period, the following relative frequencies would be obtained:

Offence committed: 600/1,000 or 60%
No offence committed: 400/1,000 or 40%

By specifying further attributes it is possible to identify a subsection of the initial population in order to determine whether they display an increased or decreased relative frequency. For example 900 of the released offenders might be male and aged between the ages of 30 and 45. If 630 of the 900 re-offend within a seven year period the following relative frequencies will reveal that the incidence of recidivism is greater where the attributes of gender and age are equal to male and 30–45 respectively. If the relative frequencies remain unchanged it is assumed the attributes have a neutral effect and therefore no association with an increase or decrease in risk.

Offence committed: 630/900 or 70%
No offence committed: 270/900 or 30%

When the data have been collected, a number of sample populations—each of which corresponds to a unique set of attributes—can be used to specify a collection or table of relative frequencies which can then be used as a basis for making probability statements and judgements about levels of risk for a specific individual, by looking for the presence or absence of certain attributes. For example given the above relative frequency of recidivism for released offenders who are male and aged between 30 and 45, researchers might infer that there is a 70 per cent chance that any released offender who is male and aged between 30 and 45 will re-offend within a seven year period or that males aged between 30–45 display a higher risk of re-offending when compared to released offenders generally. The purpose of this simplified example is to identify the process of reasoning upon which inferences are made from relative frequencies.

In practice however although the reasoning process is the same, actuarial studies will specify many more attributes beside gender and age in order to analyse recidivism rates from many different dimensions. Attributes which are used to define sample populations may be divided into those that are static and those that are dynamic. Static attributes are those that do not change with time such as an individual's gender, date of birth and criminal history, whilst dynamic factors are susceptible to change—such as an individual's, marital status, employment status or substance addiction. The *Violence Risk Appraisal Guide* (1993)[9] offers the following example of static and dynamic attributes used to assess an individual's chance of re-offending with respect to a violent offence:

(1) PCL-SV score. Indicates the presence or absence of psychopathy.
(2) Maladjustment at elementary school age.
(3) Diagnosis of personality disorder under DSM IV.
(4) Age at index of offence.
(5) Lived with both parents to age of 16.
(6) Failure on prior conditional release.
(7) Non-violent offence score.
(8) Marital status.
(9) Diagnosis of schizophrenia under DSM IV.
(10) Victim injury.
(11) History of alcohol misuse.
(12) Female victim.

For any individual it is possible to determine the presence or absence of the variables and or assign a value. The risk of an individual re-offending by committing a violent offence depends upon the number of variables to which there is a positive response with the risk increasing as more variables are found to be applicable to an individual being assessed. The psychiatrist assessing an individual will record a response to each of the 12 attributes and compare the result to the relative frequency for a sample population that has the same attributes as the assessed individual. For example person A, with the following results: high PCL-SV score, displayed maladjustment at elementary school, diagnosed with a DSM-IV personality disorder, aged 28, lived with both parents to age of 16, failed on a prior conditional release, low non-violent offence score, single, absence of a diagnosis of schizophrenia, a history of alcohol misuse and female victims. Person A might be at a higher risk of re-offending than an individual, B, with the following results: low PCL-SV score, no incidence of maladjustment at elementary school, absence of a DSM-IV personality disorder, aged 62, no failure on prior conditional release, high non-violent offence score, married, no history of alcohol misuse and no female victim. Data collected by the researchers would presumably reveal that the relative frequency or incidence of recidivism is lower for the population of individuals who display the attributes that correspond to individual

---

[9] Harris et al, *Violence Risk Appraisal Guide* (1993). The methodology for designing actuarial instruments is the same whether they attempt to predict violent or serious sexual offences. The attributes selected however may be different depending on the type of criminal behaviour being predicted.

B than for the population of individuals who display the attributes that correspond to individual A.

Limits of Statistical Inference

Categorising individuals, according to either static or dynamic attributes which correspond to sample populations that define relative frequencies, presents a number of issues. It is necessary to recognise that the data collected from research that corresponds to sample populations ultimately supports inferences about groups of individuals rather than single individuals. This distinction can be illustrated by considering the following propositions:
(i)　Smoking causes lung cancer.
(ii)　John will contract lung cancer.

The first proposition is based on a population of individuals, rather than a single individual, from which it is possible to make a generalisation that is subject to exceptions. Of the lung cancer patients surveyed in numerous statistical studies many will be habitual smokers, however not all since lung cancer can occur in either the presence or absence of habitual smoking. A relative frequency of 80% with respect to the incidence of lung cancer amongst smokers indicates that of 1,000 smokers who participated in a study, 800 developed lung cancer whilst 200 did not. It is possible to infer that any group of smokers not surveyed can be divided into two further groups, those who will develop lung cancer and those who will not, in proportions that are consistent with the surveyed sample population. Thus if the future conforms to the past then for a population of 100 non-surveyed smokers it is possible to predict, based on the statistical study, that 80 or approximately 80 smokers will develop lung cancer and 20 will not. What of inferences however with respect to a single individual rather than a group? Clearly it is not possible to divide a single individual into two categories, those with and those without, in the proportions consistent with the surveyed sample. Although for a single individual there are two possible outcomes only one will actually occur. When applied to an individual the relative frequency from a sample population serves as a probability statement that attempts to indicate which outcome is more likely to actually occur. Where each possible outcome has a rational number assigned to it, the outcome whose rational number is closest to one is more likely to occur, which in this case is lung cancer given that its value is 0.80 whilst the possibility of not contracting lung cancer is 0.20. Clearly any prediction, such as proposition (ii), about an individual smoker contracting lung cancer based on the statistical studies could be wrong. This is the impact of uncertainty.

The distinction between statements about groups and individuals with respect to relative frequencies, defined according to statistical studies, leads to a fundamental problem. For any given individual it is not possible to determine the category to which he or she will belong. It is not possible to predict whether one will belong to the group of 80 with lung cancer or the group of 20 without. The same problem clearly applies to recidivism predictions based on relative frequencies from statistical studies where it is not possible to determine for example whether a released offender with a specific collection of attributes will be one of the 70 per cent who re-offend or the 30 per cent who do not. The prediction of recidivism for a released offender like the predicted condition for a given smoker must ultimately be compared to the observed condition or behaviour in order to affirm or refute it. When a prediction is compared to the observed outcome it will fall into one of four categories: (i) True Positive, (ii) True Negative, (iii) False Positive, (iv) False Negative. In the case of recidivism a true positive is an accurate prediction that an offender will re-offend and a true negative is an accurate prediction that an offender will not re-offend. A false positive is an inaccurate prediction that an offender will re-offend and a false negative is an inaccurate prediction that an offender will not re-offend. The presence of either false positives or false negatives indicates that the particular phenomenon can not be predicted accurately which is the case for recidivism whether or not clinical or actuarial methods are employed.

In an attempt to avoid some of the problems associated with quantitative statistical statements about risk based on relative frequencies, some researchers have adopted a qualitative approach to assessing risk. Whilst a rational number between 1 and 0 is assigned to risk using a quantitative approach, a qualitative approach relies on words rather than numbers by defining categories of risk such as low, medium and high. Typically such judgements feature in clinical methods; however they may also appear in actuarial methods where different ranges of rational numbers correspond to different risk categories. Neither approach can necessarily offer accurate predictions however a qualitative approach results in a loss of precision and expresses less information. For example if an assessment that indicates there is a high likelihood that the offender will re-offend is compared to an assessment that indicates there is a 0.75 likelihood that the offender will re-offend it can be seen that the quantitative statement attempts to define the risk with more precision just as 0.756 likelihood is more precise than 0.75 likelihood. Whether risk is expressed quantitatively or qualitatively the question to be considered by the court is: what level of risk must the offender be assessed at before the sentence should be extended? Is a risk level of 0.75, indicating that the likelihood of not re-offending is 0.25, a sufficient basis for extending a sentence or is a more accurate risk level required such as 0.95? Alternatively should a sentence be extended where the risk of recidivism is judged to be high?

A second issue arises where historical information about a sample population of individuals is used to make judgements about an individual who shares a relatively small number of common attributes at the expense of ignoring distinguishing attributes that are not shared. This reveals an assumption that future individuals will behave in a manner that is consistent with the behaviour displayed by a sample population of past individuals and that the relative frequency drawn from the past sample population will remain stable over time. Inferences in statistics where individuals are characterised according to attributes that are consistent with the attributes of a sample population in statistical studies are based upon arguments of analogy. In such arguments the behaviour of something that is known may be used as a basis to make inferences about the unknown behaviour of something that is similar in certain respects. Consider the following example offered by Thomas Reid:

> We may observe a very great similitude between this earth which we inhabit, and the other planets, Saturn, Jupiter, Mars, Venus and Mercury. They all revolve around the sun, as the earth does....They borrow all their light from the sun, as the earth does. Several of them are known to revolve around their axis like the earth, and by that means must have a like succession of day and night. Some of them have moons that serve to give light in the absence of the sun, as our moon does to us. They are all in their motions, subject to the same law of gravitations, as the earth is. From all this similitude, it is not unreasonable to think, that these planets may, like our earth, be the habitation of various orders of living creatures. [10]

Reid's analogical argument attempts to make a conclusion about something that is unknown, the presence of life on other planets, based on the presence of life on earth which bears some resemblance to the other solar system planets. In the same manner psychiatrists attempt to make predictions about the unknown future behaviour of released offenders based on the known behaviour of offenders released in the past and their comparative similarities. In these types of analogies however the differences may be as important as the similarities. Although there were obvious similarities between the earth and the other observable solar system planets during Reid's lifetime, many differences have since been discovered which would suggest that the presence of carbon based life forms, such as those found on earth, is unlikely. In the same manner the relative frequencies for risk of recidivism are based on sample populations that exemplify a discrete number of common attributes. An individual with the same attributes will be assumed to represent the level of risk defined by the relative frequency of the sample population despite the fact that the individual being assessed will also possess a number of attributes that are different. These differences however which may mitigate the level of risk will be overlooked in a purely actuarial approach to risk assessment.

To compensate for the lack of emphasis on unique individual characteristics in a purely actuarial approach some psychiatrists and psychologists have adopted an actuarially informed clinical assessment which combines the methods of both. This allows the psychiatrist or

---

[10] Sir William Hamilton (ed), *The Works of Thomas Reid, D.D.* (first published 1846, 1983 ed).

psychologist to accommodate protective or mitigating factors that might be seen to decrease the likelihood of risk as determined by an actuarial assessment. Some recently developed actuarial instruments such as the HCR-20[11] have been modified to include dynamic information that requires clinical investigation. Whilst this allows important information about the individual to be considered it also introduces the weaknesses of clinical assessment methods which have already been discussed. This has an impact on the reliability of the assessment to the extent that independent psychologists or psychiatrists reach the same diagnosis or assessment of risk. That is to say that independent psychologists and psychiatrists are more likely to reach the same conclusion with respect to risk when applying actuarial methods than when applying clinical methods. As a result reliability decreases in the presence of clinical assessment methods.

Conclusion

From the limitations outlined above it should be apparent that statistical inferences are ultimately based on generalisations about populations that don't eliminate uncertainty but rather in the presence of uncertainty attempt to indicate which of two options might be seen as more likely, though not certainly, to occur. In addition such generalisations obscure the identity of the individual with the effect that differences may be overlooked. Clinical approaches on the other hand also suffer from defects that render their diagnostic and risk assessment methods unreliable, an issue which also features in actuarially informed clinical assessment. Despite the differences, all three approaches share a common goal of attempting to determine the risk that an offender poses with respect to recidivism upon release rather than attempting to predict what the offender will actually do. Given the limitations of actuarial and clinical methods of assessment, several issues require judicial consideration. Central to this consideration is the following question:

> Can clinical or actuarial methods of risk assessment yield cogent evidence, as required by the legislation, which identifies the level of risk for an offender with a high degree of probability?

Furthermore since the concept of risk implicitly accommodates uncertainty, which in this case reflects the inability to make accurate predictions about the future behaviour of released offenders, are inaccurate predictions of future behaviour an acceptable basis for extending the sentence of an offender who is otherwise entitled[12] to release?

Given the limitations outlined above it is arguable that none of the assessment methods can yield evidence which satisfies the standard of proof, a high degree of probability,[13] required by the legislation. It does not

---
11 HCR-20 (Webster, Douglas, Eaves and Hart, 1997 Version 2)
12 It follows that the requirement of risk assessment is unnecessary where a serious sexual offender is not entitled to release.
13 This phrase is not defined in the legislation, however, it is unlikely that courts would

follow that such risk assessment evidence is inadmissible for the legislation authorises the court to issue a risk assessment order to be performed by court appointed psychiatrists.[14] However the risk assessment evidence on its own is not sufficient to support a finding of dangerousness which features as only one of many factors to be taken into consideration by the court under section 13(4) of the legislation.[15] As a result the court must decide what probative value or weight should be given to the risk assessment reports conducted by the court appointed psychiatrists. In considering this question the court must critically examine the nature of the research methodology relied upon to assess risk and or make predictions about future human behaviour with respect to serious sexual offences. In doing so it should look closely at the relationship between the inferences drawn by psychiatrists and the facts or assumptions which support them. Given the problems that affect each of the methods for assessing risk and the serious consequences with respect to the outcome of an assessment it is arguable that any such evidence should be assigned a low probative value or weight.

---

accept a definition based on mathematical terms which defines probability as a rational number between 1 and 0. As such, courts are unlikely to identify a rational number between 1 and 0 that corresponds to a high degree or probability. The standard would necessarily be greater than that required for civil trials, beyond the balance of probabilities, and more closely resemble the criminal standard of proof.

14 See *Dangerous Prisoners (Sexual Offenders) Act* 2003, ss8(2), 9, 11.

15 Section 13(4) identifies ten such factors which must be taken into consideration by the court.

HUMAN CLONES AND INTERNATIONAL HUMAN RIGHTS

Kerry Lynn Macintosh*

For several years, the United Nations (U.N.) has struggled with the question of whether and how to regulate human cloning. Despite widespread agreement that reproductive cloning should be banned, member states are divided on the question of whether research cloning should be allowed to continue. Some believe that stem cells harvested from cloned embryos could be used for medical research and therapies.[1] Others argue that it is immoral to create embryos that have no chance at life, solely to harvest their cells for the benefit of others.[2]

Unable to bridge this ideological divide, the Sixth Committee (Legal) of the General Assembly abandoned the effort to draft an international convention against human cloning, and established a Working Group to draft a non-binding declaration instead.[3]

During this process, Honduras proposed the United Nations Declaration on Human Cloning (Declaration). The proposal called upon member states to "prohibit all forms of human cloning inasmuch as they are incompatible with human dignity and the protection of human life."[4] In other words, the Declaration condemned both research and reproductive cloning.[5]

On February 18, 2005, the Sixth Committee voted 71 to 35 with 43

---

* Professor of Law, Santa Clara University. I am deeply grateful for the advice I have received from Professors June Carbone, Dinah Shelton, Barbara Stark, and Beth Van Schaack. Their expertise in the field of international human rights has helped me enormously.

1 In accordance with this view Belgium proposed an international convention against reproductive cloning only. Twenty-two other U.N. members joined Belgium, including China, France, Greece, Japan and the United Kingdom. *See* U.N. GAOR, 59th Sess., 516th mtg. at 3–5, U.N. Doc. A/59/516 (Nov. 19, 2004).
2 Consistent with this view, Costa Rica proposed an international convention against all human cloning. Sixty-one other members of the U.N. joined Costa Rica, including Australia, the United States, and many countries in Latin America and Africa. *See id.* at 1-3
3 *See id.* at 7.
4 U.N. Gen. Assembly, Sixth Comm., Working Group Established Pursuant to Gen. Assembly Decision 59/547 to Finalize the Text of a United Nations Declaration on Human Cloning, *Report of the Working Group Established Pursuant to General Assembly Decision 59/547 to Finalize the Text of a United Nations Declaration on Human Cloning*, Annex I, subsec. b, U.N. Doc. A/C.6/59/L.27/Rev.1 (Feb. 23, 2005).
5 Thus, the Declaration went farther than the earlier Universal Declaration on the Human Genome and Human Rights, which provided: "Practices which are contrary to human dignity, such as reproductive cloning of human beings, shall not be permitted." UNESCO Gen. Conf. Res. 29 C/Res. 16, art. 11, *reprinted in* Records of the General Conference, UNESCO, 29th Sess., 29C/Res. 19, at 41 (1997); adopted by the U.N. General Assembly in the Universal Declaration on the Human Genome and Human Rights, G.A. Res. 53/152, U.N. GAOR, 53d Sess., 152d mtg., U.N. Doc. A/RES/53/152 (Mar. 10, 1999).

abstentions to recommend to the General Assembly the adoption of the Declaration.[6] This outcome was a big disappointment to advocates of research cloning. Belgium immediately declared that it did not feel bound by the decision, and the United Kingdom declared that research cloning would continue to be permitted there.[7]

Despite such protests, on March 8, 2005, the General Assembly voted 84 to 34 with 37 abstentions[8] to approve the Declaration.[9] The United States and Australia were among those countries voting in favor of the Declaration.

The Declaration seems likely to provoke debate on a number of points. First, it does not define human dignity or explain why both research and reproductive cloning are incompatible with human dignity.[10] This offers scholars, politicians, and others a golden opportunity to offer their own interpretations.

Second, international human rights treaties and prior declarations have been carefully worded to avoid any explicit recognition that unborn children have a right to life.[11] The Declaration, by contrast, characterizes

---

6 *See* U.N. GAOR, 59th Sess., 516th mtg. at 5, U.N. Doc. A/59/516/Add.1 (Feb. 24, 2005).

7 *See* Associated Press, *U.N. Committee Adopts Cloning Resolution*, Fox NEWS, Feb. 19, 2005, http://www.foxnews.com/printer_friendly_story/0,3566,148134,00.html.

8 *See* Press Release, General Assembly, General Assembly Adopts United Nations Declaration on Human Cloning by Vote of 84-34-37, U.N. Doc. GA/10333 (Mar. 8, 2005), *available at* http://www.un.org/News/Press/docs/2005/ga10333.doc.htm [hereinafter U.N. Press Release].

9 *See* G.A. Res. 59/280, Annex, U.N. GAOR, 59th Sess., 280th mtg., U.N. Doc. A/RES/59/280 (Mar. 23, 2005).

10 After voting on the Declaration, many U.N. representatives made public statements but did not elaborate on the relationship between cloning and human dignity. *See* U.N. Press Release, *supra* note 9. Unfortunately, documents leading up to the approval of the Declaration are not particularly illuminating. Committee reports during the abortive effort to produce an international convention reflect a consensus that reproductive cloning raises moral, religious, ethical and scientific concerns, and has far-reaching implications for human dignity. However, the reports do not lay out arguments or specific facts in support of this consensus. See U.N. Gen. Assembly, Sixth Comm., Working Group on an International Convention Against the Reproductive Cloning of Human Beings, *Report of the Working Group on an International Convention Against the Reproductive Cloning of Human Beings*, Annex II, U.N. Doc. A/C.6/57/L.4 (Sept. 30, 2002); U.N. Gen. Assembly, Ad Hoc Committee on an International Convention against the Reproductive Cloning of Human Beings, *Report of the Ad Hoc Committee on an International Convention against the Reproductive Cloning of Human Beings*, ¶ 11, U.N. GAOR, 57th Sess., Supp. No. 51, U.N. Doc. A/57/51 (Feb. 25, 2002). Perhaps U.N. diplomats framed cloning in terms of human dignity because that concept is broad enough to encompass a wide range of arguments against both reproductive and research cloning. *See, e.g.*, WHO.int, A Dozen Questions (and Answers) on Human Cloning, http://www.who.int/ethics/topics/cloning/en/ (last visited May 9, 2005) (listing a hodgepodge of anti-cloning arguments under the heading of dignity).

11 *See* Philip Alston, *The Unborn Child and Abortion under the Draft Convention on the Rights of the Child*, 12 HUM. RTS. Q. 156, 161, 178 (1990); Dinah Shelton, *International Law on Protection of the Fetus*, in ABORTION AND PROTECTION OF THE HUMAN FETUS 1, 14 (Stanislaw J. Frankowski & George F. Cole eds., 1987). For example, in the "Baby Boy" case, the Inter-American Commission on Human Rights found that legalized abortion did not violate the right to life guaranteed in the American Declaration of Rights and Duties of Man (ADRDM). The Commission reasoned that the drafters had rejected language that would have explicitly extended the right to life to the unborn. The Commission also rejected the

experimentation on cloned embryos as incompatible with the protection of human life. In so doing, it implicitly challenges the non-status of the unborn in international human rights law.[12]

Third, the Declaration seems to assume that laws against cloning can actually stop cloning. If this assumption is correct, no human clones will be born. However, if the laws cannot stop cloning, human clones are destined to be born in any event. What impact will anti-cloning laws have on those human clones?

This essay examines this third and most crucial question. It is my thesis that anti-cloning laws are counterproductive. They will serve primarily to stigmatize human clones as duplicative, defective, and unworthy of existence, based on their immutable genetic characteristics. This is not only unjust, but runs counter to the fundamental principle of non-discrimination in international human rights law.

1. No Matter What the U.N. Does, Research Cloning Will Continue.

My analysis begins with research cloning; any industry that involves the creation of cloned human embryos is a likely forerunner of reproductive cloning.

There is strong political support for research cloning among three groups. First, scientists claim that stem cells derived from cloned embryos could provide medical therapies that match a patient's own genetic structure. This holds out the tantalizing prospect that research cloning could lead to cures for Alzheimer's disease, cancer, diabetes, multiple sclerosis, and spinal cord injuries, among others. Of course, at this early stage, there is no proof that research cloning will produce such wonder therapies, but, so long as there is a chance of alleviating human suffering, research cloning will find a constituency among medical specialists and their patients.

Second, a broader group of scientists and secular humanists considers scientific knowledge to be an important good. These individuals are attracted to the possibility that research cloning will add to human knowledge. Lastly, venture capitalists and entrepreneurs are interested in research cloning. If the technology can produce viable medical therapies, they can make enormous amounts of money.

The U.N. Declaration on Human Cloning stands against these political forces. Its purpose is persuasion: national governments can take the

---

claim that the ADRDM must be interpreted as barring abortion when considered in light of its related treaty, the American Convention on Human Rights. The Convention included language protecting the right to life "in general" from the moment of conception, but this was a compromise designed to accommodate existing laws that permitted legalized abortion. See White v. United States, Case 2141, Inter-Am. C.H.R., Resolution No. 23/81, OEA/Ser. L/V/II.54, doc. 9 rev. 1 (1981).

12 *Cf.* JOHN CHARLES KUNICH, THE NAKED CLONE: HOW CLONING BANS THREATEN OUR PERSONAL RIGHTS 136 (2003) (arguing that research cloning reopens the question of when life begins for purposes of the U.S. Constitution).

Declaration home and tell lawmakers that the international community wants them to enact laws against all cloning.[13]

However, the Declaration was not supported by a true majority of the 191 member states of the General Assembly. Thirty-six members were absent and did not vote. Of the members who did vote, nearly as many abstained or voted against the Declaration as voted in favor. Dissenters included many European and Asian countries that have the technology to engage in research cloning. This striking lack of consensus undermines the value of the Declaration in international law[14] and undercuts its ability to influence national legislative debates on cloning.

More importantly, since the Declaration is non-binding, if dissenting member states refuse to ban all cloning, the U.N. will not impose sanctions against them. Thus, the Declaration cannot stop research cloning.

Some might argue that the Declaration is still very important, for it can serve as the first step towards an international treaty against all human cloning. Judging by recent efforts, however, the successful drafting of a treaty may be years or even decades away. By the time the U.N. manages to draft a treaty, many member states will have established research cloning industries and refuse to sign. Other states may sign the treaty but not ratify, particularly if no reservations are permitted. Finally, unless the treaty includes strong enforcement provisions, even states that ratify may not have an incentive to enact national implementing legislation that will offend some political constituencies.

In sum, a treaty may never exist, but even if it does, there will be no meaningful international restrictions on research cloning in much of the world.

2. The Growth of the Research Cloning Industry Greatly Increases the Likelihood that Reproductive Cloning Will Be Perfected and Human Clones Born.

While the U.N. hesitates, the business of research cloning continues apace. In 2004, South Korean scientists shocked the world by asserting that they had cloned human blastocysts, that is, advanced embryos containing hundreds of cells.[15] Using innovative protocols, the South Koreans claimed to have produced blastocysts from eggs at rates of up to 29 percent.[16] They also said they had harvested and cultured a line of embryonic stem cells

---

13 The Declaration calls upon member states immediately to adopt and implement national legislation to effectuate its principles. *See* G.A. Res. 59/280, supra note 10, para. e.
14 *Cf.* Texaco Overseas Petroleum Co. v. Libyan Arab Republic, 17 I.L.M. 1 (1978) (Int'l Arbitral Award of Jan. 19, 1997) (arbitrator gave no weight to certain provisions in the Charter of Economic Rights and Duties of States because industrialized countries with market economies had abstained or voted against them).
15 *See* Woo Suk Hwang et al., *Evidence of a Pluripotent Human Embryonic Stem Cell Line Derived from a Cloned Blastocyst*, 303 SCIENCE 1669 (2004).
16 *See id.* at 1670.

from one of 30 blastocysts.[17] The stem cell line had a normal karyotype (that is, a complete diploid set of chromosomes).

Unfortunately, as this essay goes to press, the authenticity of the 2004 South Korean experiment has been called into doubt.[18] However, research cloning is progressing in the United States, despite the opposition of President George Bush and the American delegation to the U.N. American researchers were among the first to succeed in cloning early human embryos,[19] and politicians in several states have rushed to create a legislative framework that promotes their efforts.

For example, in 1997, the California State Legislature enacted a law that placed a five year ban on reproductive cloning only. In 2002, the Legislature voted to make the ban on reproductive cloning permanent.[20] In a nod to the state's wealthy and powerful biotechnology lobby, however, the Legislature did not ban research cloning. Connecticut, Massachusetts, New Jersey, Rhode Island, and Virginia have similar laws that ban reproductive cloning but permit research cloning.[21]

In 2004, California voters approved a referendum that established a new state agency: The California Institute for Regenerative Medicine (CIRM).[22] The purpose of CIRM is to regulate and fund stem cell research, including research on cloned human embryos. The referendum also authorized issuance of general obligation bonds to finance this research, up to 3 billion dollars, subject to an annual limit of 350 million dollars. Research scientists and biotechnology entrepreneurs and investors are sure to be attracted by this taxpayer-funded pot of gold.

Technically, CIRM is prohibited from funding reproductive cloning research. Of course, few mainstream scientists are interested in reproductive cloning in any event. To protect their own research interests, they routinely denounce reproductive cloning, asserting that it is inefficient and unsafe.

Politicians have taken up the same cry, frequently justifying proposed laws against cloning on safety grounds. The U.N. Declaration on Human Cloning is consistent with this trend; it expresses concern about the serious medical and physical dangers that human cloning implies for the individuals involved,[23] and calls on member states to prohibit all forms

---

17 *See id.*
18 In early 2005, Hwang Woo Suk claimed he had created 11 stem cell lines that matched patient DNA. Subsequent tests showed this claim was false. Results from independent tests of Hwang's 2004 experiment are pending. *See* Rick Weiss, *None of Stem Cell Lines Scientist Said He Created Exists*, S.F. CHRON., Dec. 30, 2005, at A16.
19 *See* Jose B. Cibelli et al., *The First Human Cloned Embryo*, 286 SCI. AM. 44 (2002) (reporting the first creation of a cloned human embryo that grew to six cells).
20 *See* CAL. BUS. & PROF. CODE § 2260.5 (West 2003) and §§ 16004, 16105 (West 2004); CAL. HEALTH & SAFETY CODE §§ 24185, 24186, 24187 (West 2004).
21 *See* Conn. Public Act 05-149 (2005); 2005 Mass. Adv. Legis. Serv. 27 (Law. Co-op.); N.J. STAT. ANN. § 2C:11A-1 (West 2004); R.I. GEN. LAWS §§ 23-16.4 to -4 (2003); VA. CODE ANN. §§ 32.1-162.21, 32.1-162.22 (Michie 2003).
22 CIRM Home Page, http://www.cirm.ca.gov (last visited Sept. 23, 2005).
23 *See* G.A. Res. 59/280, *supra* note 10, Annex, at 2.

of human cloning on the ground that they are incompatible with the "protection of human life".[24]

Safety concerns have some basis at present. In adult cell cloning experiments performed on animals through 2001, the percentage of live births to embryos transferred ranged from 0.32 to 11 percent.[25] The vast majority of failures occur at the earliest stages, when eggs do not develop into embryos, or embryos do not produce a pregnancy.[26] Once a pregnancy is established, some fetuses do miscarry, posing risks to surrogate mothers.[27] Of cloned animals that make it to birth, a few die, and others suffer from physical abnormalities.

The reasons for cloning failures are unclear. More than one factor may be involved, and some factors may not be inherent in cloning. For example, large offspring syndrome (LOS) involves fetal overgrowth, abnormal placentas, fluid accumulation, and cardiovascular abnormalities. LOS has been observed, not only in animal clones, but also in animals conceived through routine in vitro fertilization. Scientists believe that LOS results when embryos are damaged during laboratory culture.[28] The syndrome does not occur in human in vitro fertilization, causing some researchers to conclude that it will not occur in human cloning.[29]

Other scientists theorize that cloning failures can be traced to so-called reprogramming errors. To explain in simple terms, each cell in the body of an adult animal includes the entire genetic "blueprint" for that animal. Each cell has taken on a specialized function that involves the expression of just a few genes. Skin cells express the genes necessary to create and maintain skin. Heart cells express the genes necessary to create and maintain a heart. For reproductive cloning to work, when the nucleus of a specialized adult cell is inserted into an egg, the egg must "reprogram" the nucleus so that it returns to an embryonic pattern of expression. If some of the genes required for proper embryonic development are not expressed properly, the clone cannot develop or may be unhealthy once born.[30]

But reprogramming errors threaten research cloning, too. Epigenetic abnormalities in cloned embryos could lead to unreliable experimental data and dangerous flaws in medical therapies derived from those embryos. Abnormal expression of certain genes can even cause tumors.[31]

---

24 *Id.* para. b. This language is also broad enough to condemn research cloning, which involves the deliberate creation and destruction of human embryos.
25 *See* COMM. ON SCI., ENG'G, & PUB. POLICY, NAT'L ACADS., SCIENTIFIC AND MEDICAL ASPECTS OF HUMAN REPRODUCTIVE CLONING 114-19 app. b, tbl.1 (2002) [hereinafter NAS Report].
26 *See id.*
27 *See id.* at 40.
28 *See id.* at 41.
29 *See* J. Keith Killian et al., *Divergent Evolution in M6P/IGF2R Imprinting from the Jurassic to the Quaternary*, 10 HUM. MOLECULAR GENETICS 1721 (2001).
30 *See* NAS Report, *supra* note 26, at 43; Konrad Hochedlinger & Rudolf Jaenisch, *Nuclear Transplantation, Embryonic Stem Cells, and the Potential for Cell Therapy*, 349 NEW ENG. J. MED. 275, 276-77 (2003).
31 *See* Susan M. Rhind et al., *Human Cloning: Can It Be Made Safe?*, 4 NATURE REVS. GENETICS 855, 862 (2003).

Some research scientists have tried to minimize these risks, arguing that competent cells are selected for the culture. In other words, the process of deriving stem cell lines from embryos tends to weed out cells with epigenetic abnormalities, which simply die in the Petri dish.[32] That may be true sometimes, but selection does not guarantee that therapies derived from cloned embryos will be safe.

Therefore, other research scientists, including Dr. Ian Wilmut, advocate a new approach to cloning experiments. They reason that clones may suffer from epigenetic abnormalities for a variety of reasons, some of which are not intrinsic to cloning. Scientists need to design controlled studies that can "disentangle" factors such as donor cell type, culture media, embryo manipulation, and nuclear transfer protocols from factors that are specific to cloning as such.[33] This will enable scientists to develop new protocols and strategies for the creation of cloned embryos without epigenetic defects.

Note the irony: To learn how to make medical therapies from stem cells, scientists must first learn how to create healthy human embryos at the blastocyst stage, when stem cells can be harvested. However, the creation of healthy human embryos is the first and most crucial step in reproductive cloning. This is because human embryos ordinarily implant in the lining of the uterus shortly after they grow into blastocysts.[34] If scientists engaged in research cloning can learn to create embryos without epigenetic abnormalities, they will eliminate the main scientific barrier to safe reproductive cloning. At that point, the first live birth of a human clone will be just a uterine transfer and nine months away.

3. Human Clones Will Not Be Copies.

Looking to the future, if reproductive cloning becomes possible and reasonably safe, and human clones are born, what will they be like?

Regrettably, the public, media, and politicians are full of wrong answers to this key question. Many people believe that cloning technology can be used to make duplicates of existing or dead persons.

This "identity fallacy" manifests itself throughout the cloning debate. Some arguments are obviously absurd. For example, it is not possible to replicate Adolf Hitler, Osama bin Laden, or any other dangerous megalomaniac.[35]

However, cloning opponents often advance other arguments that are grounded in the identity fallacy.[36] Although it is hard to identify the policy

---

32 *See* Hochedlinger & Jaenisch, *supra* note 31, at 281.
33 *See* Rhind, *supra* note 32, at 859-61.
34 *See* SHERMAN J. SILBER, HOW TO GET PREGNANT WITH THE NEW TECHNOLOGY 80-81 (Warner Books 1991).
35 *See, e.g.*, NAT'L BIOETHICS ADVISORY COMM'N, CLONING HUMAN BEINGS: REPORT AND RECOMMENDATIONS OF THE NATIONAL BIOETHICS ADVISORY COMMISSION 69 (1997) [hereinafter NBAC REPORT].
36 *See, e.g.*, CAL. ADVISORY COMM. ON HUMAN CLONING, CLONING CALIFORNIANS?: REPORT OF THE CALIFORNIA ADVISORY COMMITTEE ON HUMAN CLONING 24-27 (2002); PRESIDENT'S COUNCIL ON BIOETHICS, HUMAN CLONING AND HUMAN DIGNITY: AN ETHICAL INQUIRY 102-04, 111

origins of the U.N. Declaration on Human Cloning with any precision, here are some arguments that might underlie its conclusion that reproductive cloning is contrary to human dignity:

- Human clones will lack individuality and will suffer psychological damage as a result of being cloned.
- Human clones will not have an open future. They will be doomed to relive the lives of their DNA donors.
- Parents[37] of human clones will hold unreasonable expectations for them.
- Families of human clones will transgress generational boundaries and become dysfunctional. Mothers will give birth to daughters who are sisters; fathers will sexually abuse daughters who are duplicates of their wives.
- Existing persons will be cloned involuntarily and lose their individuality as a result.
- Cloning will be used to copy individuals who have superior physical or mental traits. Cloning will crush the spirit of egalitarianism and usher in a new era of eugenics that will rival the Nazi drive to produce Aryan supermen.

Space constraints preclude a thorough critique of the foregoing arguments in this essay. In a nutshell, however, the arguments fail because the identity fallacy is scientifically false.

Nature produces her own clones every day, using a rather primitive method. If a single fertilized egg splits in two, identical twins are conceived. Due to their origin in a single fertilized egg, the twins share the same nuclear and mitochondrial DNA.[38] They also are gestated in the same womb (though micro-environments within the womb can vary), and ordinarily are raised in the same family following birth. Despite these common genetic, biological, and environmental influences, each member of an identical twin pair is a unique individual. Indeed, twin researchers have found that the heritability of intelligence, cognitive skills, and personality traits is only about 50 percent.[39]

(2002) [hereinafter COUNCIL REPORT].

37   When it comes to cloning and human clones, it is important to define what one means by the term "parent". In this essay, I use the term to refer to any person who uses cloning to produce a child, so long as he or she plans to raise the child as his or her own. This broad usage is appropriate for two reasons. First, a person who decides to have and raise a child is playing the social role of parent. Second, as I explain in section 5 below, cloning is likely to emerge as an assisted reproductive technology that helps the infertile and others have genetic offspring. At least one and often both members of a marriage or partnership are likely to qualify as biological and legal parents of their cloned offspring. For a more thorough discussion of this point, *see* KERRY LYNN MACINTOSH, ILLEGAL BEINGS: HUMAN CLONES AND THE LAW 236 n.2 (2005).

38   Every human egg contains mitochondria, that is, tiny structures that produce energy within human cells. *See* BRUCE ALBERTS ET AL., MOLECULAR BIOLOGY OF THE CELL 30 (4th ed. 2002). Mitochondria have their own DNA, which is inherited down the maternal line.

39   *See* Nancy L. Segal, *Human Cloning: Insights from Twins and Twin Research*, 53 HASTINGS L.J. 1073, 1076 (2002).

Scientists clone differently. To create embryos, they take nuclear DNA from the cells of an adult (DNA donor), and inject it into donated eggs that have had their own chromosomes (but not mitochondria) removed beforehand. One or more embryos must then be inserted into the uterus of a woman for nine months of gestation and eventual birth.

These scientific facts establish two important points. First, a human clone cannot emerge from the womb as an adult; he or she will be a baby. Second, the creation processes for identical twins and human clones differ significantly, with the following results.

Unlike identical twins, human clones and their DNA donors will share the same chromosomes, but not the same mitochondria. Since mitochondria process energy, this could lead to differences in muscle, heart, eye, brain, or other body systems that use a lot of energy.[40] Human clones also will be gestated in different uteri than their DNA donors, leading to differences in how their common genes are expressed.[41] Finally, human clones will grow up in different families, eras, and cultures than their DNA donors, contributing to the development of different psychological traits, tastes, and values. As a result, human clones will differ from their DNA donors even more than identical twins differ from each other.[42] In some cases, they may not even look the same as their DNA donors.[43]

In sum, there is no scientific basis for the identity fallacy or any of the arguments that flow from it. Cloning will not flood the world with evil dictators, pathetic copies, duplicate wives, or arrogant supermen,[44] simply because it *cannot*. Human clones will be individuals, and their parents, friends, and society will have no rational reason to treat them as anything less.

Some might concede this point, yet argue that cloning must be banned because people are *not* rational. According to this point of view, no matter what the truth is, people will *think* human clones are copies, leading to unreasonable expectations, psychological damage, and discrimination.

---

40 *See* NAS Report, *supra* note 26, at 26.
41 *See* David S. Moore, The Dependent Gene: The Fallacy of "Nature vs. Nurture" 117-28 (2001).
42 *See*, e.g., Kunich, *supra* note 13, at 124.
43 Differences could be particularly marked in the case of a female baby. As the baby developed in the womb, each cell would randomly switch off one of her two X chromosomes. This X inactivation would not be influenced by whatever happened to the DNA donor when she was a developing embryo. *See* Macintosh, *supra* note 38, at 24-25; *see also* Tae Young Shin et al., A Cat Cloned by Nuclear Transplantation, 415 Nature 859 (2002) (reporting the birth of the first cloned kitten, Cc, who had different fur patterns than her DNA donor).
44 Concerns about the eugenic potential of cloning are misplaced for an additional reason. Even if a superior genome could be replicated in the bodies of human clones, these individuals would be vastly outnumbered by the teeming hordes of ordinary people born through sexual reproduction. *See* Gregory Pence, Who's Afraid of Human Cloning? 130 (1998). Regression to the mean would be inevitable – defeating the eugenic program – unless governments across the globe enacted coercive laws requiring asexual reproduction in preference to sexual reproduction. That is the stuff of science fiction novels, not serious public policy debate.

Human clones may indeed become victims of misunderstanding, since ignorance surrounding cloning runs very deep. Nevertheless, enacting anti-cloning laws is a counterproductive strategy.

To explain why, I offer here a brief historical analogy. For centuries, there were laws in the United States that made it a crime for a person of one race to marry a member of another race.[45] These laws sought to prevent the existence of mixed-race children,[46] who the white majority believed to be physically and mentally inferior.[47] Some proponents of the laws even argued that mixed-race children should not be born because they would suffer from social stigma.[48]

The California Supreme Court was the first to issue a decision invalidating such laws.[49] It rejected the argument that mixed-race children should not exist because they would suffer from the stigma of inferiority: "If they do, the fault lies not with their parents, but with the prejudices in the community and the laws that perpetuate those prejudices by giving legal force to the belief that certain races are inferior."[50]

Now, consider the argument that human clones should not exist because bigots might treat them like copies. This reasoning improperly uses prejudice to justify more prejudice[51] in the form of anti-cloning laws that give legal force to the belief that human clones are copies. Since human clones are likely to be born, no matter what laws say, it is important to choose a more effective means of combating the identity fallacy and its ill effects; scientific education would be a good start.

4. Human Clones Will Not Be Manufactured Products

Given the emphasis on human dignity in the Declaration, there is another anti-cloning argument that deserves special mention here.

The United States was a strong supporter of the Declaration. Three years before the Declaration was approved, the President's Council on Bioethics issued a report strongly condemning reproductive cloning. The report suggested that children who are "begotten" (that is, conceived through sexual reproduction) are gifts from God; as such, they stand as the equal of their parents in dignity and humanity. By contrast, cloning is a human project that treats children as manmade objects designed to genetic order. This violates human dignity.[52]

Thus framed, human dignity is a religious or moral argument which

---

45 *See* Harvey M. Applebaum, *Miscegenation Statutes: A Constitutional and Social Problem*, 53 GEO. L.J. 49, 50 (1964).
46 *See id.* at 64.
47 *See, e.g.*, Scott v. State, 39 Ga. 321, 324 (1869).
48 *See, e.g.*, State v. Brown, 108 So. 2d 233, 234 (La. 1959).
49 *See* Perez v. Sharp, 198 P.2d 17 (Cal. 1948). Nearly 20 years later, the U.S. Supreme Court held that anti-miscegenation laws violated the equal protection and due process rights of interracial couples. See Loving v. Virginia, 388 U.S. 1 (1967).
50 *Perez*, 198 P.2d at 26.
51 *See* PENCE, *supra* note 45, at 46.
52 *See* COUNCIL REPORT, *supra* note 37, at 8-10, 104-07.

is not capable of scientific proof.[53] However, this argument can also be interpreted as a warning against bad consequences: cloning will encourage parents to view their children as manmade products.

This warning runs counter to available evidence. Opponents of in vitro fertilization argued that it would objectify children, yet "test tube babies" function well and are not different psychologically from children who were adopted or conceived through sexual intercourse.[54]

Nevertheless, the President's Council on Bioethics has argued that cloning objectifies human beings to a much greater degree than other reproductive technologies, because it begins with a specific end product in mind and is tailored to produce that product.[55] As if this were not enough, cloning, even if practiced on a small scale, allegedly involves a paradigm shift from procreation to manufacturing, which threatens to impair the dignity of humankind as a whole.[56]

Such arguments rest on the premise that cloning can deliver a specific end product. In fact, as explained in section 3 above, cloning cannot do so, since human clones are not copies. No one has any scientifically valid reason to view cloned children as products, or to consider humankind objectified in some grander sense. Such perspectives are attributable not to cloning, but to abject ignorance of what cloning can accomplish, and perhaps even to the ill-conceived dignity argument itself.

5. If Reproductive Cloning Can Be Perfected, there Will Be a Demand for the Technology. Reproductive Cloning Cannot Be Stopped.

If reproductive cloning cannot manufacture specific end products, why would anyone want to use it? Where is the demand for the technology?

The answer is simple. Since all cloning can do is produce babies, asexual reproduction is a new assisted reproductive technology that can be used to conceive genetic offspring. It will appeal to three categories of persons for whom sexual reproduction is not possible or practical.

Some men and women lack functional sperm or eggs, making sexual reproduction with their partners impossible. To take advantage of reproductive technologies ranging from artificial insemination to in vitro fertilization these disabled individuals must use sperm or eggs donated by third parties. Cloning will offer them an opportunity to conceive and bear their own genetic offspring instead.[57]

Other men and women are fertile and healthy, but carry unexpressed

---

53 *See* NBAC Report, *supra* note 36, at 49.
54 *See* Susan Golombok et al., *The European Study of Assisted Reproduction Families: The Transition to Adolescence*, 17 Hum. Reprod. 830 (2002).
55 *See* Council Report, *supra* note 37, at 106.
56 *See id.* at 107.
57 *See, e.g.*, Mark D. Eibert, *Human Cloning: Myths, Medical Benefits and Constitutional Rights*, 53 Hastings L.J. 1097, 1101 (2002).

genetic disorders in their chromosomes. Sexual reproduction is a gamble for them; it could produce a child with a new genome in which the disease is expressed. Asexual reproduction will enable these carriers to sidestep the risk, and have a child with a genome that has already been proven not to express the disease.[58]

Finally, gay and lesbian couples cannot reproduce sexually without using sperm or eggs donated by third parties. Some of these couples may prefer to reproduce without having to use genes that come from individuals who are not a part of their families. Cloning will give them the chance to do so.[59]

Laws against reproductive cloning can reduce but not eliminate this demand for two reasons. The first is the ease of international travel. For years, infertile men and women have traveled to other countries to obtain egg donation, cytoplasm transfer, and other controversial fertility services and treatments that are restricted or forbidden in their homelands.[60] This history suggests that men and women who are interested in reproductive cloning will simply pack their bags and travel to jurisdictions where the technology is safe and legal. Once conception has occurred, cloning patients can come home pregnant and tell family and friends that they succeeded due to prayer, luck, or stress reduction.

Granted, nations can craft their anti-cloning laws in an attempt to block such travel. For example, although the United States does not yet have a federal law against cloning, the proposal that has achieved the most political success in recent years prohibits importing the product of cloning.[61] This presumably includes not only stem cell treatments derived from cloned embryos, but also cloned fetuses and newborns.

However, detecting violations of such laws will be a challenge. A pregnancy initiated through cloning will proceed like any other pregnancy. Moreover, newborns that strongly resemble one parent are common. Thus, absent widespread and intrusive genetic testing, authorities cannot be sure which pregnancies and newborns resulted from cloning, making enforcement difficult and incomplete.

If reproductive cloning were banned worldwide, the ability to clone abroad legally would be eliminated. However, a worldwide ban does not seem probable at this time. The inability of the U.N. to regulate cloning in any meaningful fashion increases the odds that motivated individuals will travel to get the cloning technology they need.

---

[58] *See, e.g.*, John A. Robertson, *Liberty, Identity, and Human Cloning*, 76 TEX. L. REV. 1371, 1379 (1998).
[59] *See* id. at 1380.
[60] *See, e.g.*, Debora Spar, *Reproductive Tourism and the Regulatory Map*, 352 NEW ENG. J. MED. 531 (2005).
[61] *See* H.R. 1357, 109th Cong. § 2 (2005). The House of Representatives passed a nearly identical bill in 2003 by a strong vote of 249 to 155. See H.R. 534, 108th Cong. § 2 (2003); Edward Epstein, *House Passes Bill to Prohibit Human Cloning*, S.F. CHRON., Feb. 28, 2003, at A3. A companion bill failed to clear the Senate, due to opposition from senators who support research cloning.

The second reason laws will fail to stop reproductive cloning is that a black market is likely to emerge. Research cloning experiments will train scientists and laboratory assistants to create healthy cloned embryos. Publications will make the information available to a wide audience, including fertility doctors. This increases the odds that providers will offer reproductive cloning to those able to pay a price that corresponds to the legal risks involved.

Given the debate over the morality of research cloning, it is even possible that cloning opponents will engage in reproductive cloning. Today, those who consider themselves pro-life supporters protest in front of abortion clinics; tomorrow, they may rescue cloned embryos from destruction and implant them in the wombs of volunteers who wish to serve as adoptive parents.[62]

6. Human Clones Will Be Entitled to the Same International Human Rights as Other Human Beings.

If reproductive cloning becomes scientifically possible, and cannot be stopped by law, it follows that human clones will be born around the world. The next task of this essay is to determine what international human rights these individuals will enjoy.

The U.N. Charter is a logical starting point. Pursuant to this multilateral treaty, the U.N. is bound to promote "universal respect for, and observance of, human rights and fundamental freedoms for all without distinction as to race, sex, language, or religion."[63] Nations that are members of the U.N. are obligated to take action to achieve those goals.[64]

The Charter does not define human rights and fundamental freedoms. However, shortly after the U.N. was formed, the General Assembly adopted the Universal Declaration of Human Rights (UDHR).[65] The UDHR commands more respect than the average non-binding declaration. Some international lawyers view it as an authoritative interpretation of the Charter, such that member states have the obligation to promote respect for and observance of the rights stated therein.[66]

In addition, there are two international treaties that create binding legal obligations for those member states that have signed and ratified them. Together with the U.N. Charter and the UDHR, the *International*

---

62 Services already exist to locate adoptive parents for surplus embryos created and frozen in the course of in vitro fertilization. For example, Nightlight Christian Adoptions offers a Snowflakes Embryo Adoption Program. Snowflakes Embryo Adoption Program Home Page, http://www.nightlight.org/snowflakeslanding.asp (last visited Sept. 24, 2005).
63 U.N. Charter art. 55, para. c.
64 *See id.* art. 56.
65 Universal Declaration of Human Rights, G.A. Res. 217A, U.N. GAOR, 3d Sess., 1st plen. mtg., U.N. Doc. A/810 (Dec. 12, 1948).
66 *See, e.g.,* Filartiga v. Pena-Irala, 630 F.2d 876, 883 (2d Cir. 1980); Thomas Buergenthal, *International Human Rights Law and Institutions: Accomplishments and Prospects*, 63 Wash. L. Rev. 1, 9 (1988).

Covenant on Civil and Political Rights (ICCPR)[67] and the *International Covenant on Economic, Social and Cultural Rights*[68] round out an international bill of rights.

Let us consider how some basic provisions in this international bill of rights might apply to human clones born in defiance of anti-cloning laws.

Cloning transmits nuclear DNA. If a DNA donor is human, his or her clone must be human also.[69] Article 1 of the UDHR proclaims that all "human beings" are born free and equal in dignity and rights. Thus, human clones are equal in dignity and rights to humans born through sexual reproduction.[70]

The UDHR and the ICCPR build on equality by enshrining a principle of non-discrimination. Legal experts believe non-discrimination holds a particularly high status in international law.[71]

The language of both documents is similar.[72] As a treaty, the ICCPR arguably carries greater weight than the UDHR. Thus, for purposes of discussion, this essay focuses on the ICCPR, which states in article 2:

> Each State Party to the present Covenant undertakes to respect and to ensure to *all individuals* within its territory and subject to its jurisdiction the rights recognized in the present Covenant, without distinction of any

---

[67] International Covenant on Civil and Political Rights, *opened for signature* Dec. 16, 1966, 999 U.N.T.S. 171 [hereinafter ICCPR]. The United States signed and ratified the ICCPR but declared that the treaty was not self executing. The ICCPR has no legal effect in the United States because implementing legislation has never been introduced. See Barbara Stark, *Baby Girls from China in New York: A Thrice-Told Tale*, UTAH L. REV. 1231, 1236 n.21 (2003).

[68] *International Covenant on Economic, Social and Cultural Rights*, opened for signature Dec. 16, 1966, 993 U.N.T.S. 3 [hereinafter ICESCR].

[69] Article 1 of the Universal Declaration on the Human Genome and Human Rights reinforces this conclusion; it provides that "[t]he human genome underlies the fundamental unity of all members of the human family." Universal Declaration on the Human Genome and Human Rights, *supra* note 6, art. 1. Those who bear an entirely human genome should, at a minimum, qualify for status as human beings. Thus, human clones present an easy case. I do not mean to imply that genetics should be the sole or determining factor in more difficult cases, such as human/animal hybrids. In such a case, a richer analysis that also considered developmental and cultural factors would be necessary.

[70] Similarly, the Universal Declaration on the Human Genome and Human Rights provides that "[e]veryone has a right to respect for their dignity and for their rights regardless of their genetic characteristics." *Id.* art. 2(a). This indicates human clones are entitled to respect for their dignity and rights even though they share nuclear DNA with another person. *See* KUNICH, *supra* note 13, at 64.

[71] *See* Dinah Shelton, *Human Rights and the Hierarchy of International Law Sources and Norms: Hierarchy of Norms and Human Rights: Of Trumps and Winners*, 65 SASK. L. REV. 299, 310-11 (2002); *see also* Bertrand G. Ramcharan, *Equality and Nondiscrimination*, in THE INTERNATIONAL BILL OF RIGHTS, THE COVENANT ON CIVIL AND POLITICAL RIGHTS 246, 247 (Louis Henkin ed., 1981) (equality and non-discrimination are bedrock principles in the international law of human rights).

[72] The UDHR provides: "Everyone is entitled to all the rights and freedoms set forth in this Declaration, without distinction of any kind, such as race, colour, sex, language, religion, political or other opinion, national or social origin, property, birth or other status." *See* Universal Declaration of Human Rights, *supra* note 66, art. 2.

kind, such as race, colour, sex, language, religion, political or other opinion, national or social origin, property, *birth or other status*.[73]

"All individuals" must include human clones, because human clones are human beings. Therefore, states must not deprive a human clone of ICCPR rights because he or she is black, or female, or Jewish—and so on.

More significantly, states must not deprive a human clone of ICCPR rights because he or she is a human clone.

I reach this conclusion for two reasons. First, article 2 prohibits distinctions based on birth. Presumably, this language protects the rights of children born to parents who are not married to each other.[74] However, the word "birth" is broad enough also to protect the rights of human clones born to parents who have reproduced asexually.

Second, article 2 prohibits distinctions based on "other status". In other words, distinctions must not be made on the basis of a status that is comparable to any of the enumerated statuses.[75]

Race is the first status listed in article 2. Race is an immutable characteristic which the individual does not choose and cannot change. Since a person is not responsible for his or her race, it is unjust to deprive him or her of rights based on that status.

Moreover, race does not impair one's ability to contribute to, or participate in, human society. Race does not undermine the intrinsic worthiness of an individual, or eliminate his or her claim to membership in the human family. If the purpose of the ICCPR (and UDHR) is to guarantee certain rights to human beings, it makes sense that rights cannot be denied on the basis of the irrelevant status of race.

Reasoning by analogy, the defining biological characteristic of a human clone is that he or she shares nuclear DNA with another person. DNA is not chosen and cannot be changed; it is acquired upon conception and is immutable. It would be unjust to deprive human clones of human rights based on their genetic status.

Further, status as a human clone does not affect one's ability to contribute to, or participate in, human society. As explained in section 3 above, human clones are not the soulless copies of science fiction, but individuals who are fully human in every respect. Nor does status as a human clone undermine the intrinsic worthiness of an individual, or eliminate his or her claim to membership in the human family. If the purpose of the ICCPR (and UDHR) is to guarantee certain rights to human beings, it makes sense that rights cannot be denied on the basis of the irrelevant fact that one person shares nuclear DNA with another.

---

73 *See* ICCPR, *supra* note 68, art. 2, § 1 (emphasis added).
74 *Cf.* Marckx v. Belgium, 31 Eur. Ct. H.R. (ser. A) (1979) (legal distinctions made between legitimate and illegitimate children violate the *Convention for the Protection of Human Rights and Fundamental Freedoms*, which guarantees rights without discrimination grounded on birth).
75 *See* Ramcharan, *supra* note 72, at 256.

I conclude that the basic principle of non-discrimination entitles human clones to all the rights and freedoms enumerated in the ICCPR and UDHR, without distinction based on their birth via asexual reproduction or status as human clones.[76]

7. Anti-Cloning Laws Violate the Principle that Laws Should Not Be Discriminatory.

For purposes of this essay, the most significant right to which human clones are entitled is set forth in article 26 of the ICCPR, which provides:

> All persons are equal before the law and are entitled without any discrimination to the equal protection of the law. In this respect, the law shall prohibit any discrimination and guarantee to all persons equal and effective protection against discrimination on any ground such as race, colour, sex, language, religion, political or other opinion, national or social origin, property, birth or other status.[77]

Unlike article 2, which prohibits discrimination only with respect to rights enumerated in the ICCPR, article 26 has a broader scope.[78] As the Human Rights Committee has noted:

> In the view of the Committee, article 26 does not merely duplicate the guarantee already provided for in article 2 but provides in itself an autonomous right. It prohibits discrimination in law or in fact in any field regulated and protected by public authorities. Article 26 is therefore concerned with the obligations imposed on States parties in regard to their legislation and the application thereof. *Thus, when legislation is adopted by a State party, it must comply with the requirement of article 26 that its content should not be discriminatory.* In other words, the application of the principle of non-discrimination contained in article 26 is not limited to those rights which are provided for in the Covenant.[79]

---

76 These rights and freedoms should help to protect human clones from the sort of abuse frequently depicted in science fiction. For example, Article 8, § 1, of the ICCPR and Article 4 of the Universal Declaration of Human Rights provide that no one shall be held in slavery or servitude. Similarly, Article 6 of the ICCPR and Article 3 of the Universal Declaration of Human Rights recognize that every human being has the right to life. Therefore, scenarios in which human clones are enslaved or killed for their vital organs are unrealistic. *See, e.g.*, THE ISLAND (Dreamworks 2005).
77 *See* ICCPR, *supra* note 68, art. 26.
78 Article 26 of the ICCPR differs from article 7 of the Universal Declaration of Human Rights, which provides: "All are equal before the law and are entitled without any discrimination to equal protection of the law. All are entitled to equal protection against any discrimination *in violation of this Declaration* and against any incitement to such discrimination." Some might read the emphasized clause in the second sentence of article 7 as limiting the principle of non-discrimination to rights enumerated in the Universal Declaration of Human Rights. *See, e.g.*, Karl Josef Partsch, *Fundamental Principles of Human Rights: Self-Determination, Equality and Non-Discrimination*, in 1 THE INTERNATIONAL DIMENSIONS OF HUMAN RIGHTS 61, 71 (Karel Vasak & Philip Alston eds., 1982). However, such a reading would render article 7 redundant with article 2 of the Universal Declaration of Human Rights. The first sentence of article 7 is broader; the language assures entitlement without discrimination to equal protection of the law. This language could be read consistently with article 26 of the ICCPR as prohibiting discriminatory laws in general.
79 Human Rights Committee, *Report of the Human Rights Committee, General Comment No. 18: Non-discrimination*, Annex VI, para. 12, U.N. GAOR, 45th Sess., Supp. No. 40, U.N.

Thus, article 26 prohibits laws that discriminate on the base of race and other enumerated grounds. For the reasons given above, this includes laws that discriminate against human clones on account of their birth via asexual reproduction or status as human clones.

Article 26 does not define the concept of "discrimination". However, the Human Rights Committee has offered a helpful interpretation:

> [T]he term "discrimination" as used in the Covenant should be understood to imply *any distinction, exclusion, restriction or preference* which is based on any ground such as race, colour, sex, language, religion, political or other opinion, national or social origin, property, birth or other status, *and which has the purpose or effect of nullifying or impairing the recognition, enjoyment or exercise by all persons, on an equal footing, of all rights and freedoms.*[80]

Let us apply this concept to the topic at hand. To start with the most obvious example, states must not enact laws that exclude human clones from schools, parks, transportation, and other public facilities. Such exclusion would harm the dignity of human clones and would serve no legitimate governmental purpose.

Fortunately, this kind of discrimination is unlikely to occur because it would be very difficult to implement. Unlike race, status as a human clone is not readily apparent, and cannot be verified absent genetic testing. It would not be an easy thing to identify a human clone and eject him or her from a train or school.

However, it does not follow that human clones will be safe from discriminatory laws. *Those who are born will be victimized by the very same anti-cloning laws that sought to prevent their existence in the first place.*

At first glance, this claim may seem extraordinary or even absurd. On their face, anti-cloning laws prohibit only the use of an unpopular technology; the laws do not mention human clones explicitly.

Surely, however, the ICCPR must prohibit laws that are facially neutral but discriminatory in effect and purpose.[81] Otherwise, states could find devious ways of eviscerating the protection against discriminatory laws that Article 26 is intended to provide. Therefore, it is necessary to examine anti-cloning laws for evidence of discriminatory effect and purpose.

a) Anti-cloning Laws Have a Discriminatory Effect. Consider the legal status of sexual reproduction. Though the law occasionally prohibits sexual intercourse in certain contexts, it does not prohibit sexual reproduction as such. Indeed, the right to procreate and found a family has been identified as a fundamental human right.[82] As a result of this

---

Doc. A/45/40 (Oct. 4, 1990) (emphasis added), *reprinted in Compilation of General Comments and General Recommendations Adopted by Human Rights Treaty Bodies*, U.N. Doc. HRI/GEN/1/Rev. 7, at 146, 148 (May 12, 2004) [hereinafter *General Comment No. 18*].
80 *See* id. para. 7 (emphasis added), *reprinted in* U.N. Doc. HRI/GEN/1/Rev. 7, at 147.
81 *Cf.* JOHN E. NOWAK & RONALD D. ROTUNDA, CONSTITUTIONAL LAW § 14.4, at 621 (5th ed. 1995) (facially neutral laws violate the U.S. Constitution when designed to discriminate against minority groups).
82 *See, e.g.,* ICCPR, *supra* note 68, art. 23, § 2; see also Skinner v. Okla. *ex rel.* Williamson, 316 U.S. 535, 541 (1942).

laissez faire attitude, humans born through sexual reproduction steadily increase in number. They do not suffer legal burdens on account of their origin in sexual reproduction.

By contrast, anti-cloning laws ban asexual reproduction outright. To the extent they can be enforced, the laws will reduce the number of human clones who are conceived, gestated, and born. For purposes of this essay, I will assume that embryonic human clones do not qualify as "persons" entitled to protection against discrimination.[83] However, cloned babies and children born in defiance of cloning bans are entitled to such protection. Thus, it is important to identify the burdens that anti-cloning laws will impose on them from the moment of their birth. Due to space constraints, I describe only two of these burdens here.

Whenever parents are imprisoned for the crime of cloning, their cloned babies and children will suffer. Torn away from those who loved and wanted them the most, and cut off from financial support, the innocent will be forced to depend on the not so tender mercies of the foster care system. This is a cost that is seldom mentioned or recognized in the cloning debate.

Some parents will evade detection and conviction. However, anti-cloning laws will impose a second burden on cloned children that is just as harmful as parental loss: legal stigma.

Laws have an expressive function; that is, through their various prescriptions and prohibitions, laws articulate the values of the democratic society that enacts them. To identify the values that anti-cloning laws express, we must look to the policy arguments used to justify their enactment.

When closely examined, many of these arguments turn out to have little to do with cloning *qua* cloning. Instead, the arguments focus on human clones, claiming that this class of human being must not be allowed to exist because its members have bad traits that endanger their own happiness and the happiness of others.

Chief among these bigoted arguments is the identity fallacy and its claim that human clones are copies. Variations on the fallacy stereotype human clones as lacking in individuality, autonomy, and emotional balance. Fear of eugenic cloning further stereotypes human clones as superior, arrogant, and dangerous.

Anti-cloning laws based on identity arguments reinforce these ugly stereotypes. Moreover, since individuality is an essential human trait, the laws also stigmatize human clones as less than human.

Exaggerated safety arguments against cloning are no less problematic.[84]

---

83 *Cf.* Shelton, *supra* note 12, at 10 (article 6 of the ICCPR provides a right to life without taking a textual position on when life begins).
84 For a more complete account of how safety arguments have been exaggerated and influenced by considerations that have nothing to do with science, *see* MACINTOSH, *supra* note 38, at 44-69.

Ignoring the constant improvements in cloning technology, opponents insist that human clones will necessarily suffer from terrible birth defects. Anti-cloning laws based on such safety arguments stigmatize human clones as sick and deformed.

Finally, the structure of anti-cloning laws is stigmatizing, in and of itself. Most laws are written as flat bans with no sunset clause, no provision for periodic legislative review, and no exceptions. Criminal and civil penalties are severe.[85] This draconian approach expresses the ugly idea that human clones are a disaster in the making that must be stopped at all costs.

Legal stigma is not a trivial burden. Because laws reflect the will of the electorate, the ideas they express are particularly powerful. Once the laws mark them as duplicative, dangerous, and deformed, human clones will be at increased risk of emotional distress, ostracism, discrimination in housing and employment, and victimization at the hands of vigilantes.[86]

b) Anti-cloning Laws Have a Discriminatory Purpose. Anti-cloning laws reflect not only a discriminatory effect, but also a discriminatory purpose.

As the identity and safety arguments reveal, many people have prejudged human clones as duplicative, dangerous, and deformed. But those who want to stop human clones have limited options. As explained above in section 6, once human clones come into existence, they will be entitled to the same human rights as other human beings. No democratic government could openly conduct a pogrom against them without generating a strong international protest.

Instead, anti-cloning laws attempt to solve the "problem" through a program of *existential segregation*: that is, they criminalize cloning technology in an effort to prevent human clones from coming into existence in the first place.

Granted, this is not traditional apartheid—no human clones are being excluded from schools, transportation, or other public facilities. Nevertheless, existential segregation is discrimination, repackaged in a clever new form. It eliminates the need for apartheid by attempting to stop the unpopular class at its inception.

Some readers might disagree with my argument that anti-cloning laws deliberately discriminate against human clones. They might argue that lawmakers intend only to exclude human clones from life, and not to harm them once they are born. This objection rings hollow, however. Human clones will suffer legal burdens that flow directly from the laws that target them for non-existence prior to birth. If lawmakers are willing to inflict such burdens as part of their program of existential segregation, it is appropriate to ascribe those burdens to their original discriminatory intent.

Other readers might assert that lawmakers want to stop cloning for reasons that have nothing to do with the traits of human clones. They

---

85 *See id.* at 76-88.
86 *See id.* at 122-23.

might argue that it is the *act* of cloning that is wrong, because it usurps God's domain (creation), treats humans as objects of manufacture, and endangers the health of egg donors and gestational mothers.

All of these same arguments have been raised against in vitro fertilization. Opponents on the right and left have complained for decades that in vitro fertilization is an act of hubris that offends God, objectifies children and endangers egg donors and gestational mothers. Yet, in vitro fertilization is uncontroversial and remains legal.

To discover why lawmakers treat cloning so differently, one must subtract out the arguments that the two technologies have in common, and look for a factor that is unique to cloning. What remains is the identity fallacy. Any law based on the identity fallacy is based on false and prejudiced beliefs about human clones and is discriminatory.

c) Discrimination Against Human Clones Is Not Justified. Although article 26 of the ICCPR prohibits discriminatory laws, the Human Rights Committee has explained that this does not require the elimination of all legal distinctions:

> Finally, the Committee observes that not every differentiation of treatment will constitute discrimination, if the criteria for such differentiation are reasonable and objective and if the aim is to achieve a purpose which is legitimate under the Covenant.[87]

There are few, if any, legitimate reasons for the frantic drive to legislate human clones into nonexistence. As explained in section 3 above, human clones can never be copies of anyone, good or bad. This single scientific fact holds the power to invalidate each and every argument that is traceable to the identity fallacy. This includes the fear that cloning might be used for eugenic purposes, thereby condemning us all to relive the horrors of the Nazi era.

The argument that cloning is a form of manufacturing human life fails to the extent that it is rooted in the identity fallacy.[88] If cloning cannot produce copies, it cannot produce designer products; there is no scientifically valid reason for parents to view their cloned children as products or for the rest of us to believe that our humanity has been diminished.

What about safety concerns? States have a legitimate interest in protecting the health of mothers and children.[89] However, it is important

---

[87] *General Comment No. 18, supra* note 80, para. 13.
[88] Some might counter that the injury to human dignity lies in the act of employing human rather than divine means to achieve conception. This is a religious argument; in the United States, it would not be recognized as a legitimate governmental interest. *See* Lawrence v. Texas, 539 U.S. 558, 578 (2003).
[89] Indeed, some might argue that states have a treaty obligation to ban cloning in order to protect the health of mothers and newborns. They might point to the ICESCR, which recognizes a right of everyone to the enjoyment of the highest attainable standard of physical and mental health, and requires states to reduce the rate of stillbirths and infant mortality and ensure the healthy development of the child. *See* ICESCR, *supra* note 69, art. 12, §§ 1 and 2(a). However, any such argument would be flawed. Let us begin with mothers. Women (and men) have a right under article 23, § 2 of the ICCPR

to remember that human reproduction is inherently inefficient and risky.

In sexual reproduction, 75 percent of all conceptions fail to implant or spontaneously abort.[90] Late term miscarriages, stillbirths, neonatal deaths, and maternal deaths occur.[91] Birth defects in newborns are common, ranging from 4 to 12 percent of births, depending on the age of the mother.[92] Many of these tragic outcomes happen because sexual reproduction is a cruel gamble; it produces many failed genomes for every successful one.

By contrast, cloning uses genomes that already have proven their ability to create healthy babies. Coupled with scientific advances, this fact suggests that outcomes could one day move into the same range that is tolerated for sexual reproduction.

Yet, most anti-cloning laws are flat bans that do not provide for periodic legislative review so that safety improvements can be taken into account. Given the prospects for improvement, such laws are a disproportionate means to the end of safety.[93]

Moreover, when there are legitimate concerns about the safety of new medical technologies, governments usually respond with temporary regulations, and not with blanket prohibitions. The fact that cloning has

---

to found a family. For those unable to reproduce sexually, cloning provides an alternative means of founding a family. Women will not be getting pregnant by accident; they will have considered and assumed the risks of gestating clones. Therefore, even if cloning is hazardous, it seems unreasonable to deny women the right to make their own decisions regarding a matter that involves not just their health, but also their reproductive freedom. Banning cloning to protect the right to health of newborns is even more problematic. The right to health is not a right to be healthy. *See* U.N. ESCOR, Comm. on Econ., Cultural, and Soc. Rts., *General Comment No. 14: The Right to the Highest Attainable Standard of Health*, ¶ 8, 22d Sess., U.N. Doc. E/C.12/2000/4 (2000), *reprinted in Compilation of General Comments and General Recommendations Adopted by Human Rights Treaty Bodies*, U.N. Doc. HRI/GEN/1/Rev. 7, at 86, 88 (May 12, 2004). This is good, for a right to be healthy could be used to justify eugenics laws designed to prevent the birth of physically or mentally flawed offspring.
90 *See* Lee M. Silver, Remaking Eden: Cloning and Beyond in a Brave New World 43 (1997).
91 *See* Macintosh, *supra* note 38, at 65.
92 *See* Lee Silver, *Public Policy Crafted in Response to Public Ignorance is Bad Public Policy*, 53 Hastings L.J. 1037, 1043 (2002).
93 In an effort to render safety a permanent barrier, the President's Council on Bioethics has argued that there is no ethical way to make reproductive cloning safe through experimentation because the cloned child cannot consent to his participation. *See* Council Report, *supra* note 37, at 91-94. This argument glosses over important questions. Ethics guidelines for medical research typically protect "human subjects": that is, living individuals, rather than embryos or fetuses. *See* Basic HHS Policy for Protection of Human Research Subjects, 45 C.F.R. § 46.102(f) (2005). By the time a cloned child is born and becomes a human subject entitled to protection under the guidelines, the "experiment" is already complete. Nor is it clear that reproduction qualifies as "research" subject to ethical guidelines. If it does, sexual reproduction also must be unethical, since the outcome is uncertain for the baby involved. Perhaps parents can be said to consent on behalf of their child, but that principle applies to cloning also. Finally, even if initial attempts at reproductive cloning can be classified as unethical, the realities of cloning make them likely to occur somewhere in the world. Once those initial efforts prove cloning safe, a cloning ban cannot be justified on safety grounds.

been treated so differently indicates that something other than safety lies at the heart of opposition to cloning. A leading culprit is the identity fallacy and the instinctive revulsion it inspires toward human clones. We must not allow safety to be used as an excuse for discrimination against the members of an unpopular class in violation of article 26.

To summarize this section, anti-cloning laws are inconsistent with the fundamental principle of non-discrimination enshrined in the international bill of rights. Far from being necessary to protect human dignity, the laws are a greater affront to human dignity than is cloning itself, for they discriminate against human clones based on their genetic characteristics.[94]

8. Conclusion

During the 20th century, many states enacted laws that relegated racial minorities and other unpopular groups to separate public facilities, or worse, concentration camps. The U.N. has devoted much of its work to ensuring that such inequities never happen again. Toward that end, the international bill of rights has enshrined the principle of non-discrimination.

The 21st century presents new challenges. Researchers are working to perfect embryo cloning, and there are people who need cloning to reproduce. Taken together, these facts suggest that human clones will be born in the near future.

If the non-discrimination principle is to retain its vitality in the new millennium, it must be interpreted to prohibit laws that attempt to exclude the members of an unpopular class from existence—at least, whenever scientific and social realities indicate that some members of the class are bound to be born despite the laws. Laws that seek to implement existential segregation are profoundly stigmatizing and impair the recognition, enjoyment or exercise by all persons, on an equal footing, of all rights and freedoms.[95]

Therefore, the U.N. has made a serious error in calling upon member states to ban cloning. To protect the principle of non-discrimination against further erosion, the U.N. should immediately rescind its Declaration.

If member states disapprove of cloning, they should consider alternative strategies. For example, the U.N. could work to educate the public about what cloning can and cannot do. Honest information about current safety risks could help discourage the infertile and other prospective parents from cloning prematurely. As for the rest of the public, debunking the identity fallacy should be enough to ensure that the vast majority lose interest in cloning altogether.

---

[94] See Universal Declaration on the Human Genome and Human Rights, supra note 6, art. 2(b); see also Oscar Schachter, *Human Dignity as a Normative Concept*, 77 AM. J. INT'L L. 848, 852 (1983) (dissemination of negative stereotypes of groups offends human dignity).
[95] See General Comment No. 18, supra note 80, para. 7.

Education is important for another reason. Unlike stigmatising laws, education holds the power to shatter demeaning and dehumanizing stereotypes about human clones. This is important, for if human clones are destined to exist, human dignity requires that we welcome them as equal members of our human family.

IF I ONLY HAD A HEART!
The Australian Case of Annetts and the Internationally Confounding Question of Compensation in Nervous Shock Law

Yega Muthu*, Ellen Geraghty+ and Barbara Hocking^

The question of when to award compensation for nervous shock is one faced by many jurisdictions across the common law world, yet approaches to the issue have been markedly divergent. This is particularly apparent in the context of secondary victims (such as parents) who bring an action for nervous shock suffered as a result of the serious injury or death of a loved one (such as a child) in a traumatic event.

In this area of law a key requirement for recovery has been that of "sudden sensory perception" of the ill-fated event or at least the "aftermath" of the event which caused the death or serious injury of the loved one. This requirement is a legal one, and one not grounded in science. "Shock" has enabled the law to draw boundaries around the potential for indeterminate liability in this area, and has led to the technical exclusion of parents who may have suffered even "agonisingly protracted" awareness of their loved one's fate.

This paper examines the decisions of the *Annetts and Anor v Australian Stations Pty Ltd*[1] and *Tame v Morgan*[2] in the High Court of Australia and asserts that this requirement of the law of nervous shock has long been overdue for change. We commend the recent decision of the High Court to "dramatically extend the right of a plaintiff to sue for psychiatric injury"[3] and dispense with requirement of "sudden shock" and "direct perception". Instead, the High Court in *Annetts,* a case fully demonstrating an "agonisingly protracted" awareness of their son's death by the suffering parents, preferred the "reasonable foreseeability" test. We also discuss the

---

* LLB(Hons), LLM (Staffordshire), PhD (Macquarie), Lecturer, Faculty of Law, UTS.
+ BSc, currently completing LLB (Macquarie).
^ BA, LLB (Monash), DipGrad LegStuds (Sthlm), LLM (Lond), PhD (QLD), Senior Lecturer, Faculty of Law, QUT.
1 (2002) 211 CLR 317.
2 (2002) 211 CLR 317.
3 P Hunt, "Liability for Psychiatric Injury Extended" (2002) 40 (November) *Law Society Journal* 62.

more recent High Court decision in *Gifford v Strang Patrick Stevedoring Pty Ltd* [4], where the High Court applied the test and concluded that a duty may be owed to those persons in a close relationship with an injured person, despite their not directly perceiving the event. We commend the emergence at common law of what Professor Des Butler has termed "the new landscape for recovery for psychiatric injury in Australia",[5] and as part of that, further commend the New South Wales Parliament's dramatic move to codify these changes in the *Civil Liability Act 2002* and its subsequent refinement of them in the *Civil Liability Amendment (Personal Responsibility) Act 2002*.

Prior to *Annetts,* the requisite elements for establishing a claim in nervous shock law in Australia were that the plaintiff:

1. suffer from a recognised psychiatric illness
2. be a person of reasonable fortitude at the time of commission of the tort
3. be subject to a sudden or nervous shock
4. have directly perceived the accident or its immediate aftermath.

These criteria created significant differentials between compensability for psychiatric as opposed to physical injury and were inconsistently applied and controversial.[6] However, *Tame* and *Annetts* dramatically reformed the Australian law of nervous shock, significantly removing most of the technical differences between physical and psychological injury. These reforms were then partially overturned by the legislative reforms born of the "Insurance Crisis" of 2002.[7]

When handing down their decisions, their Honours all expressed their awareness of the insurance crisis and the ramifications of their decisions. Chief Justice Gleeson, for example, set out his question in terms of "reasonableness", providing a link between legal conceptions of responsibility, contemporary social conditions and standards, and meanwhile setting it out so that it acted as a limiting factor upon recovery.[8] In *Tame* and *Annetts* the Court abolished the "nervous/sudden shock rule", the "direct perception" rule and the "normal fortitude" rule.[9]

The result was an expansion of the range of circumstances in which a person suffering psychiatric injury may recover as a result of the abolition of the "direct perception" rule and the "sudden shock" requirement;[10] but the plaintiff was still required to show their membership of a class of persons who should have been within the reasonable contemplation of

---
[4] (2003) 214 CLR 269.
[5] D Butler, "Gifford v Strang and the New Landscape for Recovery for Psychiatric Injury in Australia" (2004) 12 *Torts Law Journal* 108–27.
[6] I Freckelton, "New Directions in Compensability for Psychiatric Injuries" (2002) 9(2) *Psychiatry, Psychology and Law* 271–83, at 271.
[7] Ibid 272.
[8] Ibid 273.
[9] David Davies, "Pure Psychiatric Injury—Recovery for Compensation" (2003) 23(8) *Proctor* 24.
[10] Ibid 23.

the defendant as sufferers of psychiatric injury if receiving news of the distressing event by telephone or other medium.[11]

The old laws governing negligently inflicted psychiatric injury are the remnants[12] of the judiciary of the past—"There is now, however, an indication of a change of judicial attitude brought about by a better understanding of mental illness and its relationship to shock."[13] However, this judicial progress has arguably been curtailed by the legislature.[14]

Nervous Shock Law

A. Defining Nervous Shock

Nervous shock is the traditional name for psychiatric illness, the best known of which in this context is post-traumatic stress disorder.[15] Post-traumatic stress disorder is defined as the development of characteristic symptoms following exposure to an extreme traumatic event.[16]

It is important to distinguish between the two classes of victim in nervous shock cases: those directly affected by a negligent act, as a result of which psychiatric injury is suffered, are known as primary victims.[17] Secondary victims are those family members, rescuers, bystanders and others who suffer psychiatric injury as a result of what has happened to someone else.[18] Cases involving primary victims are relatively straightforward personal injury matters. It is with cases involving secondary victims, in which the plaintiff must prove the closeness of their relational tie, that this paper is concerned.[19] Nevertheless, this approach

---

11 Ibid.
12 Peter Semmler QC, "Testing the Limits of Liability for Psychiatric Injury" (2002) 51 *Plaintiff* 37.
13 L Dunford and V Pickford, "Is There a Qualitative Difference Between Physical and Psychiatric Harm in English Law?" (1999) 7 *Journal of Law and Medicine* 39–40.
14 As Seeto notes, "[t]o move away from the flexibility of the common law position and categorically define who may claim, as the legislation does, is regrettable." Nicole Seeto, "Shock Rebounds: Tort Reform and Negligently Inflicted Psychiatric Injury" (2004) 26 *Sydney Law Review* 293, 300.
15 L Dombek and A Fisher, above n 9, 6.
16 According to the revised fourth edition of the *Diagnostic and Statistical Manual of Mental Disorders* (DSM-IV-TR), there are five major identifiers of post-traumatic stress disorder: a stressor event, re-experiencing symptoms, avoidance behaviour, a numbing of general responsiveness and arousal. The individual must experience a disturbance and impairment of their life as a result of exposure to the stressor event. American Psychiatric Association, *Diagnostic and Statistical Manual of Mental Disorders (Text Revision)* (4th ed, 2000) 463.
17 An example of such a primary victim is where an individual is run down by a car and suffers post-traumatic stress disorder as a result. See also B A Hocking and A Smith, "From Coultas to Alcock and beyond. Will Tort Law Fail Women?" (1995) 11 *Queensland University of Technology Law Journal* 120.
18 L Dombek and A Fisher, "Post Disaster Management" (Paper presented at Exeter College, Oxford, 10 September 1997) 6. (Copy on file with authors).
19 Previously as demonstrated in *McLoughlin v O'Brien* (1983) 1 AC 410, once relational proximity has been established, plaintiffs must face the often greater hurdle of proving physical proximity to the accident in time and space. In a legal sense this has meant that the plaintiff must either have experienced the accident or witnessed its immediate aftermath. This requirement of physical, temporal and relational proximity to a traumatic event has strictly limited the success of numerous nervous shock cases in the past and

was abandoned by the High Court of Australia in *Annetts* and *Tame* as arbitrary and artificial to follow.

B. Disparity Between Science and the Law

The common law has adopted a much narrower view of "compensable harm" than the science of psychiatry. Its usual restrictions include:

(i) Comparing the claimants' reaction to trauma with the standard of ordinary phlegm or normal disposition, unless the defendant is aware of the plaintiff's inherent susceptibilities.[20]

(ii) In the English jurisdiction, taking proximity factors such as space and time, as a requirement, into account and balancing these factors against whether it is just, fair and reasonable to impose a duty on the defendant.[21] Whereas in Australia, such a requirement is not a precondition for recovery for the negligent infliction of psychiatric illness.[22]

(iii) Determining whether the defendant breached the standard of care, taking into account the degree of risk, the practical precautions taken by the defendant and the social utility of the conduct of the defendant which resulted in damage.[23]

Recovery of damages for psychiatric illness has proved to be a continuing problem for the common law. As will be seen below, numerous ideas have passed into and out of fashion with the courts in their struggle to resolve the underlying policy tensions. This has not made the situation any easier for plaintiffs. Nor has the current medico-legal mix of restrictions, which can pose insurmountable hurdles for the majority of plaintiffs. So it was with the Annetts, who were "removed" from the death of their son by the simple fact of where and how it occurred.[24]

Case in Point: Annetts v Australian Stations Pty Ltd

In August 1986, 16 year old James Annetts was employed as a jackaroo (farmhand) on a cattle station in a remote part of Western Australia. His mother had sought and obtained reassurance from the manager of the station that her son would be appropriately supervised.

Another young man, 17 year old Simon Amos, was employed in the same capacity at around the same time as James. Despite their youth and inexperience, and despite the assurances given to Mrs Annetts by the manager of the property, both the boys were sent to work alone at remote locations only seven weeks after their arrival in Western Australia. Soon after, in December 1986, the two boys went missing. It appeared that

---

continues to do so.
20 *Jaensch v Coffey* (1984) 155 CLR 549 (hereinafter Jaensch).
21 *Alcock v Chief Constable of South Yorkshire Police* (1992) 1 AC 310.
22 *Annetts v Australian Stations Pty Ltd* (2002) 211 CLR 317.
23 *Paris v Stepney Borough Council* (1951) AC 367.
24 J Dietrich, "Nervous Shock: Tame v New South Wales and Annetts v Australian Stations Pty Ltd" (2003) 11 *Torts Law Journal* 11.

they had become increasingly unhappy with the work, its hardship and isolation, and had decided to "escape" in a vehicle which they drove into the desert.[25] They met a tragic fate. Their parents were far away. They had been missing for several days before the station manager informed the police of the boys' absences. The police then telephoned Mr Annetts and informed him that his son was missing. On hearing this news, Mr Annetts collapsed and his wife took over the telephone conversation.

A number of intensive searches were undertaken to locate James and his companion, and his parents were in telephone contact with the police. The missing young men became the subject of a police investigation. James' parents travelled to the investigation scene on a number of occasions.[26]

In January 1987, James' blood-stained hat was located and shown to the boy's parents.[27]

In April 1987, Mr Annetts was informed by the police that they had found his son's vehicle, which had been bogged in the desert. Later that same day, Mr Annetts was told that two sets of remains had been found nearby. Mr Annetts identified a skeleton in a photograph shown to him as his son.

The coroner found that James died on or about 4 December 1986 in the Gibson Desert about 133 km south of Balgo as a result of dehydration, exhaustion and hypothermia. Both his parents developed psychiatric injuries as a result of their son's tragic death.

Apart from the uniquely Australian setting of the tragedy, the fact situation differs little from the range of cases that have been considered in England[28], Canada[29], South Africa[30], Ireland[31] and New Zealand[32] in this area of law. It is "the classic secondary victim case".[33]

A. A Recognisable Form of Psychiatric Illness?— The Application of the DSM Manual

As a result of the cumulative manner in which they learnt about the tragedy which claimed the life of their son, the plaintiffs in *Annetts* were diagnosed with a grief reaction and a reaction extending beyond "mere grief" to an entrenched and recognisable psychiatric condition within the ambit of the DSM Manual.[34]

---

25 See S Muirhead and B Hocking, "A Uniquely Australian Tragedy? (The Law of Nervous Shock Limps On)" (2001) 6 *Tolley's Communications Law* 111.
26 Ibid 112–13.
27 Ibid 113.
28 *White v Chief Constable of South Yorkshire* (1999) 1 AII ER 1.
29 *Devji v District of Burnaby* (1999) BCCA 599.
30 *Barnard v Satnam Bank Bpk* (1999) SA 202.
31 *Bell v Great Northern Railway Co of Ireland* (1890) 26 LR Ir 428.
32 *Van Soest v Residual Health Management Unit* (2000) 1 NZLR 179.
33 P Handford, "When the Telephone Rings: Restating Negligent Liability for Psychiatric Illness: *Tame v Morgan* and *Annetts v Australian Stations Pty Ltd*" (2001) 23 *Sydney Law Review* 598.
34 American Psychiatric Association, above n 17, 463.

B. Legal Issues Arising from Annetts

At trial and on appeal, the law "removed" the suffering of Mr and Mrs Annetts from the tragedy of their son's disappearance by virtue of the geographical distance between them and their son at the time. When the Annetts sought damages for psychiatric illness resulting from the defendant cattle station management's negligent treatment of their son while he was in their employ, they confronted the "shock" or "sudden sensory perception" obstacle of the relevant legal doctrine, as it was the way in which they came to know about the disappearance and subsequent death of their son which otherwise stymied their claim. It was their pursuit of that claim which challenged the Court to consider whether the facts were sufficient at law to give rise to an independent tortious duty of care owed by the defendant cattle station owners to the parents to exercise reasonable care and skill to avoid causing them psychological injuries. The law's history did not bode well for the suffering parents.

The History of Nervous Shock Law in Australia

Australian judges have long exercised caution in the recognition of negligently inflicted psychiatric illness.[35] Early Australian cases found liability in situations of *intentional* infliction of emotional distress,[36] but rejected *negligently* inflicted psychiatric illness. For example, in *Chester v Waverley Municipality*,[37] a mother suffered shock after seeing her dead son being lifted out of a trench. The High Court of Australia decided that a duty was not owed to her, as her injury could not have been reasonably anticipated by the defendant.[38]

---

[35] D Butler, "Media Negligence in the Information Age: A New Frontier for a New Century" (2000) 8 *Torts Law Journal* 159, 162.

[36] For example, in *Bunyan v Jordan* (1937) 57 CLR 1, the defendant's threats threw the plaintiff into an emotional state which caused a neurasthenic breakdown. It was said that the defendant, "in the course of socially worthless conduct, failed to exercise care to avoid causing nervous shock to the plaintiff" (16). It was recognised that damages may be recovered for the intentional infliction of psychiatric illness. See also H Luntz and D Hambly, *Torts: Cases and Commentary* (2002) 497. Further, in *Levi v Colgate* (1941) 41 SR (NSW) 48, the defendant, the manufacturer of a washing product, owed no duty to take precautions to a consumer sensitive to dermatitis, but only the same duty owed to a normal consumer. According to Luntz and Hambly, again at 360, "although the defendant was under no duty to take special precautions to protect the abnormal, if an abnormal plaintiff suffered loss in circumstances in which a normal plaintiff would also have suffered loss, the fact that the abnormal plaintiff suffered more loss than the normal plaintiff would not prevent the plaintiff recovering for all the losses. This argument has been applied to nervous shock as well as to physical damage".

[37] (1939) 62 CLR 1; C J Miller, "Mental Shock and the Aftermath of a Train Disaster" (1968) 31 *Modern Law Review* 92, 94; A L G, "Case Note: An Australian Shock Case" (1939) CCXX *Law Quarterly Review* 495.

[38] G L Fricke, "Nervous Shock—the Opening of the Floodgates" (1981) 7 *University of Tasmania Law Review* 113, 115. See *Abramzik v Brenner* (1967) 65 DLR (2nd) 651 (*Abramzik*). The Saskatchewan Court of Appeal denied recovery to a mother who suffered "nervous shock" on being informed by her husband that two of her children had been killed in a road accident. *Abramzik* may have been decided differently today: current legal developments would be taken into account, in particular the notion that for a mother to witnesses the immediate aftermath of an accident and suffer shock as a result would be a

A. The Law Reform (Miscellaneous Provisions) Act 1944 (NSW)

Criticism of *Chester* resulted in the passing of the *Law Reform (Miscellaneous Provisions) Act 1944* (NSW). Section 3 of the Act abrogated the *Chester* case and gave the court the authority to have regard to the negligent infliction of psychiatric illness arising from shock, and to award damages in such cases. Section 4 defined the category of allowable claimants to include members of a family who suffered psychiatric injury as a result of a loved one being negligently killed, injured or put in peril.[39]

This legislative reform seemed to encourage rather than discourage the Australian common law in developing a more open stance towards negligently inflicted psychiatric illness. Later cases saw a relaxation of the requirements of reasonable foreseeability to allow close family members to claim nervous shock after witnessing the occurrence and aftermath of accidents involving their relatives.[40] The widening of foreseeability to include "witnessing the aftermath" began in *Benson v Lee*[41], where the plaintiff was informed by a third party that her son had been knocked down by a car. The plaintiff mother rushed to the scene of the accident 100 yards away. In this case Lush J stated:

> "if within the limits of foresight something is experienced through direct and immediate perception of the accident, or some part of the events constituting it, which imparts shock, that is all . . . the law requires."[42]

Further, while foreseeability of shock of some kind was required, the precise nature of the shock suffered need not be foreseeable.[43]

B. Jaensch v Coffey[44]

Similar issues were discussed by the High Court in the landmark case of *Jaensch v Coffey*[45] In this case, the plaintiff saw her injured husband in

---

common experience of mankind which would therefore be compensable.

[39] Similar legislation is in force in the Australian Capital Territory (*Law Reform (Miscellaneous Provisions) Act 1955*, ss 17, 22, 23, 24(1)(5), 32 clarifies the requirements for post-traumatic stress disorder and categories of claimants; D Butler, "Nervous Shock at Common Law and Third Party Communications: are Australian Nervous Shock Statutes at Risk of Being Outflanked?" (1996) 4 *Torts Law Journal* 120 and the Northern Territory (*Law Reform (Miscellaneous Provisions) Act 1956*, s 23, 24, 25(5) clarify the requirements for post-traumatic stress disorder and categories of claimants).

[40] For example, both a brother who watched his infant sibling involved in a terrible accident and their mother, who was summoned to the aftermath, recovered damages in *Storm v Geeves* (1965) Tas SR 252.

[41] (1972) VR 789.

[42] Ibid.

[43] *Mount Isa Mines Ltd v Pusey* (1970) 12 CLR 383. In this case, the plaintiff attempted to rescue workmates who had been badly burnt by an electric arc while working on a switchboard. As a result of this incident, the plaintiff suffered schizophrenia. The plaintiff was awarded damages on the basis that, "what the defendant had to foresee was the occurrence of the class of injury, mental disorder, rather than the particular illness." N J Mullany and P R Handford, "Moving the Boundary Stone by Statute: the Law Commission on Psychiatric Illness" (1999) 22 *University of New South Wales Law Journal* 350.

[44] (1984) 155 CLR 549.

[45] Ibid; Y Muthu, "Negligent Infliction of Psychiatric Illness: An Area which Remains to

a combination of events which led her to suffer psychiatric illness. The High Court of Australia dealt with the definition of the "aftermath" of an accident, the observation of which could give rise to a claim of nervous shock. It was found that the "aftermath" of an accident should not be restricted to the actual site of the injurious event.[46] Instead, it extended to the hospital during the period of the immediate post-accident treatment of the person physically injured by the tortfeasor.[47] It is important to note that in this decision the Court was prepared to contemplate recovery where a plaintiff was so devastated by being told of an accident involving family members that he or she was unable to attend the various scenes.

The majority of the Court allowed recovery in *Jaensch*. However, Deane J sought to impose a new test for the establishment of a duty of care, in addition to the test of reasonable foreseeability. This test was the test of proximity.

C. Proximity

The notion of proximity is concerned with closeness in space, time and relationship. In *Jaensch,* Deane J concurred with the speech of Lord Wilberforce in the English case of *McLoughlin v O'Brian*[48], in which closeness of time and space were identified as important elements in establishing liability.[49] According to Deane J, a duty of care could be established in cases of physical proximity (closeness of space and time), circumstantial proximity (close or overriding relationships) or causal proximity (close or direct causal relationships between acts and injuries or losses).[50] In such cases the defendant's negligence must be a proven primary and continuing cause[51] of the plaintiff's psychiatric illness.[52]

Thus, according to Deane J, to establish a duty of care one must prove:

(i) The reasonable foreseeability of a real risk of that harm of the kind suffered by the plaintiff or a member of that class;

(ii) The existence of the requisite element of proximity in the relationship between the parties and;

---

be Clarified?" (1999) 4 *Malayan Law Journal* clxxvii.
46 D Mendelson, "The Defendant's Liability for Negligently Caused Nervous Shock in Australia—Quo Vadis?" (1992) 18 *Melbourne University Law Review* 16, 37; R Atkinson, "... of the Tort of Negligence" (1987) *Queensland Law Society Journal* 237.
47 D Mendelson, above n46. The High Court noted that, in view of today's fast and efficient ambulance services, it would be anomalous to allow recovery only to those plaintiffs who could "beat the ambulance to the scene of the accident," per Deane J (1984) 58 ALJR 426, 462; F A Trindade, "The Principles Governing the Recovery of Damages for Negligently Caused Nervous Shock" (1986) 45 *Cambridge Law Journal* 476, 498–99.
48 (1983) 1 AC 410 (*McLoughlin*).
49 C Witting, "A Primer on the Modern Law of '"Nervous Shock'" (1998) 22 *Melbourne University Law Review* 62, 72.
50 (1984) 155 CLR 549, 584–85; D Butler, "Proximity as a Determinant of Duty: the Nervous Shock Litmus Test" (1995) 21 *Monash University Law Review* 159, 161.
51 In other words, was it the predominant causal factor that led to the illness?
52 Deane J acknowledged that arbitrary lines of demarcation often need to be drawn with respect to time and space which are otherwise infinite.

(iii) The absence of any statutory provision or common law rule . . . which operates to preclude the imposition of such a duty of care in the circumstances of the case.[53]

Deane J's approach was essentially an expansion and adaptation of the existing English approach which had been adopted in that country in *Anns v Merton London Borough Council*.[54] In Anns, in the leading judgement of Lord Wilberforce (with which the majority of the House of Lords concurred), it was held that a duty of care would exist where a relationship of sufficient proximity existed for the relevant harm to be foreseeable by the defendant and where there were no considerations which might reduce or negate the duty he owed to the plaintiff.[55]

Brennan J took a different approach to the question of duty of care in *Jaensch*. Whilst appreciating the objective aspect of the foresight test, Brennan J "stressed that it was a question of fact whether a set of circumstances might induce psychiatric illness."[56] Time and distance were viewed as matters going to causation and reasonable foresight, which were not matters of policy which limited liability.[57]

Brennan J also drew a distinction between the sudden sensory perception of an event as opposed to learning of an event in less confronting circumstances during its aftermath.[58] His Honour held that it was more plausible that persons would find difficulty in coping with, and would suffer injury as a result of being engaged in a traumatic event than in hearing about the involvement of others in such an event.[59]

D. Critical Analysis of Proximity in the English and Australian Jurisdictions following *Jaensch*

While Deane J stood alone in *Jaensch* on his formulation of proximity, subsequent decisions of the court saw a growing acceptance—and later criticism—of the concept.[60]

The notion of proximity was further developed in the case of *Sutherland*

---

53 J Keeler, "The Proximity of Past and Future: Australian and British Approaches to Analysing the Duty of Care" (1989) 12 *Adelaide Law Review* 93, 97.
54 (1978) AC 728 (*Anns*).
55 (1978) AC 728. 751–52, per Lord Wilberforce.
56 D Gardiner, "*Jaensch v Coffey*, Foresight, Proximity and Policy in the Duty of Care for Nervous Shock" (1985) 1 *Queensland University of Technology Law Journal* 69, 75.
57 Ibid 75. This approach was also taken in *Brice v Brown* (1984) 1 All ER 997, per Stuart-Smith J, 1007.
58 C Witting, "A Primer on the Modern Law of 'Nervous Shock'" (1998) 22 *Melbourne University Law Review* 62, 72.
59 Similarly in *Nader v Urban Transit Authority* (1985) 2 NSWLR 501, the defendant was held liable for the psychiatric injury suffered because it was of a kind that was foreseeable, though foresight of the extent of the injury was not required.
60 D Butler, "Mass Media Liability for Nervous Shock: a Novel Test for Proximity" (1995) 3 *Torts Law Journal* 75, 76. In *Sutherland SC v Heyman* (1985) 157 CLR 424, Deane J restated the approach he had first formulated in *Jaensch v Coffey*. It is really a three stage approach, namely, reasonable foreseeability, proximity and policy. Emphasis typically falls on the second stage, "proximity".

Shire Council v Heyman.[61] In this case, Deane J restated the three stage approach he had first formulated in *Jaensch*. In the same case, Brennan J rejected the *Anns* two stage approach, arguing that it allowed for massive extensions of liability and that its vague "considerations to the contrary" were an inadequate limit to liability. In his judgement, Brennan J expressed his preference for the "incremental" approach whose roots were essentially in the categorical approach to law.[62]

In *Hill v Van Erp*[63], the notion of proximity was criticised for its failure to provide a discrete legal principle.[64] In the High Court of Australia, Dawson J expressed reservations about proximity's role as "a unifying theme".[65] He opined that the concept of proximity embodies "the proposition that in the law of negligence, reasonable foreseeability of harm may not be enough to establish a duty of care'[66] and that a process of reasoning—which might be viewed as a formal incorporation of policy considerations into the process of legal reasoning—must be gone through in order to limit it.[67]

In the English case of *Caparo plc v Dickman*,[68] the criticisms of *Anns* offered by Brennan J were accepted by the House of Lords. In this case, the House of Lords did not search for a general overarching principle but reverted to the categories approach.[69] However, Lord Bridge argued that new situations should be considered in three stages, the first two of which bore a remarkable resemblance to the approaches in *Anns* and *Jaensch*. The considerations at each stage are:

(i)   foreseeability;
(ii) proximity; and
(iii) notions of fairness, justice and reasonableness.

Lord Bridge noted that:

> The concepts of proximity and fairness embodied in these additional ingredients are not susceptible of any such precise definition as would be necessary to give them utility as practical tests, but amount in effect to little more than convenient labels to attach to the features of different specific

---

61 (1985) 157 CLR 424; J Allen and M Dixon, "Notes: Foreseeability Sinks and Duty of Care Drifts: the High Court visits Rottnest" (1993) 23 *Western Australian Law Review* 320, 324.
62 The categorical approach allows modest extensions to the law by analogy with established categories.
63 (1997) 188 CLR 159; B Feldthusen, "Liability for Pure Economic Loss: Yes, but Why?" (1999) 28 *University of Western Australia Law Review* 84, 118.
64 See also *San Sebastian Pty Ltd v The Minister* (1986) 162 CLR 340, *Burnie Port Authority v General Jones Pty Ltd* (1994) 179 CLR 520 and *Bryan v Maloney* (1994) BCL 279, in which further erosion of the proximity criterion took place.
65 *Hill v Van Erp* (1997) 188 CLR 159, 160.
66 (1997) 188 CLR 159. See also D G Gardiner, above n 63, 69; D Ipp, "Negligence—Where Lies the Future?" (2003) 23 *Australian Bar Review* 5.
67 (1997) 188 CLR 159, 206, 220. In *Gala v Preston* (1991) 172 CLR 243, Brennan, Dawson and Toohey JJ concentrated specifically on policy considerations instead of principle to deny relief to a drunken teenager who was injured when the driver of a car in which the teenager was joyriding lost control of the car which then collided with a tree.
68 (1990) 2 AC 605.
69 (1990) 2 AC 605, 617–18 per Lord Bridge.

situations which, on a detailed examination of all the circumstances, the law recognises pragmatically as giving rise to a duty of care of a given scope.[70]

In Australia, Kirby J favoured *Caparo*'s three stage approach in *Pyrenees Shire Council* v *Day*.[71] Although criticism of proximity as the determining test was continuing to grow, the favoured approach after *Pyrenees Shire Council* involved considerations of foreseeability, proximity and policy.[72] Subsequently, in *Perre* v *Apand Pty Ltd*[73], McHugh J of the High Court of Australia expressed objections to *Caparo*. He argued that given the inherent uncertainty about the meaning of proximity, it should not be given greater weight than other factors. He further argued that the *Caparo* three stage approach threatened to deprive the law of such certainty as it already had regarding the concepts of fairness, justice and reasonableness, and offered little practical guidance to practitioners.

McHugh J acknowledged that whatever formula was used, in grey areas the court would have to exercise its discretion. In such circumstances, he maintained justice and morality should be employed only when principle had failed to provide an answer. This caveat reflected the objections which had been made earlier in regard to *Anns* in England.

Ultimately, McHugh J stated that "Deane J's concept of proximity... is no longer seen as the unifying criterion of duties of care"[74] as "it is a category of indeterminate reference par excellence".[75]

Nonetheless, the proximity criterion remains material in determining the existence of a duty of care. In *Modbury Triangle* v *Anzil*,[76] Kirby J referred to the "failed notion of proximity" but also commented that: "As a measure of factors relevant to the degree of physical, circumstantial and causal closeness, proximity is the best notion yet devised by the law to delineate the relationship of 'neighbour'."

In *Sullivan v Moody*[77] the High Court of Australia categorically rejected the notion of proximity as a general criterion for the determination of a duty of care because it offered little practical guidance. The High Court also rejected the three stage approach adopted by Lord Bridge in the House

---

70 (1990) 2 AC 605, 618.
71 (1998) 192 CLR 330. Kirby J considered competing approaches and argued that the three stage approach in *Caparo*, while not perfect, was better than any of the others. This preference was reiterated in *Perre v Apand* (1999) 73 ALJR 1190 and was applied again in *Crimmins v Stevedoring Industry Finance Committee* (1999) 167 ALR 1.
72 C Phegan, "The Tort of Negligence into the New Millennium" (1999) 73 *Australian Law Journal* 885, 886, 891.
73 (1999) 198 CLR 180; B McDonald and J Swanton, "Foreseeability in Relation to Negligent Infliction of Nervous Shock" (1995) 69 *Australian Law Journal* 945.
74 (1999) 198 CLR 180, 210; similarly, in *Spence v Perry* (1990) ATR 81, Derrington J attempted to apply the test of causal proximity but the Full Court rejected the proximity criterion. The judge in question tried to hold the defendant liable for psychiatric illness suffered by a mother three years after the relevant accident.
75 (1999) 198 CLR 180, 210.
76 (2000) 205 CLR 254.
77 (2001) 207 CLR 562.

of Lords decision in *Caparo Industries plc v Dickman*[78] which involved the notions of fairness, justness and reasonableness and which the Court felt did not represent the law in Australia. The court stated that what was required was the development of principles capable of general application.

The High Court did acknowledge that "proximity" might still be relevant as a factor when considering areas of economic loss and psychiatric illness. Nevertheless, in the recent decisions of the High Court of Australia in both *Annetts v Australian Stations Pty Ltd*[79] and *Tame v Morgan*,[80] which will be discussed later in this piece,[81] the majority of the High Court of Australia stated that proximity was not a precondition for recovery in a psychiatric illness case. This was essentially a reiteration of what the Western Australian Supreme Court stated in *Annetts v Australian Stations Pty Ltd*[82] and what the New South Wales Court of Appeal stated in *Morgan v Tame*.[83] Spigelman CJ in *Tame* confirmed that the concept of proximity was no longer to be regarded as a unifying principle, however, it remained a material consideration in determining the existence of a duty of care.[84]

E. The Aftermath Principle

According to the aftermath principle, secondary victims who have viewed only the aftermath of a traumatic event rather than the traumatic event itself, are permitted to recover damages. In *Jaensch v Coffey*, Deane J expanded the previous definition of "aftermath" which referred only to the "events at the scene after an accident, including the extraction and treatment of the injured," noting that in a modern society, "the aftermath also extends to the ambulance taking the injured person to the hospital for treatment and to the hospital itself during the period of immediate post-accident treatment."[85]

This development of the notion of "aftermath" suggested that the closeness of the relationship between the primary victim and any secondary victims played a greater part than geographical proximity in determining whether a duty of care was owed and whether psychiatric injury was foreseeable.[86]

---

78 (1990) 2 AC 605.
79 (2002) 211 CLR 317.
80 (2002) 211 CLR 317.
81 (2000) NSWCA 121 <http://www.lawlink.nsw.gov.au> at 25 August 2000 (Copy on file with author). In another case, *AMP v RTA and Anor* (2001) NSWCA 186 (2 August 2001), the issue was whether an employer was liable to a deceased employee's widow for psychiatric illness suffered by her as a result of the employee's depression and suicide. The plaintiff was awarded $101,895 in damages for nervous shock. The defendant and insurer appealed. The appeal was allowed. On appeal, it was held that considerations of policy and value judgements indicated that deliberate self infliction of harm should generally be seen to break the causal link. Thus no duty was owed to the plaintiff to prevent her from suffering mental trauma. It was held that there was no causation as the injury was too remote in law.
82 (2000) 23 WAR 35.
83 (2000) 49 NSWLR 21. See also *Dandashli v Dandashli* (2000) NSWCA 273.
84 (2000) 49 NSWLR 21.
85 *Jaensch v Coffey* (1984) 155 CLR 549, 607.
86 P Handford, "When the Telephone Rings: Restating Negligent Liability for Psychiatric

While the question of whether a plaintiff who was merely told of an accident could recover damages was left open by Gibbs and Deane JJ, they commented that it is difficult to see why a rule based on public policy should preclude recovery for psychiatric injury sustained by a wife and mother who is so devastated by being told on the telephone that her husband and children have all been killed that she is unable to attend the scene while permitting recovery for the reasonably, but perhaps less readily foreseeable psychiatric injury sustained by a wife who attends at the scene or its aftermath at the hospital when a husband has suffered serious but not fatal injuries.[87]

However, the Court noted that there was no binding authority which compelled it on this issue, neither was there an existing legal principle which excluded reasonably foreseeable damage to a person who suffered nervous shock without being in sight or hearing of the relevant event. This caution has been reflected in post-*Jaensch* cases which have called on courts to consider the aftermath test in relation to the notion of proximity.

In the New South Wales Court of Appeal decision of *Campbelltown City Council v Mackay*,[88] Kirby P, as he then was, questioned the rule that liability in an action for nervous shock could only arise where shock arose from a sudden sensory perception. In his judgement, Kirby P considered that the law was predicated upon a scientific anachronism which had long since ceased to be scientifically justified, and commented: "It is artificial to imprison the legal cause of action for psychiatric injury in an outmoded scientific view about the nature of its origin."[89]

This gentle movement away from the requirement of a plaintiff's presence at the scene of an accident or its immediate aftermath was recognised by the South Australian court in *Pham v Lawson*.[90] In that case, the Court noted that this movement should be incremental and adaptive to current legal circumstances and that it should not be used as a yardstick by any means.

Nonetheless, in the New South Wales case of *Knight v Pederson and Ors*,[91] damages were recovered by the child of a parent killed by a negligent act, even though the child was out of sight and hearing when the parent was killed.

The question of recovery for claims for nervous shock occasioned by communication has since been left open by the High Court. In *Coates v Government Insurance Office of New South Wales*[92] Kirby P stated that it would be artificial to restrict recovery to a direct perception of the occurrence of

---

Illness: Tame v Morgan and Annetts v Australian Stations Pty Ltd" (2001) 23 *Sydney Law Review* 600.
87 (1983) 155 CLR 549, 551–552, 595–596.
88 (1989) 15 NSWLR 501.
89 (1989) 15 NSWLR 501, 503.
90 (1997) 68 SASR 124.
91 [1999] NSWCA 333.
92 (1995) 36 NSWLR 1 (*Coates*).

the tort, or to its immediate aftermath. In today's world, shock occasioned by the communication, by telephone or by oral message, of an event after it had taken place, should be seen as foreseeable and directly related to the wrong sued upon as if the vulnerable observer had received the shocking perception by his or her own eyes or ears. In this case, Kirby P again stated that the actual perception rule was a product of outmoded notions of psychology and psychiatry, which was used by the courts as the basis of a policy shield against expanding the liability of wrongdoers for the harm they cause.

F. Appellate Court Decisions After Jaensch

Since *Jaensch v Coffey*, claims have been allowed in situations where a plaintiff has merely heard about an accident involving loved ones.[93] For example, in *Petrie v Dowling*,[94] damages were recoverable for the plaintiff's shock and consequent illness, which arose after the receipt of distressing news.[95]

In *Sloss v New South Wales*,[96] the New South Wales Supreme Court allowed recovery to a mother who suffered "shock" as a result of hearing

---

[93] D Partlett, "Negligence—Limits of Liability for Nervous Shock Negligently Caused—Reasonable Foreseeability and Proximity as Criteria for Duty of Care" (1985) 59 *Australian Law Journal* 44.

[94] (1989) Aust Torts Rep 80–263. See also D Butler, "Identifying the Compensable Damage in 'Nervous Shock' Cases" (1997) 5 *Torts Law Journal* 67, where the author cites *Coates v Government Insurance Office of New South Wales* (1995) 36 NSWLR 1. In this case, Kirby P rejected the submission of the defendant that an individual who was not present at the scene or aftermath of an accident and was informed about the accident by telephone or a later message should not be entitled to recover. Kirby P opined that the relevant rule was in part a product of 19th century notions of psychology and psychiatry. "The suggested rule is hopelessly out of contact with the modern world of telecommunication. If any judge has doubts about this, he or she should wander around the city streets and see the large number of persons linked by mobile telephones to the world about them. Inevitably such telephones may bring, on occasion, shocking news, as immediate to the senses of the recipient as actual sight and sound of a catastrophe would be. This is the reality of the world in which the law of nervous shock must operate." Similar to this case is *Reeve v Brisbane City Council* (1995) 2 Qd R 661. Although it is acknowledged that not every novel claim succeeds, the law with regards to psychiatric illness is cautiously being assimilated into the law on injury generally, as stated in *Pham v Lawson* (1997) 68 SASR 124. D Butler, "Case Notes: *Pham v Lawson*: Widening the Sphere for Bystander Recovery for Nervous Shock" (1998) 6 *Torts Law Journal* 195.

[95] (1989) Australian Torts Reports 80–263. The Supreme Court of Queensland applied the obiter comments of Deane J in *Jaensch v Coffey* (1984) Aust Torts Rep 80–300. In *Quayle v State of New South Wales* (1995) Aust Torts Rep 81–367, the plaintiff suffered psychiatric trauma on receipt of the news that his wife had suffered irreversible brain damage whilst in an abortion operation. The plaintiff succeeded on the grounds of suffering shock and providing care for his wife thereafter. N J Mullany, "Recovery for Psychiatric Injury by Report: Another Small Step Forward" (1996) 4 *Tort Law Review* 96. In *Gifford v Strang Patrick Stevedoring Pty. Ltd.* [2001] NSWCA 175 (14 June 2001), a widow and her children failed in their claim for nervous shock pursuant to *Workers Compensation Act 1987* s151and *Law Reform (Miscellaneous Provisions) Act 1944* s4 because they could not sustain evidence of a demonstrable psychological condition resulting from learning about the father's death. Also see *Stergiou v Citibank* [1999] FCA 1321 (24 September 1999) and *Kavanagh v Akhtar* (1998).

[96] [1999] NSWSC 995, <http://www.lawlink.nsw.gov.au> at 6 October 1999 (Copy on file with author).

of the death of her son, who had been incarcerated. The defendant, the state of New South wales, did not contest that it owed a duty of care to the prisoner, but it refused to accept liability for the nervous shock suffered by the plaintiff mother. The judge found that the state's duty of care extended to all persons in sufficient emotional proximity to suffer nervous shock. However, this duty did not extend to recovery for economic loss which had resulted from an effect on the plaintiff's mental state so adverse that she was unable to run her business.[97]

Three other cases followed *Sloss* in the superior courts. In *State of New South Wales v Seedsman*,[98] a police officer in charge of investigating crimes against children suffered from post-traumatic stress disorder as a result of exposure to the nature and brutal reality of those crimes. No form of counselling or therapy was provided by the Police Service to alleviate any stress, anxiety or depression the officer may have had. The court allowed recovery for the negligent infliction of psychiatric illness.[99]

In *Tame v Morgan*,[100] the plaintiff suffered psychotic depression[101] upon learning that a police officer had made a report in which she was recorded as having been drinking when in fact she had not. The plaintiff succeeded in the District Court, receiving damages in the sum of $115,000. However, the decision was overturned in the New South Wales Court of Appeal, on the basis that it was not reasonably foreseeable that an individual in the plaintiff's position would have suffered the kind of injury complained of. The plaintiff had lost again.

Subsequently, in *Annetts*, having failed at first instance, Mr and Mrs Annetts took their case to the Western Australian Supreme Court of Appeal.[102] It was accepted in evidence that Mr and Mrs Annetts' son went missing from his place of employment and that shock was sustained by the boy's parents as a result of learning of their son's disappearance and eventual death.[103] The Court considered the problems confronting the law of psychiatric illness in this area and found that there was no binding

---

97 Y Muthu, "Sloss v State of New South Wales: Pathological Grief Disorder" (2000) 4 *Malaysian Journal of Law and Society* 169, 172.
98 [2000] NSWCA 119,<http://www.lawlink.nsw.gov.au> at 25 August 2000 (Copy on file with author). Previously in *Gillespie v Commonwealth* (1991) 104 ACTR 1, an employer was required to prepare an employee who was transferred from one embassy to another embassy in a foreign country to a less stressful post. In this case, the plaintiff suffered from post-traumatic stress disorder as result of being transferred to a foreign embassy, however, the employer had complied with the required formalities.
99 D Butler, "Voyages in Uncertain Seas with Dated Maps: Recent Developments in Liability for Psychiatric Injury in Australia" (2000) 9 *Torts Law Journal* 4.
100 (2000) 23 WAR 35.
101 The illness suffered by the plaintiff, designated psychotic depression, included paranoia and anxiety.
102 [2000] WASCA 357 <http://www.austlii.edu.au> at 22 August 2001; I Freckelton, "Compensability for Psychiatric Injury: An Opportunity for Modernisation and Reconceptualisation" (2001) 9 *Journal of Law and Medicine* 137.
103 [2000] WASCA 357, (21 November 2000) <http://www.austlii.edu.au> at 22 August 2001 (Copy on file with author).

Australian authority[104] supporting recovery for psychiatric damage caused solely by learning of a distressing event by telephone.[105]

The Court noted that whether any duty of care was owed by the defendant station owner to Mr and Mrs Annetts was a matter of fact, and commented that the finding of an existing duty of care was always more likely where the plaintiff was at the scene of a traumatic event and so perceived the injury to the loved one. Otherwise the existence of the duty of care became less likely as the criteria for its existence became more remote.[106] The chances of Mr and Mrs Annetts' case succeeding were not good.

The defendant cattle station knew that the plaintiffs' son was young, had had little experience as a jackaroo and that his parents were concerned about his safety and wellbeing. Strong concern for the young man's wellbeing had been communicated to the cattle station by the mother and assurances given by the servants or agents of the pastoral station as to his wellbeing. While they were not physically proximate to their son at the time of his disappearance and death, surely it was clearly foreseeable that the parents could suffer trauma possibly amounting to psychiatric injury if harm befell their son as a consequence of the defendant's negligence. As Lord Oliver commented in the English case of *Alcock v Chief Constable of South Yorkshire*,[107]

> The traumatic effect on a mother of the death of her child is as readily foreseeable in a case where the circumstances are described to her by an eye witness at the inquest as it is in a case where she learns of it at a hospital immediately after the event.[108]

Nonetheless, as suggested by its earlier comments, the Court finally took a traditional line, noting that: "The circumstances of the case show that the psychiatric injury claimed was not based upon a sudden sensory perception as the parents were not directly involved."[109]

Similarly, Ipp J held that:

---

104 at para [23] Ipp J stated, "On the basis of the direct perception requirement, the appellants have not established the requisite degree of proximity under either of the scenarios I have postulated. Apart from the occasion (in January 1987) when Mr Annetts saw a blood covered hat belonging to James, and when he identified James' remains (from a photograph seen some five months after his death), they did not directly perceive the consequences of the respondent's breach of duty. I do not consider the two instances I have mentioned as satisfying the requirement."
105 M Stauch, "Risk and Remoteness of Damage in Negligence" (2001) 64 *Modern Law Review* 191, 192. The court considered proximity in terms of time and space and concluded that learning about the death, which led to the shock sustained, was outside the temporal and geographical aftermath of the accident.
106 (2000) 23 WAR 35, 61.
107 (1992) 1 AC 310.
108 [2000] WASC 104 <http://www.asutlii.edu.au/cgi-bin/disp.pl/cases/wa/WASC> at 17 July 2001 (Copy on file with author) 13.
109 [2000] WASC 104 <http://www.asutlii.edu.au/cgi-bin/disp.pl/cases/wa/WASC> at 17 July 2001 (Copy on file with author) 13 6, 7.

On the basis of the direct perception requirement, the appellants have not established the requisite degree of proximity under either of the scenarios I have postulated. Apart from the occasion (in January 1987) when Mr Annetts saw a blood covered hat belonging to James, and when he identified James' remains (from a photograph seen some five months after his death), they did not directly perceive the consequences of the respondent's breach of duty. I do not consider the two instances I have mentioned as satisfying the requirement.[110]

It had been 18 years since the High Court of Australia last had the opportunity to examine the law pertaining to psychiatric illness in *Jaensch*. As Des Butler observes, the triumvirate of cases recently decided by the High Court—*Tame v New South Wales*; *Annetts v Australian Stations Pty Ltd* and *Gifford v Strang Patrick Stevedoring Pty Ltd* "provided the opportunity for the court to settle an area of common law which for long has been bristling with contentious issues and to provide guidance for lower courts which have for some time struggled to divine the law from ageing and imperfect High Court authorities."[111]

G. Annetts and Tame on Appeal to the High Court

The full court of the High Court heard the merits of *Annetts*[112] concurrently with the case of *Tame*,[113] on appeal from the New South Wales appellate court.[114] They had to consider, in *Annetts*, whether the defendant station owners owed James Annetts' parents a duty of care, and in *Tame*, whether a duty was owed by the defendant to a person involved in a motor vehicle accident who was wrongly named by the police as having a blood alcohol level three times the legal limit and who consequently suffered shock.

In determining whether there was duty in each case, the Court reflected on existing common law in relation to psychiatric injury. The common law required the presence of three factors in addition to the basic standard that psychiatric injury be a reasonably foreseeable result of the respondent's actions. These factors were:

(i) Normal fortitude: The foreseeability must be of psychiatric injury occurring in a person "of normal fortitude" rather than a person with a more fragile psyche.

   (ii) Presence of sudden shock: The psychiatric injury must have been caused by a sudden shock to the senses.
   (iii) Direct perception: The injured person must have perceived directly a distressing phenomenon or its aftermath.[115]

---

110 [2000] WASCA 357 (21 November 2000) <http://www.austlii.edu.au> at 22 August 2001 (Copy on file with author).
111 Butler, above n.5 (2004), p. 108, citing *Jaensch v Coffey* (1984) 155 CLR 549 and *Mount Isa Mines v Pusey* (1970) 125 CLR 383.
112 *Ibid* s 1.
113 *Ibid* s 1.
114 Both cases were heard on 4 and 5 December 2001 and judgement was handed down on 5 September 2002.
115 P Handford, above n 33, 610.

These tests, which firmly distinguish the common law surrounding psychiatric injuries from the looser standards which prevail for other forms of injury, have evolved on the basis of the fact that injury to the mind is not observable. As a result, there is a perceived danger of encouraging exaggerated or false claims. However, in the past these tests have proved to be inflexible and inappropriate in certain factual scenarios.

The judges in *Annetts* and *Tame* differed in their opinions and delivered separate judgements. However, the High Court effectively disposed of the requirements for "sudden shock" and "direct perception of a distressing phenomenon."[116] *Annetts* itself effectively showed that psychiatric injury could arise from anxiety or stress over a prolonged period as well as from a sudden event, and the majority of the court (Glesson CJ, Gaudron J, Gummow J, Kirby J and Hayne J) recognised this, arguing that the "sudden shock" mechanism should not be maintained as, "Cases of protracted suffering, as opposed to 'sudden shock', [could] raise difficult issues of causation and remoteness of damage. Difficulties of that kind are more appropriately analysed with reference to the principles of causation and remoteness, not through an absolute denial of liability."[117]

The court differed on whether the "normal fortitude" test should be preserved. The majority agreed that the test should be retained: a respondent could not be expected to foresee the consequences of his or her actions on a person, perhaps such as Mrs Tame, who was of less-than-normal psychological fortitude. Despite the divergence of opinion on whether or not the test should have been kept, a definition of the test was agreed upon. This definition stated that, once it had been proved that it was reasonably foreseeable that a person of normal fortitude would have suffered psychiatric illness in the relevant circumstances, the defendant would be held liable for the entire illness suffered by the plaintiff, even if the plaintiff had an "eggshell psyche".[118]

The majority also held that the injury suffered by the plaintiff must be a *recognisable* psychiatric disorder as defined in the DSM Manual, and as opposed to mere grief, sorrow or upset.[119]

The Annetts were granted leave to appeal. Assurances as to their son's welfare and supervision were relevant to the duty finding. The Court held that Australian Stations had breached its duty of care to Mr and Mrs Annetts by sending their 16 year old son, contrary to those assurances, out to work alone in an isolated area as a result of which he disappeared and subsequently died. The news that their son had disappeared, the uncertainty about his fate, and the eventual news of his death, caused them to suffer shock. The rationale behind this decision was that a person

---

116 *Jaensch v Coffey* (1984) 155 CLR 549, 567, per Brennan J.
117 (2002) 211 CLR 317, 389 [211].
118 (2002) 211 CLR 317, 430 [335].
119 (2002) 211 CLR 317, 388 [208].

of normal disposition would have suffered the kind of illness complained of by Mr and Mrs Annetts.[120] By contrast, the appeal in *Tame* was not allowed. The case arose from an error in a drink-driving record, which mistake was promptly rectified. However Mrs Tame considered that her reputation had been harmed and suffered psychiatric injury due to this mix up. The Court held that it could not have been within the relevant police officer's reasonable contemplation that Mrs Tame would suffer psychiatric illness as a result of the error that he made. Thus he owed her no duty of care inasmuch as Mrs Tame was specifically susceptible to the illness from which she suffered and that special susceptibility was not reasonably foreseeable. Gleeson CJ was of the view in *Tame* that any foreseeability of harm had to be reasonable, while other judges reiterated that for the purposes of cohesion in the law it could hardly impose a duty on a police officer to the subject of an investigation not to cause a person such as Mrs Tame stress in the proper pursuit of that investigation.[121]

H. The Consolidation with Gifford v Strang

The final case in the "new landscape for recovery for psychiatric injury in Australia"[122] is *Gifford v Strang Patrick Stevedoring Pty Ltd*.[123] Here the High Court ruled that an employer owes a duty of care to avoid psychiatric injury to the children of its employees. Finally we witness the demise of a rule identified some years ago by Professor Peter Cane as unacceptable: that of proving closeness of relationship. The relevant New South Wales law had already sought to remove the need for a family member to prove closeness of relationship with the relevant family member: it had been intended as "a beneficial provision expanding the ability of close family members to recover for nervous shock."[124] The deficiencies in the common law position were recognised with that statutory provision.[125] Thus it was no longer necessary to "prove" the closeness and affection of the relationship, and the High Court demonstrated an understanding of parental emotions in resolving that children-parent is a "relationship of natural love and affection."[126] It will still be necessary to consider whether a duty is owed to the person suffering psychiatric injury pursuant to the DSM diagnosis of mental disorder, supported by psychiatric testimony, but following *Annetts*, sudden shock and direct perception of the incident are no longer required.

---

120 P Hunt, "Liability for Psychiatric Injury Extended" (2002) 40 *Law Society Journal* 62, 65.
121 Butler, above n 5, 110.
122 Butler, above n 5.
123 [2003] HCA 33.
124 Butler, op. cit. (2004) 113.
125 Ibid, citing *Chester v Waverley Corporation* (1939) 62 CLR 1 and *Bourhill v Young* (1943) AC 92.
126 (2003) 198 ALR 100, 104.

Legislative Approaches

The commendable decision of the High Court in the case of *Annetts* finally brought the law of nervous shock into closer alignment with that governing claims brought over physical injury, while simultaneously placing nervous shock law on a footing more firmly based upon modern scientific knowledge. The next part of this paper discusses whether and to what extent this expansion of psychiatric illness law has been curtailed by Australian legislatures. It also discusses the approaches taken by other jurisdictions across the common law world, as well as briefly canvassing public policy considerations affecting and likely to affect the development of psychiatric illness law up to this point and into the future.

The key contention of this paper is that *Annetts* forced an overdue confrontation as to the failure of medical knowledge to inform the law in this area, as well as the need for increased communication between the disciplines of science and law. The paper concludes by arguing that, despite recent expansions of liability for nervous shock, the law has thus far failed to adequately protect the emotional rather than the physical investments of plaintiffs which, when jeopardised by the injury of a loved one, result in nervous shock. It further argues that, given recent policy concerns about compensation and insurance crises and the increase in litigation, whether the progress so far evident in the High Court's grant of leave to appeal to the plaintiffs in *Annetts* and in the *Civil Liability Act* and *Civil Liability Amendment (Personal Responsibility) Act* of 2002, is likely to change this in practice, has yet to be seen.

In 2002 changes[127] were made to the law by the New South Wales Parliament in the *Civil Liability Act*. Several significant measures to discourage actions for minor injuries were introduced.[128] The most notable included the limitation of the award of damages for legal costs,[129] a threshold for general damages, set at 15 per cent of the

---

[127] On 2 October 2002, the Federal Assistant Treasurer Senator Helen Coonan released the final report of the Review of the Law of Negligence (the *Review*). The report was authored by a panel chaired by the Honourable Justice David Ipp of the New South Wales Supreme Court and also comprising Professor Peter Cane, Associate Professor Donald Sheldon and Mr Ian Macintosh. The panel was asked to inquire into the law of negligence and to develop a series of proposals to provide a principled approach to reforming the law of negligence. The basis for these far-sighted reforms was recommendations contained in the Review of the Law of Negligence authored by another panel, similarly chaired by Justice Ipp. The Review was commissioned to provide a principled evaluation of the existing law as a blueprint to assist governments to achieve comprehensive reforms. The panel appointed to undertake the Review sought to strike a balance between the interests of injured people and those of the community at large and to impose a reasonable burden of responsibility on individuals to take care of others and to take care of themselves. The panel made 61 recommendations on specific changes that could be made to the law of negligence.

[128] Spigelman C J, "Negligence: The Last Outpost of the Welfare State" (paper presented at the Judicial Conference of Australia Colloquium, Launceston, 27 April 2002) http://www.agd.nsw.gov.au at 10 Sep 2002 (copy on file with author).

[129] E.g. no order for legal costs should be made where the award of damages is less than $30,000. Where the award is between $30,000 and $50,000, the plaintiff may recover no more than $2,500 in legal costs.

most extreme case,[130] and a $350,000 cap on general damages.[131]

The New South Wales Parliament has since introduced the *Civil Liability Amendment (Personal Responsibility) Act 2002*. This Act significantly extends the provisions of the *Civil Liability Act* and attempts to enforce the responsibility of individuals for their actions. Many of the provisions of this later Act are likely to have far-reaching consequences. The more significant provisions are the new sections 5B and 5C which are concerned with duty of care and sections 5D and 5E which cover the meaning of reasonable foreseeability and causation. Sections 16 and 17 address pain and suffering for non-economic loss. Most relevant to this paper are sections 27 and 30, which deal with mental harm.[132]

According to the *Civil Liability Amendment (Personal Responsibility) Act*, damages for psychiatric illness are limited to persons who are victims of, or present at the scene of, an accident.[133] Those persons who can recover include family members who have demonstrated a recognisable form of psychiatric disorder as opposed to mere grief, sorrow or being upset. "Family members" comprise those individuals listed within that category in the *Law Reform (Miscellaneous Provisions) Act 1944* (NSW) and include the parents, spouse (or de facto), siblings or children of a victim.

Damages may also be recovered by any individual not related to the primary victim, who has suffered a recognisable form of psychiatric disorder extending beyond a normal emotional or cultural grief reaction after witnessing a traumatic event.[134]

No recovery will be permitted where damages are otherwise restricted by the Act "or any other written or unwritten law."[135]

These legislative provisions confirm the majority decision of the High Court in *Annetts* and *Tame* which insisted that a defendant is liable for a plaintiff's psychiatric injury if the defendant ought to have foreseen that a person of normal fortitude might suffer psychiatric injury if reasonable care was not taken by them.[136] They also confirm the High Court requirement, laid out in *Annetts* and *Tame*, that the plaintiff suffer a recognisable form of psychiatric illness.[137] While this codification of the law regarding recovery for psychiatric illness is a step forward in some ways, some argue that to "move away from the flexibility of the common law position and categorically define who may claim, as the legislation does, is regrettable."[138]

---

130 *Civil Liability Act 2002*, s16(1).
131 *Civil Liability Act 2002*, s16(2).
132 <http://www.lawlink.nsw.gov.au/report/lpd_reports.nsf/pages/civil_bill_2002> at 20 November 2002 (copy on file with author). The limitation is listed on page 22 of the Report: the victim, a bystander or a close relative may recover.
133 *Civil Liability (Personal Responsibility) Act 2002*, s30.
134 *Civil Liability (Personal Responsibility) Act 2002*, s30(2)(a).
135 *Civil Liability (Personal Responsibility) Act 2002*, s30(4).
136 *Civil Liability (Personal Responsibility) Act 2002*, s32(1).
137 *Civil Liability (Personal Responsibility) Act 2002*, s31.
138 (Dyanah) Seeto, "Shock Rebounds: Tort Reform and Negligently Inflicted Psychiatric

International Perspectives on Nervous Shock Law, Proximity and the Aftermath Principle

A. England

In 1983, the year before the Australian decision in *Jaensch v Coffey*, the judgement in the case frequently known as its English twin—McLoughlin v O'Brian[139]—was handed down. At this time, Australian courts had made up for their previous sluggishness in expanding liability in nervous shock cases, and the approaches to these cases were substantially in harmony in the two jurisdictions. Since that time, however, the Australian courts have outstripped the English in their recognition of liability for nervous shock cases. Faced with a number of cases resulting from mass disasters like the Hillsborough tragedy,[140] the English judiciary has stoically been holding the line against any further expansion of liability for nervous shock.

While encouragingly considering the closeness of relationships outside those between spouses and parents and children, in the House of Lords case of *Alcock v Chief Constable of South Yorkshire Police*,[141] their Lordships refused to countenance recovery by anyone who had learnt of the disaster by any means other than direct perception of the event, or the aftermath within two hours of the event taking place, with their unaided senses.[142]

In *White v Chief Constable of South Yorkshire*,[143] the plaintiffs—secondary victims of the Hillsborough tragedy—were a number of police officers. In this case, Lord Goff established a number of important criteria for determining whether an entitlement to damages for psychiatric illness existed. These criteria were:

(i) The plaintiff must have close ties with the victim;
(ii) The plaintiff must have been present at the accident or at its immediate aftermath; and
(iii) The psychiatric injury must have been caused by direct perception of the accident or its immediate aftermath and not upon hearing about it from someone else.[144]

Lord Hoffman qualified this summary but cautioned that it should not be viewed as an exhaustive list.[145] Finally, the majority held that rescuers were owed no duty unless they had been within the area of physical danger—the police officers' claim was denied, and the law had narrowed again.

Injury" (2004) 26 *Sydney Law Review* 293, 300.
139 (1983) 1 AC 410.
140 The "Hillsborough tragedy" was the death by crushing of 95 people in 1989 and the injury of several hundred at the FA Cup semi-final held in Hillsborough. The tragedy resulted from a decision by the police to open up a barrier to speed admission to the semi-final.
141 (1992) 1 AC 310.
142 (1992) 1 AC 310.
143 (1999) 2 AC 455, 472, discussed in (2000) 23 WAR 35, 56.
144 (2000) 23 WAR 35, 36.
145 (1999) 1 All ER 1.

In its 1995 *Consultation Paper on Liability for Psychiatric Illness*, the Law Commission reviewed the current English law on psychiatric injury.[146] In that paper, the Commission identified the key criteria which the court will apply, specifically:

(i) The plaintiff must suffer a recognised psychiatric illness such as post-traumatic stress disorder or pathological grief disorder. As in Australia, mental distress alone is insufficient: *Hicks v Chief Constable of the South Yorkshire Police*.[147]

(ii) Where the plaintiff is a secondary victim, the psychiatric illness must be shock induced (*Sion v Hampstead Health Authority*[148]) and the result of the direct perception of an event or its immediate aftermath;

(iii) The plaintiff must also be able to prove a sufficient degree of physical and emotional proximity.[149]

There are poignant reminders in *Annetts* of the "seriously doubted" first instance decisions of the English courts in *Hevican v Ruane*[150] and *Ravenscroft v Rederiaktiebolaget Transatlantic*.[151] Those decisions allowed recovery by the suffering yet "distant" families (one son had been working far away on an oil-rig in the North Sea). Both cases were overturned on appeal. Whereas, by way of contrast, the somewhat similar case of *Annetts* (which involved an Australian version of vulnerable young men at work in relevantly remote situations) failed before the two lower courts, with the Full Court of the Supreme Court of Western Australia particularly restrictive in upholding the decision of the trial judge.[152] Yet this case has now contributed on appeal to the High Court to an emerging landscape of psychiatric injury.

For the moment, however, the English common law in regard to nervous shock has "all the hallmarks of a legal system learning from experience and trying to adjust to the changing demands of a more litigious society. Courts are in fact making it up as they go along."[153]

B. South Africa

Pertinent to the subject matter of this piece is the South African decision of *Barnard v Santam Bpk*.[154] In this case, a 13 year old boy was killed in a bus accident; the appellant mother suffered psychiatric injury upon being informed by her husband (who had himself received the information over the telephone) of the death of her son. Deputy Chief Justice Van Heerden cited the comments of Kirby J in *Coates* in a judgement which rejected the

---

146 English Law Commission, London, *Consultation Paper on Liability for Psychiatric Illness* No 137, 1995.
147 (1992) 2 All ER 65. This case involved a claim for damages which arose from the Hillsborough disaster.
148 Unreported, 27 May 1994.
149 L Dombek and A Fisher, above n 11, 6–7.
150 (1991) 3 All ER 65.
151 (1991) 3 All ER 73.
152 Butler, above n 5, 111.
153 L Dombek and A Fisher, above n 11, 6–7.
154 (1999) 1 SA 202.

notion that all hearsay victims of psychiatric illness should be excluded from seeking damages. It was further held that notions of reasonableness and fairness did not preclude the court from finding that the respondent's negligence was the legal cause of the appellant's shock. The remaining four members of the court concurred.

This decision provides "Confirmation that negligence law can provide redress against some forms of carelessly communicated bad news."[155] The decision relied heavily on Australian authorities and was consistent with developments in the rest of the common law world. Nonetheless, the decision was downplayed by Ipp J in *Annetts* on the grounds that South African civil law was based on the law of delict, rather than tort, and was limited only by causation and public policy— proximity had no role.[156]

C. Canada

Canada has generally also taken a cautious approach to the expansion of liability for nervous shock. An example of this cautious approach is the 1999 decision of the British Colombia Court of Appeal in *Devji v District of Burnaby*,[157] in which the Court had regard to a duty of care that required "not merely foreseeability but also proximity and something more".[158] In this case the Court was not able to conclude that the psychiatric injury suffered by the plaintiff parents was reasonably foreseeable when they attended a hospital to identify the body of their daughter. The Court refused to expand the aftermath principle beyond its previous limits, or to contemplate the award of damages where direct perception was lacking, emphasising the need to maintain existing limits on liability in such cases.

D. Ireland

It was an Irish judge who first repudiated the old rule of non-recovery for nervous shock.[159] In keeping with this avant garde individual, later judgements in Ireland have shown a similar recognition of the need to develop the law in this area.

Generally speaking, the Irish judiciary has taken a more rational approach to the aftermath principle than England's.[160] They have granted recovery to a "hearsay" victim,[161] and recognised that employers owe their employees a duty to protect them from psychiatric injury.[162]

---

155 Graeme Orr, "Book Review of Barbara Hocking, *Liability for Negligent Words*" (2001) 16 *Professional Negligence* 1, 60.
156 (2000) 23 WAR 35, 60.
157 (1999) BCCA 599.
158 (1999) BCCA 599, (2003) 23 WAR 60, para 67.
159 *Bell v Great Northern Railway Co of Ireland* (1890) 26 LR Ir 428.
160 *Mullally v Bus Eireann* (1992) ILRM 722.
161 *Kelly v Hennessy* (1995) 3 IR 253. In this case recovery was permitted to a mother who was informed by telephone of an accident involving her children. The mother had later attended the hospital.
162 *Curran v Cadbury (Ireland) Ltd* (2000) 2 ILRM 343. The duty of employers to avoid psychiatric harm to employees had been denied by the House of Lords in *White*.

E. New Zealand

Also pertinent to the subject matter of this paper is the dissenting judgement of Thomas J in the recent New Zealand Court of Appeal case of *Van Soest v Residual Health Management Unit*.[163] While the majority held that reasonable foreseeability was insufficient to establish liability where other proximity requirements were absent, Thomas J was in favour of adopting reasonable foreseeability as the sole test of liability for psychiatric injury and abandoning the rules involving geographical, temporal and relational proximity.

Public Policy Considerations

In his decision in *Chester v Waverley Municipal Council*,[164] Rich J noted that "The law must fix a point where its remedies stop short of complete reparation for the world at large, which might appear just to a logician who neglected all social consequences which ought to be weighed on the other side."[165]

This "point" is the great bone of contention for judges in nervous shock cases, who are torn between the utopian ideal of fully compensating plaintiffs for their injuries and the reality of a world in which the "consequences of such lack of restraint for the rest of the community" would be dire.[166] The tension these conflicting pressures create is borne out by the numerous ideas which have come into and gone out of fashion with judges in an attempt to resolve the dilemma that they have created.

Past policy considerations which were employed to limit liability in nervous shock cases have been, and continue to be, debunked. Notions such as the lesser severity of psychiatric injury by comparison with physical injury, the fear of fraudulent claims, concern about "compensationitis", a wider class of people as potential claimants, and concerns about placing disproportionate burdens on defendants—have all been cited in the past in attempts to hold the line against a rising tide of nervous shock claims.[167]

---

163 (2000) 1 NZLR 179.
164 (1939) 62 CLR 1, 11.
165 (1939) 62 CLR 1,11. Cited in D Ipp, "Negligence—Where Does the Future Lie?" a paper given in January 2003 at the Supreme Court and Federal Court Judges" Conference. (Copy on file with author).
166 In *Chester* Rich J commented: "The attempt on the part of the appellant to extend the law of tort to cover this hitherto unknown cause of action has, perhaps, been encouraged by the tendencies plainly discernible in the development which the law of tort has undergone in its process towards its present amorphous condition. For the so-called development seems to consist in a departure from the settled standards for the purpose of giving to plaintiffs causes of action unbelievable to a previous generation of lawyers. Defendants appear to have fallen completely out of favour." *Chester v Waverley* Corporation (1939) 62 CLR 1, 11.
167 These policy considerations have been refuted (respectively) as follows: as mental attitude becomes more important, the seriousness of psychiatric injury similarly gains in importance: see H Teff, "Psychiatric Injury in the Course of Policing: a Special Case?" (1997) 5 *Tort Law Review* 184; H Teff, "The Hillsborough Football Disaster and Claims for 'Nervous Shock'" (1992) 32 *Medicine, Science and Law* 251; H Teff, "The Requirement of 'Sudden Shock' in Liability for Negligently Inflicted Psychiatric Damage" (1996) 4 *Tort Law*

Increasingly, these and similar notions are refuted or recognised as being without foundation, and so are being left to the past.

Justice Kirby has sought on many occasions to elevate the approach in *Caparo* which allows for policy articulations to come to the forefront of negligence reasoning in the High Court, but recently accepted that his view had not gained currency. Nor has the High Court been "plaintiff friendly" during the extensive statutory reform period that has followed the Ipp Report in 2002. In fact, just as some argued that the pendulum of judicial opinion had swung far too strongly in favour of the plaintiff,[168] so others argued that recent cases have simply been "continuing a trend that has been apparent since the end of 1999 [and] ... distinctly favoured defendants."[169] Indeed, Professor Luntz wrote of this trend in both 2001[170] and 2003,[171] and then again in 2004.[172]

The *Civil Liability Act* 2002 (discussed earlier in this piece, and accompanying concerns about a "compensation crisis" and increasing litigation within Australia), while not dealing specifically with nervous shock law, will presumably have an effect on the mentality of the judiciary in nervous shock cases. It has only limped from its narrow boundaries since the 1939 decision in *Chester v Waverley Council* where only Justice Evatt was capable of understanding that a reasonable mother in the shoes of that grieving mother would suffer shock. For those States where the Ipp recommendations have been adopted or considered, it is worth noting

---

Review 44; H Teff, "Tort Liability for Psychiatric Damage: The Law of 'Nervous Shock'" (1994) 10 *Professional Negligence* 108. While concerns about fraudulent claims for psychiatric illness are difficult for the layman (including the judiciary) to debunk, it has been argued that a psychiatrist will be just as likely to pick up a fraudulent psychiatric illness claim as a physician would be to pick up a claim for damages for a fraudulent back injury (English Law Commission, above n 150). Concerns about compensation have been the main concern (Lord Steyn). However, the Law Commission points out that claims for damages for physical injury are just as likely to produce compensationitis, if not more likely, as sufferers of psychiatric conditions are more likely to be dissuaded from bringing actions because of the stigma associated with their conditions, the prospect of psychological assessment and the condition itself (Teff). Teff also dismisses concerns about the "wider class of claimants", arguing that psychiatric illness from accidents to other people is not that common, and less so where involvement is only with the aftermath or through the communication of a third party. In addition, the "wider class of claimants" concern suggests that those suffering psychiatric illness are not as worthy of protection as those suffering physical injury. It has been noted that "we would not refuse compensation for physical injuries just because the train was full." See H Teff, "Involuntary Participation and Survivor's Guilt" (1998) 6 *Tort Law Review* 190; H Teff, "Liability for Negligently Inflicted Nervous Shock" (1983) 99 *Law Quarterly Review* 100; H Teff, "Liability For Negligently Inflicted Psychiatric Harm: Justifications And Boundaries" (1998) 57 *Cambridge Law Journal* 91.

168   Ipp's opinion is unsurprisingly in line with the report of the panel which undertook the Review of the Law of Negligence—which he chaired—and which lead to the introduction of the *Civil Liability Act* (*NSW*) 2002.
169   Harold Luntz, "Editorial Comment: Round-up of Cases in the High Court of Australia in 2003" (2004) 12 *Torts Law Journal* 1, 1.
170   Harold Luntz, "Torts Turnaround Downunder" (2001) 1 *Oxford University Commonwealth Law Journal* 95
171   Harold Luntz, "Turning Points in the Law of Torts in the Last 30 Years" (2003) 15 ILJ 1, 22.
172   Luntz, above n 169.

this observation by Boyd: "It is arguable that s75AE of the TPA [*Trade Practices Act 1974 (Cth)*] is wider in scope than the Ipp Report's proposed doctrine of mental harm as contained in Recommendations 33, 34 and 35 ... However, it may be a reason for a plaintiff suffering from mental harm to commence proceedings under the TPA as opposed to negligence."[173]

Conclusion

A range of events is said to have prompted recent statutory attempts to roll back what some perceive to be the "juggernaut" of negligence in Australia, including the decision of the High Court of Australia in *Annetts*. A more widely suggested cause is the world-wide collapse in the insurance industry. Whatever the cause, the result was a New South Wales Parliamentary review of the law pertaining to compensation and the introduction of changes to physical and psychological injury law in the shape of the *Civil Liability Act 2002* (NSW) and the *Civil Liability Amendment (Personal Responsibility) Act 2002* (NSW).

The consequences of the *Civil Liability Act* and the *Civil Liability Amendment (Personal Responsibility) Act* and *Annetts* on the law of nervous shock in Australia are likely to be far-reaching, but whether in practice they result in an expansion of liability for nervous shock remains to be seen.

An examination of other common law jurisdictions around the world indicates that Australia is at the vanguard of the incremental expansion of liability for nervous shock. First instance and supreme court appeal decisions in *Annetts* were more in keeping with restrictive English nervous shock law than the recent radical legislative changes in New South Wales and other states in Australia. However, increasing refutation of many of the traditional policy reasons for limiting recovery bodes well for the Annetts' last chance to recover in the High Court of Australia, as does that Court's decision in granting the Annetts leave to appeal, and the subsequent codification of the rules laid out in that case in the *Civil Liability Acts* of 2002. It is only to be hoped that the recent concerns about compensation and insurance crises and increasing litigation will not act as a brake on the necessary continued expansion of liability in this area of the law.

---

[173] Guy Boyd, "Personal Injuries Law Reform: An Unintended Effect on Product Liability Claims?" (2003) II *Torts Law Journal* 262, 277. Section 75 AE of the *Trade Practices Act 1974* (Cth) deals with liability for defective goods causing injuries where loss is sustained by a person other than the injured individual.

THE TRIALS OF TENOFOVIR:
Mediating the Ethics of Third World Research

Peter J. Hammer & Tammy Sue Lundstrom*

In 2004, Phnom Penh was on the front lines of debates over HIV research. Press coverage pitted the demands of a tenacious union of sex workers against the good intentions of international researchers funded, in part, by the Bill and Melinda Gates Foundation. The headlines reveal part of the story: "Key AIDS Study in Cambodia Now in Jeopardy."[1] "Cambodia Stops Important Tenofovir Prevention Trial."[2] "Hun Sen: Don't Test Drugs on Cambodians."[3] "Cambodian Leader Throws Novel Prevention Trial into Limbo."[4] The drug at issue was tenofovir, a newer anti-retroviral commonly used to treat HIV infection. The research question was whether the drug could be used as an effective pre-exposure prophylaxis in high risk groups, such as commercial sex workers. The stakes are undeniably high. With a vaccine against HIV/AIDS still decades away,[5] attention must focus on intermediate strategies to slow the transmission of the disease, including pre-exposure prophylaxis.[6] Literally, tens of millions of lives hang in the balance.

---

* Peter Hammer, J.D., Ph.D., is a Professor of Law at Wayne State University Law School. Tammy Lundstrom, J.D., M.D., is Vice President, Chief Quality and Safety Officer, Detroit Medical Center, and Assistant Professor, Department of Medicine, Division of Infectious Diseases, Wayne State University. Professor Hammer has spent more than a decade working on Cambodian law and development matters. Doctor Lundstrom has spent a good part of her career treating poor and medically underserved HIV/AIDS patients in the Detroit community.

1 Marilyn Chase & Gautam Naik, *Key AIDS Study in Cambodia Now in Jeopardy*, WALL ST. J., Aug. 12, 2004, at B1.
2 John S. James, *Cambodia Stops Important Tenofovir Prevention Trial*, AIDS TREATMENT NEWS, July 23, 2004, at 4.
3 Corinne Purtill & Yun Samean, *Hun Sen: Don't Test Drugs on Cambodians*, CAMBODIA DAILY, Aug. 4, 2004, at 1.
4 Jon Cohen, *Cambodian Leader Throws Novel Prevention Trial into Limbo*, 305 SCIENCE 1092 (2004).
5 The World Health Organization (WHO) notes that although "more than 30 candidate HIV vaccines" are in the pipeline, none is expected to be available for use in the immediate future. WORLD HEALTH ORG. [WHO], THE WORLD HEALTH REPORT 2004: CHANGING HISTORY, at xvi (2004) [hereinafter WHO, WORLD HEALTH REPORT], *available at* http://www.who.int/whr/2004/en/report04_en.pdf.
6 For a discussion of the importance of intermediate preventative measure, see Project Inform, *The World's Most Important AIDS Research?*, PROJECT INFORM PERSP., Nov. 2004, http://www.thebody.com/pinf/nov04/research.html.

While the imperative for action is strong, so is the demand that medical research be undertaken in an ethical manner. The ethical problems raised by human experiments are complicated. They become even more complicated when the research subjects are vulnerable populations in an already resource-poor developing country. Exploitation is an ever-present risk. Safeguards must be in place to prevent the exportation of research to the Third World that would not meet basic ethical standards. This was not the problem in Cambodia. Instead, the Cambodian story illustrates the growing inability of First World medical ethics to address the demands of international research. The unfortunate result was that a well intentioned and well designed research proposal reached an impasse that led to its cancellation. How did two groups that should be allies in the battle against HIV/AIDS—sex workers and medical researchers—become pitted against each other as adversaries? It is important to understand what went wrong in Cambodia so similar problems can be avoided in the future.

This article proposes mediation as a framework to address the social and ethical tensions associated with Third World medical research. Section I examines the science behind the tenofovir trials, explaining the rationale for the study design and the logic for focusing on high risk populations. Section II details the social and political trials of tenofovir, looking at the conflicts culminating in the study's cancellation. Section III explores how the scientific and social concerns might be better mediated in light of emerging ethical principles guiding international research.

I The HIV/AIDS Crisis and the Science Underlying the Tenofovir Trials

A. The HIV Crisis and the Importance of Prevention

In discussing HIV/AIDS, a sense of urgency is unavoidable. As the World Health Organization (WHO) declares, "[t]ackling HIV/AIDS is the world's most urgent public health challenge."[7] HIV/AIDS is responsible for more than 20 million deaths in the last quarter century,[8] with five million new infections in 2003 alone.[9] "HIV/AIDS is now the leading cause of death and lost years of productive life for adults aged 15–59 years worldwide."[10] While each new HIV infection is a tragedy for an individual and a family, the ravages of the virus go beyond its effects on personal health. "In many countries, the cumulative effects of the epidemic will have catastrophic consequences for long-term economic growth and seriously damage the prospects for poverty reduction."[11] In addition, HIV infection promotes the spread of other communicable diseases, such as tuberculosis, to the

---

7 WHO, WORLD HEALTH REPORT, *supra* note 5, at xi.
8 *Id.*
9 *Id.*
10 *Id.*
11 *Id.* at 9.

population as a whole. This places great stress on public health systems that are already overwhelmed and underfunded.

One-fifth of the 34–46 million people living with HIV/AIDS worldwide are in Asia.[12] In Cambodia, estimates are that more than 1% of the adult population is infected with the virus that causes AIDS.[13] These figures highlight the need for thoughtful, creative and immediate action to diminish the spread of the virus. Appropriate interventions can make a difference, as the WHO reports. "Together, prevention, treatment and long-term care and support can reverse the seemingly inexorable progress of the HIV/AIDS epidemic, offering the worst-affected countries and populations their best hope of survival."[14] Cambodia has made important progress in implementing a number of HIV prevention measures among sex workers. "In response to these programs, condom use between sex workers and clients rose to more than 90% and the number of men visiting sex workers was halved."[15] It is estimated that these efforts have reduced HIV prevalence in the general population from predictions of 10–15% down to current projections as low as of 2–3%.[16] HIV prevalence among female sex workers is much higher, but even these numbers have been substantially reduced. A 1998 sentinel surveillance study found an HIV prevalence rate in sex workers of 42.6%, falling to 28.8% by 2002.[17]

Prevention is important, but there are serious limitations to traditional "safer sex" approaches. In many cases, as Sheila Davey found, "sex workers are unable to insist on condom use, especially if they are young, victims of trafficking, or migrants."[18] In addition to encouraging condom use, prevention alternatives that empower women and bypass male involvement must also be developed. Approaches that can be controlled by the female partner, such as microbicides, or "anti-infective gels, creams, impregnated sponges and similar devices that women apply before sexual intercourse to prevent HIV transmission"[19] are particularly important. According to the WHO:

> Epidemiological modeling based on the data from over 70 low-income countries suggests that even a partially effective microbicide is likely to have a significant impact on the epidemic: a product that is only 60% effective in protecting against HIV could avert 2.5 million new infections over a three-year period, even if it is used in only 50% of sex acts not protected by condoms, and assuming it is used by only 20% of people easily reached by existing health services.[20]

---

12 *Id.* at xv.
13 *Id.* at 3.
14 *Id.* at xv.
15 *Id.* at 13.
16 *Id.* at 12. *See also* Jon Cohen, *Thailand & Cambodia: Two Hard Hit Countries Offer Rare Success Stories,* 301 SCIENCE 1658 (2003).
17 Cohen, *supra* note 16, at 1659.
18 Sheila Davey, *Sex and Drugs Fuel Simmering AIDS Crisis in Asia and Pacific,* 79 BULL. WORLD HEALTH ORG. 1000 (2001).
19 WHO, WORLD HEALTH REPORT, *supra* note 5, at 77.
20 *Id.*

Unfortunately, the use of microbicides is not without its own problems. Because waiting time is necessary between insertion and intercourse, they could cause irritation with frequent use, which may actually increase the probability of HIV transmission per sex act. Moreover, like vaccines, microbial agents are themselves still in clinical trials.

B. Tenofovir as an HIV Prophylaxis

Other preventative strategies can give women greater control over their risk exposure. Anti-retroviral drugs are known to be effective in controlling HIV for persons already infected. Is it possible that antiviral treatment could reduce the risk of HIV transmission if taken before exposure to the virus as a form of prophylaxis? This is where the tenofovir story begins. Tenofovir is a long acting anti-retroviral drug of the reverse transcriptase inhibitor class that can be given once daily, with fewer side effects than many older agents. In a landmark study, scientists discovered that tenofovir given shortly after exposing monkeys to SIV, a simian virus similar to HIV, could prevent the monkeys from becoming infected.[21] This finding supported the theory that tenofovir could be used as a post-exposure prophylaxis for humans, and possibly as pre-exposure prophylaxis in high risk HIV-negative populations in order to prevent infection.

Substantial experience already exists with anti-retrovirals as post-exposure prophylaxis. In previous studies, the Centers for Disease Control and Prevention (CDC) determined that an older drug zidovudine (AZT) could reduce by 79% the risk of health care worker seroconversion after an occupational exposure to HIV, such as a needlestick.[22] Subsequently, the CDC recommended that health care workers sustaining exposures should receive prophylaxis with anti-retrovirals. The CDC monitors health care workers undergoing post-exposure prophylaxis. Although minor side effects such as nausea and fatigue are common, serious or lethal side effects are not.[23] The regimens in the CDC study included anti-retroviral cocktails of multiple classes of drugs, [24] increasing the potential for side effects above that of a single drug such as tenofovir. Moreover, with regard to potential side effects, tenofovir's safety profile is significantly more favorable than many of its treatment predecessors. Listed side effects for tenofovir include "nausea, vomiting, diarrhea, headache, asthenia, flatulence, and renal

---

21 Roberta J. Black, *Animal Studies of Prophylaxis*, AM. J. MED., May 19, 1997, at 39. *See also* Che-Chung Tsai et al., *Effectiveness of Postinoculaiton (R)-9-(2-Phosphonylmethoxypropyl) Adenine Treatment for Prevention of Persistent Simian Immunodeficiency Virus Infection Depends Critically on Timing of Initiation and Duration of Treatment*, 72 J. VIROLOGY 4265 (1998).
22 Denise Cardo et al., *A Case-Control Study of HIV Seroconversion in Health Care Workers After Percutaneous Exposure*, 337 NEW ENG. J. MED. 1485 (1997).
23 Ctrs. for Disease Control & Prevention, U.S. Dep't of Health & Human Servs., *Antiretroviral Postexposure Prophylaxis After Sexual, Injection-Drug Use, or Other Nonoccupaitonal Exposure to HIV in the United States: Recommendations from the U.S. Department of Health and Human Services*, 54 MORBIDITY & MORTALITY WKLY. REP. 1, 4 (2005) [hereinafter CDC, *Postexposure Prophylaxis Report*].
24 *Id.*

impairment."[25] In all but a few cases, side effects of anti-retrovirals are reversible once the drug is discontinued,[26] so the likelihood of permanent study drug-related side effects in this setting is remote.

If anti-retroviral drugs are effective as post-exposure prophylaxis, could their use be extended to certain high risk groups in a pre-exposure setting? Tenofovir is a good candidate for such a test. It has fewer side effects than other anti-retrovirals and can be taken in a once-daily dose. Researchers at the University of California at San Francisco (UCSF) and the University of New South Wales (UNSW) proposed to offer "960 HIV-uninfected female sex workers . . . either 300 mg of tenofovir or placebo daily for 1 year"[27]. The researchers would then assess, by comparing the two groups, whether tenofovir is effective as prophylaxis. Potential subjects would be tested upon enrolment to determine their HIV status. HIV-positive women would be screened out of the study at the beginning. Study participants would then be randomly assigned either to the tenofovir arm of the study and be given a daily dose of the drug for the following year, or to the placebo arm and be given a daily "sugar pill". Neither the women nor the researchers would know who was receiving tenofovir and who was receiving the placebo. "At the beginning and once a month during the trial, study subjects will receive counseling to reduce risky behavior, free condoms, and free screening and treatment for sexually transmitted diseases."[28] The experiences of patients receiving tenofovir versus those receving placebo would be compared to assess safety and side effects. The United States National Institute of Allergy and Infectious Diseases (NIAID) and the Bill and Melinda Gates Foundation funded the study. The research was to be conducted in collaboration with the Kingdom of Cambodia Ministry of Health.

Studies of pre-exposure and post-exposure prophylaxis raise different ethical and medical questions. Risk of actual HIV exposure is typically higher in the post-exposure scenario. The course of post-exposure prophylactic treatment is relatively short, making side effects less likely. Moreover, alternatives such as behavioral change are not available in the post-exposure setting. In contrast, in the pre-exposure setting, the course of treatment can be much longer, with the drug potentially being taken for an indefinite period. This increases the risk of side effects. Counseling for behavior change may be an appropriate alternative in the pre-exposure setting. Similarly, the possibility that the pre-exposure prophylaxis might actually increase risky behavior must be seriously considered. In the end, whether the individual benefits of pre-exposure prophylaxis outweigh the

---

25 *Id.* at 10.
26 *Id.* at 4.
27 Khabir Ahmad, *Trial of Anti-retroviral for HIV Prevention on Hold,* 4 Lancet Infectious Diseases 597, 597 (2004).
28 *AIDS Prevention: Study Will Test Anti-retroviral Drug Tenofovir to Prevent HIV Infection,* Drug Wk., Oct. 10, 2003, at 9.

individual risks depends critically on the individual's level of likely HIV exposure. How high is the individual's high risk group?

HIV transmission rates affect individual cost benefit analysis. They also have important implications for study design. HIV transmission typically occurs through the exchange of blood and other bodily fluids during sexual intercourse. Despite the large numbers affected worldwide, the transmission risk from a single sexual encounter is low. The CDC estimates that the transmission rate for receptive penile-vaginal intercourse is one transmission per 1,000 acts and the risk for receptive anal intercourse is slightly higher—five transmissions per 1,000 acts.[29] This low sexual transmission rate raises challenges for scientific studies of preventative measures. With low transmission rates, studies must examine very large population groups, examine outcomes over a long period, or focus on high risk groups in order to determine statistically whether the proposed intervention is effective. A study design targeting high risk groups, such as sex workers, men who have sex with men or injection drug users is likely to be less costly and to generate statistically significant results in a shorter time.

These higher risk categories, however, also correspond to vulnerable social groups. While the economic and statistical desire to focus on high risk groups is understandable, testing the preventative efficacy of tenofovir on a group like Cambodian sex workers raises important ethical concerns. What medical treatment will be provided study participants for possible side effects of the drug during and after the study? What will happen to the women screened out at the beginning who learn for the first time that they are HIV-positive? What will happen to the women in either the tenofovir or placebo arm who become HIV-positive during the course of the study? Could participation in the study lead participants to engage in more risky behavior, a particularly important question for those in the placebo arm? Can one effectively recruit research subjects and obtain meaningful informed consent in a vulnerable population, such as Cambodian sex workers, where cultural, language, and socio-economic factors differ so dramatically from those applying to the people conducting the research?

II The Social and Political Trials of Tenofovir

The Cambodian Women's Network for Unity (WNU) was at the center of the tenofovir dispute. Understanding the history and mission of the organization helps place the tenofovir controversy in perspective. WNU describes itself as a "grassroots representative collective of Phnom Penh based Sex Workers. The network seeks to promote the rights of Sex Workers to earn a living in a safe environment, free from exploitation and social stigma."[30] The organization was founded in 2000 and is reported

---

29 CDC, *Postexposure Prophylaxis Report*, supra note 23, at 7.
30 This background information is taken from the organization's website. Women's Network for Unity Home Page, http://www.womynsagenda.org/Program/SWs/SWNU.html

to have approximately 5,000 members. Notions of individual and group empowerment are central organizational themes. While the specter of HIV is ever present in the lives of Cambodian sex workers, there are dangers far more immediate, such as daily threats of violence and abuse from clients, the police and brothel owners.

Groups like WNU are on the front lines of efforts to improve condom use and introduce safer sexual practices. As WNU reports, demanding safer sexual practices begins with building the individual self esteem of its members:

> The network has made significant achievements since its inception in 2000—sex workers have improved their attitudes to healthcare and approaches to HIV/AIDS prevention; improved their client negotiation skills; gained the courage to speak out about their problems; engaged in information sharing from workshops on HIV/AIDS and sex worker rights with their friends and peers. Together they have achieved solidarity and the collective strength that comes from one voice. They have an understanding of the value of their lives, and the importance of HIV/AIDS prevention.[31]

Preventative measures such as the promotion of condom use have been very effective in bringing down rates of HIV infection in Cambodia.[32] The participation of groups like WNU is central to the success of these efforts.

Exploitation is a daily fact of life for marginal groups in Cambodia. Trust is difficult to earn and skepticism is a necessary trait for survival. When rumors first started circulating about proposed medical research targeting Cambodian sex workers, the sex workers naturally turned to WNU. WNU adopted a proactive role. They pursued a negotiating position that sought to protect the rights and dignity of the sex workers as potential research subjects. WNU's specific concerns are outlined in a background statement issued in conjunction with a March 29, 2004 press conference.[33] These concerns reflect a sophisticated understanding of international ethical standards governing medical research in developing countries.

The WNU Statement raises three substantive concerns and two procedural objections. The substantive concerns will be addressed first. WNU was concerned about (1) the availability of medical treatment for side effects, both during and after the study period; (2) the access to tenofovir as a prophylaxis for sex workers in the future if the study proved the drug's efficacy in preventing HIV infection; and (3) the danger that the study may encourage higher risk practices, particularly for those in the placebo control group. While not specifically raised in the Statement,

---

(last visited Oct. 7, 2005).
31 *Id.*
32 For a discussion of Cambodia's success in improving safe sex practices and reducing HIV transmission amongst sex workers, *see supra* notes 15-17 and accompanying text.
33 Women's Network for Unity, Background to WNU Press Conference on Tenofovir Trials in Cambodia on March 29, 2004, http://www.womynsagenda.org/Program/SWs/WNU/wnu29mar04.pdf [hereinafter WNU Background Statement].

a natural concern also existed for the women who would be screened out of the study after learning that they are HIV positive and the women who become HIV positive during the course of the trials. As of 2004, access to anti-retroviral treatments in Cambodia for those infected with HIV was minimal to non-existent.[34]

Most media attention focused on WNU's demand for continuing medical coverage for potential adverse side effects. In the press, this was often portrayed as a demand for lifetime insurance, suggesting either the unreasonableness or the naïveté of the sex workers. This is not correct. The WNU demand for long term medical guarantees was limited to study-related side effects.

> The Network wants insurance against possible side effects of Tenofovir for 30 years or more and not just health care for the duration of the trial. When the researchers are finished and leave Cambodia who will take responsibility for sex workers and their families who may be suffering longer term side effects?"[35]

The WNU demand resonates with ethical standards designed to govern international clinical research. CIOMS Guideline 19 addressing the "Right of injured subjects to treatment and compensation," provides as follows:

> Investigators should ensure that research subjects who suffer injury as a result of their participation are entitled to free medical treatment for such injury and to such financial or other assistance as would compensate them equitably for any resultant impairment, disability or handicap. In the case of death as a result of their participation, their dependants are entitled to compensation. Subjects must not be asked to waive the right to compensation.[36]

The ethical norm is clear: Researchers should be responsible for study-related side effects.

WNU's demands for insurance reveal a deeper psychological concern and underscore a basic breakdown in communication with study researchers. A demand for insurance is reflective of underlying conditions of uncertainty. There are ways to address uncertainty other than through the provision of insurance, such as providing credible information regarding the risks of future side effects. The WNU Statement reflects an incomplete understanding of the actual risk of side effects. It correctly notes that tenofovir as pre-exposure prophylaxis has only been tested in animals and

---

[34] Hopefully, HIV therapies will be more widely available in the future. *See* WHO, "3 BY 5" PROGRESS REPORT 19 (2004), *available at* http://www.who.int/3by5/ProgressReportfinal.pdf (discussing efforts to increase availability of avtiretroviral treatments in Cambodia).
[35] WNU Background Statement, *supra* note 33.
[36] *See* COUNCIL FOR INT'L ORGS. OF MED. SCIS., INTERNATIONAL ETHICAL GUIDELINES FOR BIOMEDICAL RESEARCH INVOLVING HUMAN SUBJECTS, Guideline 19 (2002) [hereinafter CIOMS, Guidelines], available at http://www.cioms.ch/frame_guidelines_nov_2002.htm. *See also* World Med. Ass'n [WMA], *World Medical Association Declaration of Helsinki, Ethical Principles for Medical Research Involving Human Subjects*, princ. 29 (2004) [hereinafter WMA, *Declaration of Helsinki*], available at http://www.wma.net/e/policy/pdf/17c.pdf.

that the drug has not been tested on HIV-negative humans.[37] Similarly, the Statement correctly notes the known side effects of the drug, ranging from "diarrhea, nausea, [and] weakness to major liver and kidney failure and 'brittle bone' disease."[38] Not acknowledged, however, is the fact that there is substantial clinical experience with tenofovir in HIV-positive persons and with post-exposure prophylaxis. The likelihood and severity of tenofovir's side effects are known with some degree of certainty.

Recognizing this, the researchers likely felt that the chance of long term side effects was remote and, therefore, that insurance was not necessary. The question, however, is how could this sentiment be credibly conveyed to the women of WNU? In business, sellers with superior information will often extend warranties (a form of insurance) to convey their assurances of product safety and reliability. In the presence of asymmetric information, sellers who are unwilling to warrant their goods are rightly met with skepticism. From this perspective, the WNU demand for insurance for future side effects actually functioned as a test of the researchers' veracity. WNU asked "If the researchers are so sure that this drug is safe for HIV-women to take, in the short and long term, why don't they commit to insurance for us and our families? If we get sick or can't work it can be the difference between life and death for our families."[39]

This reasoning is sound from an economic perspective, but it is also a classic form of Cambodian logic—reasoning in the form of a question. If one focuses only on the question or the demand, one misses the basis of what is often a persuasive argument.[40] Dismissing the demand for insurance without providing credible alternative mechanisms to convey the actual likelihood of future risks simply added to WNU skepticism and distrust.

WNU's second substantive demand was for access to tenofovir after the study, if the drug proved to be effective at preventing HIV infection.

> If our members agree to take the risk, which may one day benefit people in richer countries and the drug company, then we deserve adequate protection to our future lives and families. The high cost of this drug means that even if it is successful in preventing HIV/AIDS, Cambodian sex workers will most likely never be able to afford it.[41]

---

37 WNU Background Statement, *supra* note 33.
38 *Id.*
39 *Id.* (quoting Kao Tha, President of Women's Network for Unity).
40 A similar example of Cambodian logic can be found in the Press Release accompanying WNU's June 15, 2004 Press Conference: "If they are so sure this drug is safe, why don't they send their own sisters and daughters to test it? They have a lot more money than sex workers and have protection if the drug makes them sick. Also, if it was their sisters or daughters, they would be a lot more honest about the risks and side effects." Press Release, Women's Network for Unity, Women's Network for Unity Protests Drug Trial Recruitment Tactics (June 21, 2004), http://www.womynsagenda.org/Program/SWs/WNU/wnu21june04.pdf [hereinafter June 21st Press Release].
41 WNU Background Statement, *supra* note 33.

Again, this demand resonates with emerging international standards and expectations. CIOMS Guidelines 10 and 21 seek to ensure that the benefits of the research are made *reasonably available* to the populations supporting the research efforts. CIOMS Guideline 10 addresses "Research in populations and communities with limited resources".

> Before undertaking research in populations or communities with limited resources, the sponsor and the investigator must make every effort to ensure that: (1) the research is responsive to the health needs and the priorities of the population or community in which it is to be carried out; and (2) *any intervention or product developed, or knowledge generated, will be made reasonably available for the benefit of that population or community.*[42]

Similarly, CIOMS Guideline 21 "Ethical obligations of external sponsors to provide health care services", states that "external sponsors are ethically obligated to ensure the availability of . . . services that are necessary as part of the commitment of a sponsor to make a beneficial intervention or product development as a result of the research *reasonably available to the population or community concerned*."[43] The tenofovir researchers did little to respond to WNU's demand.

WNU's third substantive concern dealt with was the effects the trials might have on inducing high risk behavior. WNU warned that women involved in the trial would not know if they are taking the drug or a placebo and may mistakenly think that condom use is not necessary. Alternatively, they might take greater risks with clients in order to increase their income.

> We believe that even if the experiment participants are given counseling or condoms many young women will still believe that they are safe from HIV infection as long as they are involved in the experiment. Condom use is our most effective and cheapest protection from HIV/AIDS and we are worried women will stop using them because they think they are protected by the drug.[44]

The possibility that a prophylaxis could undermine safe sexual practices is a serious concern and one under express examination in the tenofovir studies of gay men planned in San Francisco and Atlanta.[45] The problem of adverse behavior change amongst sex workers in Cambodia is even more complicated and the potential dangers more real. The women have

---

[42] CIOMS, GUIDELINES, *supra* note 36, Guideline 10 (emphasis added). *See also* WMA, *Declaration of Helsinki, supra* note 36, princ. 30 ("At the conclusion of the study, every patient entered into the study should be assured of access to the best proven prophylactic, diagnostic and therapeutic methods identified by the study."); Christine Grady, *The Challenge of Assuring Continued Post-Trial Access to Beneficial Treatment*, 5 YALE J. HEALTH POL'Y L. & ETHICS 425 (2005).
[43] CIOMS, GUIDELINES, *supra* note 36, Guideline 21 (emphasis added).
[44] WNU Background Statement, *supra* note 33.
[45] Sabin Russell, *Antiviral Drug Used to Treat AIDS to be Tested as Vaccine*, S.F. CHRON., Dec. 1, 2004, at A9. In studies performed in the Untied States and Brazil among homosexual men, the availability of post-exposure prophylaxis did not appear to increase sexual risk-taking behaviors. *See* CDC, *Postexposure Prophylaxis Report, supra* note 23, at 4.

direct economic incentives to take risks because payment is often higher for unsafe services, such as intercourse without a condom. Moreover, WNU members are subject to the demands of pimps, brothel owners and clients in an environment where they have limited means of self protection. The type of education, counseling and oversight provided to both the tenofovir and the placebo arms of the study are critical aspects of ethical study design.[46]

Even more significant than WNU's substantive concerns may be the procedural objections raised by the organization. WNU demanded (1) the right to information and (2) that the researchers enter into a series of discussions with them as a legitimate stakeholder in the process. "WNU believes that all sex workers who participate in the trial have the right to ask questions and be fully informed about the risks and to demand better medical and financial protection."[47] "WNU plans to continue outreach activities to its members on this issue and have further meetings, workshops and press conferences to negotiate protection for its members' health and human rights."[48]

Information is critical to any notion of informed consent. Traditional research ethics envision a dyadic relationship between the researcher and the research subject. The research subject is typically viewed as an isolated, autonomous decision maker. This model is inadequate when addressing the ethical demands of research subjects who are vulnerable groups in developing countries. Study design should incorporate a broader community education component and aspire to a level of transparency that will facilitate the development of trust. In this process, space must be made at the table for other important stakeholders. In addition to informed consent, the ability to credibly convey information, such as the likelihood and severity of side effects, could have addressed substantive concerns like the need for long term insurance.

Unfortunately, healthy communication was lacking in Cambodia. The situation deteriorated even further as study implementation began. On June 15, 2004, the WNU held a press conference objecting to practices researchers were allegedly using to recruit sex workers into the study. "A number of sex workers have reported that when they were approached by recruiters, they refused to provide the name of the drug and would say

---

[46] A substantive concern not raised by WNU but deserving consideration is the possible promulgation of tenofovir resistance in those sex workers receiving the drug who go on to become HIV-positive. Resistance to most anti-retrovirals occurs rapidly if used as single drugs therapy in treating known positive patients. If widespread tenofovir resistance developed it would undermine the drug's use both as a prophylaxis and as a therapeutic treatment. It is true that utilizing a single drug therapy for prophylaxis would leave other classes of HIV drugs available for treatment of study participants who developed tenofovir-resistant HIV infection. This assumes, however, that these women would be lucky enough to have access to therapeutic treatment in the first place.
[47] WNU Background Statement, *supra* note 33.
[48] *Id.*

only that it is good for the sex workers and has no side effects."[49] "Some sex workers have been told that the drug will prevent HIV and not being clear and honest that the drug is experimental and its effectiveness for HIV prevention and long-term side effects is not known."[50] It is impossible to verify these claims using outside sources. There is no doubt that given cultural, linguistic and socio-economic barriers, obtaining legitimate "informed consent" in this setting presents a difficult challenge. It is interesting to observe, however, how closely WNU's objections echo previous complaints by the US Food and Drug Administration against Giliad Sciences, Inc., the manufacturer of tenofovir. The FDA has warned that Giliad was making misleading and exaggerated claims regarding the efficacy of tenofovir and failing to properly warn patients about side effects in treating HIV/AIDS.[51] Illustrating WNU's sophistication, as well as how much smaller the Internet can make the world, the FDA warnings were known by WNU and a copy of the Warning Letter was posted on their website. At a minimum, statements made during trial recruitment and their similarity to misstatements by the drug's manufacturer in the United States added to the growing atmosphere of distrust.

Ethical issues regarding the Cambodian tenofovir trials gained international attention at the July 2004 International AIDS Conference in Bangkok when ACT-UP Paris sprayed fake blood on Giliad posters and complained about the inadequacy of counseling and safe sex education being built into the trials.[52] To the surprise of all, Prime Minister Hun Sen called an end to the tenofovir trials on August 4, 2004.[53] "Cambodia is not a trash bin country," the Prime Minister declared, stating that "[t]hey should not conduct experiments with Cambodians. They should do it with animals."[54] Towards the end of the year, the focus shifted from Cambodia to Cameroon, where an identical study of tenofovir was underway. Similar ethical questions were raised, leading to a postponement of the African trials.[55] Those trials have been resumed and there is increasing pressure in Cambodia to restart the cancelled tenofovir study.[56] On March 4, 2005, WNU sent a letter to Prime Minister Hun Sen opposing efforts

---

49 June 21st Press Release, *supra* note 40.
50 *Id*.
51 Warning Letter from Thomas W. Abrams, Dir., Div. of Drug Mktg., Adver. & Commc'ns, U.S. Dep't of Health & Human Servs., to John C. Martin, President & Chief Executive Officer, Gilead Scis., Inc. (July 29, 2003), *available at* http://www.womynsagenda.org/Program/SWs/WNU/fda29july03.pdf.
52 James, *supra* note 2, at 4.
53 Purtill & Samean, *supra* note 3, at 1.
54 *Id*.
55 U.N. Integrated Reg'l Info. Networks, *Cameroon: Clinical Trials of Anti-HIV Drug on Sex Workers in Question*, INTEGRATED REGIONAL INFO. NETWORKS, Jan. 27, 2005; *see also* U.N. Integrated Reg'l Info. Networks, *Cameroon: Government Suspends Trial of AIDS Drug*, INTEGRATED REGIONAL INFO. NETWORKS, Feb. 4, 2005.
56 Allen Myers, *Cambodia: Sex Workers Fight Proposed Drug Trial*, GREEN LEFT WKLY., Mar. 23, 2005, http://www.greenleft.org.au/back/2005/620/620p18.htm ("The Cambodian government is under pressure to allow a controversial trial of the anti-HIV drug tenofovir.").

to restart the trials.[57] The letter continued to complain that researchers have not "provided information and documents related to the trial," and asked, regardless of the fate of the tenofovir study, for the creation of "a community committee to supervise the ethics of any clinical trials" that might be conducted in the future.[58] Whether it is the trials of tenofovir or some other drug in some other country, the dilemmas of conducting medical research in developing countries are here to stay.

III Mediating the Ethics of Third World Research

A dangerous misconception is that a study that meets the ethical strictures of the first world will necessarily satisfy the ethical needs of the third world. The reality is much more complex. A study protocol obtaining Institutional Review Board (IRB) approval in the U.S. or Australia cannot simply be exported to a country like Cambodia. Substantial differences in economic resources and prevailing medical standards between rich and poor countries create many obvious challenges. Less appreciated, however, is the fact that first world IRBs play a very specialized ethical function that is necessarily predicated upon a network of other social institutions capable of addressing ancillary social needs. This permits a complex division of labor, whereby certain social and medical concerns can be removed from the purview of "research ethics". Comparable institutional networks do not exist in most developing countries. Consequently, the ancillary considerations that can be ignored in developed countries cannot be ignored in developing countries. Ethical third world research must therefore address a range of social and political issues not typically associated with the "ethics" of first world medical research. Furthermore, when addressing this broader range of social concerns, the very process of ethical review must itself take on more the characteristics of well functioning political processes, namely transparency, accountability and legitimacy.

What exactly does this mean? Research in the first world takes place against a backdrop of robust civic institutions and elaborate social systems dedicated to providing citizens comprehensive therapeutic care. This permits research ethics to perform a highly specialized institutional function and to do so in a realm that can legitimately ignore a range of difficult ancillary social and political questions. For example, whether a placebo design research protocol is ethical depends upon its incorporation of the prevailing standard of care. In the first world, determining the standard of care is largely a positive undertaking: what is the best alternative treatment a research subject would receive if they were not part of the study? The constraints determining the best alternative treatment in the developed world are largely matters of technology, not economics.

---

57 *See* Letter from Kao Tha et al., Secretariat of Women's Network for Unity, to Samdech Hun Sen, Prime Minister, Cambodia (Mar. 4, 2005), *available at* http://archives.healthdev.net/sex-work/msg00556.html.
58 *Id.*

When research is exported from the first to the third world, however, and when the prevailing standard of care is lower due to economic rather than medical constraints, defining the acceptable standard of care for research unavoidably takes on normative dimensions. Research ethics in this environment confronts issues that become increasingly social and political in nature.[59]

Once this is acknowledged, many mainstays of traditional medical ethics are called into question. Is it possible to address disparities in medical resources between first and third world standards of care in a responsible way without creating "undue inducements"? Similarly, it is well established in the developed world that researchers have no ethical obligation to treat non-study-caused medical problems, but merely refer such persons to existing clinical resources. This standard is defensible where medical services are generally available, but is far more contestable when no alternative treatment exists because of a lack of medical and financial resources. Even those who might continue to defend the absence of an affirmative duty to provide care as "ethical", must feel uncomfortable about such a position in an HIV/AIDS prophylaxis study where those who become HIV positive during the course of research have no realistic access to care and anti-retrovirals. On the other hand, any effort to provide medical care for non-study-related problems would face the first world criticism that such care would be an unethical inducement, undermining the validity of participant informed consent. There are no easy answers, but these tensions highlight the shortcomings and inadequacies of existing ethical standards.

The trials of tenofovir are illustrative in this regard. The standard first world ethical position is articulated as follows:

> Mary Fanning, associate director for clinical research at the National Institute of Allergy and Infectious Diseases, says offering volunteers 30 to 40 years of care, as the protest group demands, wouldn't pass an ethics test because it is an "undue inducement." Incentives "so enormous" could entice volunteers to enroll in a study regardless of the risks, she says, tainting the informed consent process.[60]

The inadequacy of this reasoning is suggested by ethics blogger Stuart Rennie with a boxing analogy:

> In this corner, the sex workers union demanding 30 to 40 years of medical care for sex workers in the study who acquire HIV. In that corner, Mary Fanning, associate director of clinical research at NIAID, countering that offering such compensation would be tantamount to undue inducement, would invalidate voluntary informed consent, and hence would be, um,

---

[59] The commentary on Guideline 11: Choice of Controls in Clinical Trials of the INTERNATIONAL ETHICAL GUIDELINES FOR BIOMEDICAL RESEARCH INVOLVING HUMAN SUBJECTS provides a window into these contentious issues. *See* CIOMS, GUIDELINES, *supra* note 36, Guideline 11 cmt.

[60] Chase & Naik, *supra* note 1, at B1. As should be clear from the earlier discussion, WNU was not demanding 30–40 years of free medical care, but simply assurances of long term post-study treatment of study induced side effects.

unethical. In this corner, ACT-UP Paris claiming that the $3 offered to prospective participants already constitutes unethical inducement, and calling for the immediate termination of Viread [tenofovir] trials worldwide until participants were assured of effective HIV prevention education and resources, and received access to adequate treatment and care in the event of HIV infection. In that corner, Ward Cates of Family Health International (the North Carolina-based non-profit health organization overseeing the Cambodia and Cameroon trials) arguing that the human rights of study participants were respected, because the care being offered to them was well above the standard of care in Cambodia. Any reasonable sex worker, it seems, would be better off joining the trial than plying her trade outside it (but isn't that, um, undue inducement?).[61]

The WNU demands were not radical or irrational. The Union's demands reflected recognized standards of international medical ethics as articulated in the CIOMS Guidelines. As such, the impasse in Cambodia was not simply a failure of a team of first world researchers to take seriously the concerns of a union of sex workers. The trials of tenofovir illustrate the basic inability of existing research infrastructures to address a much broader range of contemporary ethical demands.

Under emerging international standards, researchers who choose to work in developing countries are called upon to take on new social responsibilities. For example, CIOMS Guidelines 10 and 21 require that future benefits derived from the research be made "reasonably available" to study participates.[62] Consistent with these standards, WNU sought assurances that if tenofovir were proven effective as an HIV/AIDS prophylaxis, sex workers in Cambodia would be assured future access to the drug. While perhaps originally grounded in ethical concerns, assuring future access also raises political and economic concerns. In this new environment, the lines between ethical, social and political responsibilities start to become blurred. Not surprisingly, therefore, asking even basic questions about how such ethical commitments are to be operationalized suggests how ill equipped traditional IRBs are to address these issues. These are social, as well as ethical concerns. Properly addressing these questions will require new processes that will increasingly take on characteristics that look more civic than ethical in nature.

The commentary to CIOMS Guideline 10, which deals with how the benefits of research are to be made *reasonably available* to the study community, is revealing in this regard.

> When an investigational intervention has important potential for health care in the host country, *the negotiation* that the sponsor should undertake to determine the practical implications of "responsiveness," as well as the "reasonable availability," *should include representatives of stakeholders in the host country*; these include the national government, the health ministry, local health authorities, and concerned scientific and ethics groups, *as well as*

---

61 Posting of Stuart Rennie to The Gilead Saga, American Journal of Bioethics Editors Blog, http://blog.bioethics.net/2005/02/gilead-saga.html (Feb. 18, 2005).
62 CIOMS, Guidelines, *supra* note 36, Guidelines 10, 21.

representatives of the communities for which subjects are drawn and non-governmental organizations such as health advocacy groups.[63]

The lesson is clear. New institutional processes are necessary to work in conjunction with traditional ethical review boards to implement these responsibilities. These processes must be undertaken in a manner that openly acknowledges and accommodates their social and political dimensions.

Until more formal institutions are developed, it is natural to think of mediation as a framework to address these questions. It is also clear, however, that mediation will face a number of difficult challenges. Mediation is a process-oriented solution. This stands in sharp contrast to the substantively proscriptive nature of traditional ethical review. Identifying legitimate mediation partners, who can speak for the study subjects, and defining the rights and entitlements of the disparate stakeholders will be problematic. Beyond providing informed consent and agreeing to comply with the study protocol, research subjects are not traditionally viewed as "stakeholders" in the research process. Mediation will be more complicated, contentious and participatory than traditional ethical research review and approval. This can be difficult and unpredictable. Those who think that time and money will be saved by exporting research to the third world need to think again, at least if they are committed to conducting research in a responsible manner.

If mediation is to be successful, there are a number of prerequisites. To begin with, the relevant stakeholders must be identified and engaged. Participants in the process have to approach the exercise in good faith. Norms of healthy communication, mutual respect and full disclosure of information need to be encouraged. True understanding will require a willingness of participants to sympathetically engage the concerns of other stakeholders. Furthermore, mediating the more expressly social dimensions of third world research will require processes that serve more political and not scientific functions. To be effective, these mechanisms need to be modeled in accordance with the standards of well functioning civic institutions. Is the system open? Is the system accountable? Is the system legitimate?

Judged by these standards, the failings of the Cambodian tenofovir trials become evident. The challenges were to prevent the exploitation of a vulnerable social group, to make adequate assurances for the medical treatment of study-related side effects, and to ensure future access to any treatment proven efficacious in the study. Addressing these concerns called for an effective mediation exercise. The CIOMS speaks of the need to include a wide range of stakeholders in these deliberations, including groups like WNU.[64] This is particularly true when the research subjects

---

[63] *Id*. Guideline 10 cmt. (emphasis added).
[64] *Id*.

are vulnerable groups who are likely to be disenfranchised from existing political processes.[65] Even in developed countries with strong traditions of representative democracy, there is little reason to have faith that government ministries can effectively represent the interests of socially marginalized groups like sex workers, gay men and IV drug users.

It is impossible to appreciate fully from second hand press reports why the impasse between the researchers and the WNU could not be resolved. We can only offer some educated guesses. The researchers appeared to treat their mandate as a fait accompli and to view their previous IRB approval as a basis for not having to re-examine the ethical and social concerns raised by WNU. This mind set is probably representative of most medical researchers. IRB review in developed countries is a rigorous process. In the minds of the researchers, all of the important ethical questions had already been resolved. From this perspective, WNU was viewed as a potential public relations problem that had to be managed, but not as a group that had to be seriously engaged. This posture, however, fails to appreciate that there are important social and political dimensions to third world medical research that must be negotiated and resolved in the country where the research is to take place, not in the country of funding sponsorship. From this standpoint, the impasse leading to the cancellation of the study was nearly unavoidable. No mediation can be successful when one of the central stakeholders fails to acknowledge that there is anything that requires discussion and resolution.

Reflective of this denial was the failure of researchers to be forthcoming with information. The limited access to information is troubling even from the perspective of traditional informed consent. Informed consent presupposes the disclosure of appropriate information. Whether one is dealing with WNU as a group, or its individual members, prospective study participants have the right to ask fundamental questions about the study and to be given access to relevant information. This was not done in Cambodia. We believe it is fair for research subjects to ask for and be provided copies of the study protocol. We also believe that it is fair to ask for and receive copies of minutes of IRB meetings or summaries of IRB discussions that purportedly addressed and resolved "ethical" issues relating to the study. This level of transparency will make the first world IRB process more accountable as a civic institution, as well as provide the information needed to facilitate truly informed consent. Information

---

65   It was not enough for the researchers to work collaboratively with the Cambodian Ministry of Health. Cambodia is at best a fledgling democracy, whose government institutions face daily struggles with corruption. *See, e.g., Rotten at the Core: Graft is Slowing Cambodia's Return to Better Health*, ECONOMIST, Feb. 17, 2005; *World Bank Warns Corruption Could Threaten Cambodian Economy*, THAI PRESS REPS., Feb. 16, 2005 ("World Bank President James Wolfensohn says the three greatest obstacles to Cambodia's growth are 'corruption, corruption, corruption.'"). As is true in many developing countries, the healthiest and most proactive forms of civic society are often found in the non-governmental organization (NGO) community.

and transparency are also essential for building the cooperation and trust necessary for successful mediation.

Groups like WNU cannot and should not be ignored. As the WHO recognizes in its "3 by 5" initiative, if progress is to be made in the war against AIDS, more, not less involvement of civil organizations will be required.[66] Civil organizations need to be able to advocate for vulnerable populations from which they draw their members, even if such advocacy challenges traditional ethical constructs and regulatory processes. WNU is not the first civic organization to challenge traditional research regimes. In the United States, organizations like ACT UP were responsible for accelerating the pace of change in AIDS research.[67] Researchers should view WNU's participation as a stimulus that could help redefine considerations for ethical third world research, rather than as an impediment to study recruitment. In the future, this strategy would necessitate involving civil organizations like WNU at the early planning stages of the research. In accordance with CIOMS Guidelines, these groups should be engaged in discussions as to what type of care should be provided during the study and on what care is necessary on an ongoing basis to address study-related side effects. The end result would be to create allies rather than adversaries.

The goals of HIV researchers, sex workers and health care providers are the same. There is a collective need to take pragmatic steps to curtail the spread of the virus and to provide effective, compassionate medical care to those already infected with the disease. What happened to the tenofovir trials in Cambodia is regrettable. At the same time, the conflict helps focus much-needed attention on the political and social demands of third world research, demands that traditional research ethics and IRBs are ill equipped to address. It is not possible to know whether a mediation framework could have overcome the problems that led to the cancellation of the Cambodian research. The cancellation of the Cambodian study, however, suggests that future researchers must more effectively engage groups like WNU if important HIV/AIDS research is to succeed.

---

66 WHO, WORLD HEALTH REPORT, *supra* note 5, at 26. The "3 by 5" initiative is a multidisciplinary partnership, the goal of which is to provide needed HIV treatment to 3 million HIV-infected individuals in the developing world by the end of 2005. *Id.* at xii. The program acknowledges that "[p]olitical commitment and national ownership of programmes are essential." *Id.* at xiii. The program emphasizes the role that "associations of people living with HIV/AIDS and their advocates, faith-based organizations, and other groups such as trade unions" play in HIV/AIDS treatment and prevention strategies in developing countries, and welcomes their participation. *Id.* at 43.

67 The WORLD HEALTH REPORT states that "[g]roups such as the AIDS Coalition to Unleash Power (ACT UP), formed in the USA in 1987, combined a successful advocacy strategy with the building of a formidable scientific knowledge base, which enabled members to become informed participants in medical research and the policy-making process. During the 1980s and 1990s, these groups won increased funding for antiviral drug research, increased AIDS services budgets at federal, state and local levels, an accelerated testing process for drugs, and expanded access to experimental drugs for people not accepted into clinical trials." *Id.* at 46.

REVIEW

Ian Ellis-Jones

Michael Head and Scott Mann:
Law in Perspective: Ethics, Society and Critical Thinking,
UNSW Press, Sydney, 2005

In the introduction to this book the authors state that the principal aim of the book, which has been designed "first and foremost, as an introductory textbook",[1] is to "encourage critical, responsible and creative thinking about law as a system of ideas and as a social institution".[2]

The book is divided into three main sections. The first section, "Logic, Science and Law", seeks to explore the interrelationships between those three disciplines. The second, "Ethics, Social Theory and Law", discusses what the authors regard as the "principal theoretical approaches to the nature and social role of law". The third, "Law and Contemporary Social Problems", seeks to evaluate the role played by the law in the alleviation or exacerbation of major social conflicts.

I found the first two sections of the books the most interesting, perhaps because I share with the authors a deep concern that learning to think in the thought forms of a lawyer requires, among other things, the ability to think logically and in an ethically acceptable fashion. Sadly, all too many law courses these days neglect these two areas. Little, if any, time is spent on logic and legal reasoning in any principled sense, and our approach to ethics tends to focus almost entirely on the legal rules made by or on behalf of the professional bodies regulating the actual conduct of the legal profession, rather than exposing law students to the range of ethical theories that have been expounded over the years.

The authors make it clear[3] that they see substantial dangers in both legal positivism (with its "strongly disciplinary and black-letter approach") and the epistemological anarchy of "faddish postmodern deconstructions lacking in all substantive content". What is required, according to the authors, is for students to master "basic tools of critical thinking and analysis at the earliest possible stage of their studies".[4] I couldn't agree more and, if I had my way, I would make the study of logic and basic philosophy an essential part of any law degree as it once was in some

---

1 p. 1.
2 p. 1.
3 p. 2.
4 p. 2.

places. Being very much of an Andersonian realist,[5] I do not, however, accept the authors' working definition of logic as "the science that evaluates arguments".[6] Logic is not so much a body of rules, principles and methods for evaluating and constructing arguments as a description of how things are related to each other. In other words, logic is about *things*, not thought. Logical thinking means relating (that is, putting together or distinguishing) different pieces of information about facts or alleged facts. In that sense, logic is a description of reality. Logic helps us to find facts and see the connections between one set of facts and another. It teaches us that a fact can be explained *only* as following logically from other facts occurring on the same level of observability. Even opinions and ideas can be said to be true or false when attention is directed, *not* to the opinion or idea itself, but to the thing that the opinion or idea or value is *of*. The test of a true opinion or idea is to see whether or not something *is* the case.

The authors rightly assert[7] that there is no special kind of logic called "legal logic". They also assert, somewhat self servingly, that while logic has "undergone continuous development and evolution for more than 2,000 years" few contemporary Australian law texts have kept abreast with those developments. True, there are many schools of logic, but I remain unconvinced that there is more than one way in which we can speak meaningfully about the universe other than by means of the Aristotelian propositional form. (Call me old fashioned but I am firmly of the opinion that good old fashioned Aristotelian logic has never been bettered.) Although the authors are to be commended for providing an informative, intelligible and workable overview of the basic rules of applied logic that are relevant to legal thinking, they don't make it all that clear what school or schools of logic they're endorsing, although what they generally do expound[8] is, for the most part, not inconsistent with traditional Aristotelian logic and should prove very useful both to law students and legal practitioners.

The part of the book dealing with ethics[9] is extremely good in its exposition of the inherent weaknesses of both moral relativism and the "command" theory of ethics. As regards the former, the authors make the valid point that just "because there are differences between the values of different cultural groups does not mean that there are no correct answers."[10] Good stuff, but, regrettably, the authors, whilst admirably

---

5 C.f. John Anderson (1893–1962), Challis Professor of Philosophy, University of Sydney, from 1927 to 1958. Anderson's central thesis is that there is only one order or level of reality, that of ordinary things in time and space, and that a single logic applies to all things.
6 p. 11. The authors cite with approval what Patrick Hurley, in his *Concise Introduction to Logic*, 5th ed (Wadsworth, Belmont CA, 1994), wrote (on p.1), viz., that the aim of logic is to "develop a system of methods and principles that we may use as criteria for evaluating the arguments of others and as guides in constructing arguments of our own".
7 p. 15.
8 See, especially, the material on "deduction" and "induction" on pp. 23–30.
9 See, especially, ch. 8.
10 p. 164.

drawing attention to some of the inanities of the "subjectivist" view of ethics, fail to give meaningful consideration to the "objectivist" view of ethics which asserts that there *are* indeed objective moral values that do not depend upon the command theory. For example, that whatever promotes or enhances human well-being, is *intrinsically* good, can be considered to be an objective moral value. Of course, it is, as Anderson used to point out, a "relativist" mistake (that is, purporting to define something by reference to its relations to other things) to enquire as to the conditions for goodness or fairness just as it is a mistake to enquire as to the conditions for redness, for we can speak meaningfully only in terms of what are the conditions for something being fair, being good, being beautiful, being red, and so forth. However, that is not to be taken to be a question about the conditions of fairness, goodness, beauty or redness itself. For example, the features of a fair hearing in law—that is, those things that must be done in order for there to be fairness—are not what constitute a thing's fairness. They simply permit appreciation or recognition of its fairness.

Also, there are, according to the "objectivist" view of ethics, certain self evident ethical truths such as "unnecessary suffering is wrong", "equals are to be treated equally", and so forth and I would have liked the authors to deal with that matter. Their attack on the assertion in the US Declaration of Independence that there are certain "self-evident truths" as being simply the result of "the struggle of the aspiring American capitalist class against British colonial domination"[11] is, in my view, far too dismissive and cynical and sidesteps the real issue.

Be that as it may, the authors rightly and robustly expose the fundamental flaws of the command theory, more than adequately pointing out that what is "right" and "wrong" do not, and cannot, depend upon external authority or the commands or existence of God. As philosopher A.K. Stout and many others have pointed out, religion is *never* a logical basis for morality. Why? Because religion appeals to authority (God, Bible, Pope, and so forth), and the argument from authority is no argument at all and no definition of good, nor does it constitute a theory of ethics. Also, as David Hume pointed out, one can't logically derive a value judgment or normative proposition ("we ought to do X") from a factual statement ("God commands X", "X is right").

The book contains a very good description of such matters as natural law and legal positivism, with references to such notables as Locke, Austin and H.L.A. Hart. There is also an excellent treatment of "distributive justice".[12] Regrettably, the book tends to become a bit polemic and doctrinaire when dealing with such matters as Marxist theory (e.g. "capitalist production is driven by pursuit of profit"),[13] anti-terrorism measures ("a grave threat

---

11 pp. 182–83.
12 pp. 199–200.
13 p. 250.

to basic democratic measures"),[14] and the plight of asylum seekers ("In most cases they have broken no laws, and have not been convicted of any offence").[15] As regards the first mentioned matter, the authors obviously accept the classical theory of the firm that firms are solely motivated by the desire for profit maximisation, a view which seems self evidently true but which is otherwise quite simplistic in many respects. Although I personally have few, if any, problems with the views expressed by the authors in this third section of their book, the polemic tone of much of this third section of the book will alienate many more conservative readers.

Although I have a few qualms concerning the content of the book, it is nevertheless an excellent and wide-ranging introduction to the law and critical legal thinking and is suitable as a legal text commencing with first year students. I will be recommending it to my students.

---

14 p. 368.
15 p. 373.

Previous Issues of UTS Law Review

(1) The Courts and the Media
(2) Law on the Internet
(3) Legal Education in Australia
(4) Courts, Lawyers and the Internet
(5) The Public Right to Know
(6) Computerisation of the Law: Global Challenges